SHIPPING ENTERPRISE
AND MANAGEMENT
1830-1939

Thomas Harrison (1815–1888)

Shipping Enterprise and Management
1830-1939

Harrisons of Liverpool

FRANCIS E. HYDE

with contributions from

J. R. Harris and A. M. Bourn

LIVERPOOL UNIVERSITY PRESS

1967

Published by

LIVERPOOL UNIVERSITY PRESS

123 Grove Street, Liverpool 7

© Copyright 1967 by

FRANCIS E. HYDE

First published 1967

Made and Printed in Great Britain
by C. Tinling & Co. Ltd.,
Liverpool, London and Prescot.

To Marian

IN TENEBRIS OCULI, MARIANA,
MANUSQUE FUISTI:
ACCIPE IAM MUNUS
QUOD FUIT ANTE TUUM

PREFACE

WHEN Mr Brian Watson Hughes, Chairman of the firm of T. and J. Harrison commissioned the writing of a history of the Charente Steam-Ship Company Ltd, it was agreed that the resulting study should not take the form of a descriptive house history. This decision was not meant as, and did not imply, any denigratory criticism either of house histories in general or of descriptive writing in particular. Far from it. As the reader will discover there is a fair amount of the purely descriptive in this book, because description is essential to the narrative, and helps to give perspective to those chapters based on the use of economic argument or other analytical techniques. In turn, it is hoped that the latter will have given a quantitative background both to the events and to the formulation of conclusions.

The main purpose has been to pose a series of questions and to seek the answers to these questions on the business operations of a shipping firm which started from humble beginnings and, during the course of a long history, developed world-wide interests. As a result, there is an increasing emphasis on decision-taking and the entrepreneurial capacity of the Managers. This applies especially after 1884. At the end of this year, Thomas and James Harrison made a formal division of functions; the fleet, previously designated the Charente Steam-Ship Company, was created a limited company under the direct management of T. and J. Harrison. This pattern of organization, common to many other shipping companies, lends itself to analysis; in fact, the shipping industry as a whole can provide the economist with excellent models of capital growth, income flows and expectation of profit.

The Harrison archives proved to be informative and readily capable for purposes of quantitative analysis but extremely scanty of information for any qualitative assessment of personalities. Although the Minute Books, accounts and a variety of memoranda have survived in reasonably complete form, there is an almost total absence of personal data such as diaries and correspondence. Nearly all the business correspondence used came from outside sources, from agents and from a somewhat fortuitous gleaning from the records of other shipping companies. It has not, therefore, been possible to examine the personal qualities and the impact of individual characteristics on the course of events with the precision one might have wished; nor, as a result, has it been possible to infuse the narrative with lively quotations from the pens of the chief protagonists, indicating their preferences, their fears or their forthright opinions about their competitors. What has been lost in this respect, however, will, it is hoped, have been given more than adequate compensation by the use of a variety of techniques which, though impersonal in themselves, throw light upon the collective activities and the decisions of the group as a whole. In short, the nature and scope of the material to a very large extent not only determined but accentuated the approach to, and the eventual concept of, the book.

The concept of the book, apart from any consideration imposed by the nature of the source material, is a development from a series of discussions concerning the nature and value of business history. The Harvard Business School has, for many years, had such argument under review. We, in Great Britain, have more recently become involved in the controversy. The publication of Professor T. S. Ashton's *Peter Stubs* raised our academic sights; Professor Charles Wilson's *History of Unilever* and Professor T. C. Barker's *Pilkington Bros. and the Glass Industry* proved that the quality of the British product was, by academic standards, no less excellent than that of our American colleagues. As the interest in business history developed, both economists and economic historians turned their attention to widening the scope of techniques which could be applied to a better understanding of the managerial function. Professor R. L. Sayers's work on Lloyds, Dr Peter Payne's *Rubber and Railways in the Nineteenth Century*, Dr Sheila Marriner's *Rathbones of Liverpool*, Dr Eric Sigsworth's *Black Dyke Mills* and Professor A. H. John's *A Liverpool Merchant House* showed what could be done through the employment of economic concepts. Finally, through the establishment of a British journal, *Business History*, the controversy and the development of techniques were given space for ventilation.

It was in the pages of this journal that Professor B. E. Supple published a most interesting review article on the 'Uses of Business History'.[1] He argued that the business historian should not only ask

1. B. E. Supple, 'The Uses of Business History,' *Business History* IV, No. 2. June 1962, pp. 81-90.

questions and, as far as possible within the circumscription of his material, attempt to answer them; but that he should make use of a varied range of techniques, and, by so doing, seek to check and give depth to his conclusions. His primary aim must be that of investigator; and his attention should be focussed upon the use of resources not merely from the point of view of the firm itself, but of the firm in relation to its competitors and the wider background of its environment. In the ensuing discussion the relevance of regional studies was convincingly argued;[1] the relationship of a firm to its environment and the economic and social impact of the firm's activity upon that environment are obvious phenomena requiring investigation. Equally so are the complex factors determining effective action and decision-taking on the part of the entrepreneur. Most economists would agree that theories of maximization and of expectation are rational, though by no means perfect, aids to an understanding of the behaviour of businessmen.[2] Nevertheless, despite personal quirks which may often disturb the theoretical pattern, there is a general rationality among business men which can be studied and tested. In the most profitable use of his resources, the individual can only rely on his judgement to assess the future expectation of profit. Whether or not his decisions are correct can only be judged by the results over a given period. It is precisely in the nature and scope of historical evidence, and in the evaluation of such evidence by the economic historian, that the economic theorist may find a practical application of his ideas. Here is at least one reason why economists and economic historians should keep abreast of each other's developing fields of knowledge.

The following pages, as we have already said, are concerned with the activities of a shipping firm. These activities, however, have been given a varied scrutiny within the framework of the discussion outlined above. Harrisons' shipping interests are shown, not only within the context of the environment from which they sprang, namely, the port of Liverpool, but expanding to the countries throughout the world whose economies they served. Within the limits of this narrative there are comparative essays on such topics as the progress

1. P. L. Payne, 'The Uses of Business History' *Business History* V, No. 1. December 1962, pp. 11-21.
2. Francis E. Hyde, 'Economic Theory and Business History' *Business History* V, No. 1. December 1962, pp. 1-10.

of the firm in relation to its competitors, the firm's cost structure in relation to the British shipping industry as a whole and the effects on resources of fluctuations in trade. From an initial consideration of business activity there is, therefore, in this book a continuing emphasis on business enterprise. To answer the relevant question whether or not the Managers were successful as entrepreneurs, we have subjected the historical evidence to a variety of processes, economic, statistical and accounting, in the hope that, through a range of analysis, the main-springs of policy and the ensuing results might be given perspective. In the absence of a sufficient body of personal data, this is the best that we can do to arrive at an approximation of the truth.

In writing this book I have had very considerable help from my colleagues, Dr J. R. Harris, Mr Michael Bourn and Dr Sheila Marriner. While I must bear full responsibility for the concept, the use of techniques and the writing of the book as a whole, I have to thank Dr J. R. Harris and Mr Frank Neal (whose services as my research assistant were made possible by a generous grant from Messrs. T. and J. Harrison) for the collection and initial preparation of much of the source material. In particular, their visit to Tonnay Charente led to the discovery of personal records of the Williamson family and other documents relating to the early history of the firm. The drafting of this and other material by Dr Harris enabled me to give a much more comprehensive treatment to the firm's history before 1884 than would otherwise have been possible. In addition, Dr Harris's knowledge of machines and their history stimulated his interest in the technical details of the Harrison fleet. His contribution on the shipbuilding side of the business is incorporated in Section II of Chapter 8. Mr Michael Bourn's skill as an accountant is manifest in the setting out of the firm's accounts. This work (published as appendices) involved him in many hours of labour and is testimony to his high standards of accuracy and insight into those problems of management with which this book is concerned. Without his careful estimate of employed capital, his arrangement of the balance sheets and his calculation of the source and disposition of funds, it would have been extremely difficult to have made any worthwhile comparison of the firm's growth over a period of fifty-five years or of the utilization of resources. The figures which Mr Bourn has compiled were taken from the firm's annual statement of accounts; the interpretation of these figures and, consequently, any errors which may be found in this interpretation must be attributed to me. To Dr Sheila Marriner I owe a debt of gratitude not only for reading and correcting errors in the text but for her stimulating and pertinent criticism of those sections of the book involving the analysis of material within a theoretical framework. I must also acknowledge the help which I received from Mr P. N. Davies who made relevant extracts from the files of *Fairplay*.

No words can adequately express my thanks to my wife for her patient and zealous checking of discrepancies in the manuscript sources, for her accurate work on the tables in the text and for her revision of the first drafts. There is no page in the book which has not directly benefited from her inspiration and her careful criticism. Finally, to my secretary, Miss Valerie Dodd, and to Miss Dorothy Woolley and to Mrs E. Harris I make grateful acknowledgement of their skill in the preparation and in the work on the various sections of the typescript.

The University of Liverpool,   F.E.H.
    October, 1966

ACKNOWLEDGEMENTS

THE author gratefully acknowledges the helpful co-operation of the Directors of the Charente Steam-Ship Company in the writing and the publication of this book. First, for the generous financial support which made it possible for a research assistant to be employed in making a search for relevant source material; secondly, in the permission, freely given on all occasions, to use the records of the firm without restriction or hindrance.

To Mr Brian Watson Hughes the author owes an especial debt of gratitude. His initiation of the project was followed by an interest in the analysis of the material and in the writing of successive chapters. Furthermore, his remarkable memory of past events not only gave point to his criticisms, but added immeasurably to the accuracy of the narrative.

Mr John Cowan, whose long and distinguished career as a shipowner has always been combined with an active interest in the history of

Liverpool's shipping firms, gave unstinted advice and invaluable criticism at every stage in the writing of the first draft. For this, and for many other acts of kindness, the author has great pleasure in recording his thanks. Acknowledgement and thanks are also due to Mr J. K. Harrison for permission to use various collections of family papers including the most valuable correspondence of Frederick James Harrison; and to the members of the Williamson family still living in Charente, especially to Mr Richard Williamson and to Col. Tribot Laspiére for their help in tracing the records relating to the early voyages of Richard Williamson and of his son Richard Pierre; and to Mr Gordon Reid and to Mr Pat Wilson, some apology must be made for the unwarranted intrusions which were so frequently made on their daily journey by train from West Kirby to Liverpool, and thanks expressed for their patience, courtesy and active help; thanks are also due to Mr Eric Carter Braine and Mr William Marcus Graham for their notes and recollections, to Mr H. J. H. Wiseman for permission to use papers from the estate of the late Col. Eustace Harrison and to Mr J. H. Beazley for technical information about the fleet; to Mr E. N. Mayall, Mr G. A. Paton, and Miss Elizabeth Warburton for the invaluable help in collecting information; to Mr H. Bowman, Miss Marjorie Jones and Mr M. J. T. Hunton for their assistance in checking the figures in the Tables and Appendices; to Mr Scott Thomson and Mr A. R. D. Thomson for their permission to use the Staveley Taylor records and finally to Mr Rupert C. Jarvis for permission to work on the Liverpool and Scarborough Statutory Registers of Merchant Ships.

CONTENTS

PART TWO

Expansion, Competition and Financial Organization,
1885-1914

PART THREE
Management and the Allocation of Resources, 1914-39

LIST OF ILLUSTRATIONS

INTRODUCTION

LET it be stated at the outset and in the most emphatic way that this book is not a house history. It is a study of the successive attempts of business-men over a period of a century and a half to achieve efficiency in the use of resources. In so doing they promoted the economic growth not only of their own enterprise but indirectly that of a wider sector of the various economies at home and abroad which they served. In this particular case the subject for analysis is a shipping firm of high reputation and world-wide interests, T. and J. Harrison, managers of the Charente Steam-Ship Company Ltd. The techniques of analysis which are employed, however, could be applied to any firm with a body of records capable of a reasonable degree of sophisticated investigation. Nevertheless, whatever may be the nature of the exercise and whatever may be the nature of a firm's or an industry's activity, the central point of this kind of approach to an understanding of men's business motives must lie in the character and judgement of the men themselves. As decision-takers the success or failure of their policies must reflect their skill as interpreters of past events and as assessors of future expectations. In writing up their achievements the economist and the economic historian may apply their own tests. The result may be either a case study or a business history; it most certainly should not be a descriptive house history.

Having said this, however, let us hasten to add that the statement about house histories is not made in a pejorative sense. Such histories are often illuminating and useful as historical documents; but they rarely seek to ask and answer questions relating to entrepreneurship and economic progress. It is arguable that the economic historian should concern himself with facts and not with theories; but when material is scarce and unequal in content (as it often is) facts may tend to be given a subjective, rather than an objective appraisal. In such circumstances the need for a quantitative rather than qualitative assessment becomes a necessary part of the historian's checking technique. From this it is an easy step to a more scientific use of material and to the application of methods other than those purely historical. What then is the scope of business history and how should it be written in order to satisfy the widest range of interest in what it has to say?

If we start from Professor Charles Wilson's dictum that biography is an essential element in the writing of business history, it follows that the main ingredients of any study must be concerned with the minds and actions of men over periods of time and against a changing pattern of events. Knowledge is built up from a meticulous piecing together of evidence, from documents either written by the businessmen themselves or from those written by others about them. As every historian knows, the validity of such evidence is sometimes questionable because of its subjective nature. Elaborate devices have, therefore, to be used by the historian to introduce correctives and establish objectivity. In the writing of business history, however, there is an impersonal safeguard which can always be used to offset bias. The extent to which a business man can justify his actions or estimate the extent of his own abilities can usually be tested against the earning capacity of his company. How many examples are there of firms whose directorate ought to have been replaced long before retirement? How many founders of large-scale enterprises lost the initiative of an early career by their preference for greater leisure rather than sustained economic rewards? The signs of their palsied hands, their faltering steps, their waning powers and even their pig-headedness are mirrored in many a balance sheet.

Balance sheets, however, though impersonal evidence, can be just as unreliable as any other form of evidence unless the historian has taken steps to acquire some of the technicalities of the accountant. These technicalities need not be too refined or too complicated to be used as tools in the business historian's equipment; but they are essential if scientific objectivity is to be achieved. It might well be of importance, for example, to know something of the source and disposition of a firm's funds, to be able to estimate the growth of employed capital and establish the ratio of total income to that capital. It might be of greater importance to know whether the return on capital employed in the firm was, over given periods, larger or smaller than the return from outside sources of investment. One might by a variety of techniques (accountancy, statistical and theoretical) attempt a judgement as to the marginal efficiency of capital within the firm, and, by the process of discounting cash flows, make an assessment of relative investment opportunities and even, by *ex post* analysis check, expected

James Harrison (1821–1891)

earnings against actual earnings. In other words, the whole exercise of writing business history can develop from first principles through a series of rational and analytical processes. In this context biography is still an essential element but, in the process of developing the material, business history has now become economic history with a particular bias and economic history (according to the technique used) a branch of applied economics.

If, therefore, the first question which a business historian might ask is of a biographical nature, the second must concern itself with action and, following this, the investigation of causal relationships and the interpretation of the consequences of such action. In the case of the Charente Steam-Ship Company, the chief protagonists are clearly defined though the precise nature of their ideas on the conduct of business is obscured, partly because of a scarcity of private correspondence, and partly because of the cloak of anonymity covering the official records. Even so, the individual characteristics of the two Richard Williamsons, of Thomas and James Harrison in the foundation and early expansion of the firm stand out clearly; so also does the perspicacity and drive of Frederick James Harrison and John William Hughes in their efforts to combat competition and put the financial affairs of the company on a sound basis; the vision of Thomas Harrison Hughes, Frank Ward and John Watson Hughes in widening the scope of the firm's trading interests in the period before 1914; and the sagacity of Sir Harrison Hughes, John Cowan, John C. Mannings and Brian Watson Hughes in the difficult post-war years. All of these men are worthy of greater biographical detail than it has been possible to give them in this book. Nevertheless, the collective decisions which they made and the resultant effect of these decisions on the national and international aspects of Britain's shipping policy are reported and made the subject of analysis.

In the period of something more than a century there have been a number of turning points in the history of this firm. Between 1853 (the date of establishment under the title of T. and J. Harrison) and 1884 the partners pursued a policy of gradual expansion, directing their operations outwards from the wine and brandy trades along the European coastline to the establishment of trans-oceanic services. The driving force of personality was just as much an element in this expansion as the nature and profitability of the new trades. After 1885, however, the Company had to face growing competition from other powerful British and Continental steamship lines. To make progress, therefore, a greater knowledge of the economic potentialities of a rapidly changing world was essential. The decision to enter the Indian tea trade in 1889 was an example of the Managers' awareness of the nature of the competitive struggle; so too was their decision to enter the South African trade in 1902. By 1908 they had become so expert in assessing future expectations that they were able to base their investment policy upon a fairly sophisticated analysis of events. The establishment of their London office in 1910, their purchase of the Rennie fleet, and their entry upon new trade routes gave them a greater diversity of interests and a consequent spreading of risks. These developments reflected wisdom in management and were effective in promoting the growth of the firm. They are basic to an understanding of the firm's relative strength during the difficult years of the 1920s and 1930s.

It is obvious that in treating the subject matter as an exercise in decision-taking this study requires something more than a purely historical technique though, in fact, this technique is a major element in construction. The supplementary tools of accountancy, economic and statistical analysis have been used wherever possible to give depth and perspective. In short, this is a business history more in the nature of a case study than a chronological description of events. It is, as the title suggests, rather more than the history of a single firm; the magnitude of the achievement is much wider; comprehending, by implication, much that is best in the story of Liverpool's shipping enterprise.

PART ONE

Creation of a Shipping Line
1830 - 1910

Margaret and *Mariote*

CHAPTER ONE

The Pattern of Partnership 1830 - 84

I

THE year 1812 can, perhaps, be given as the date on which the Harrison history had its mainspring. In that year two marriages took place; the one at Cockerham in Lancashire where James Harrison, farmer and landowner, of Garstang, married Ann Hodgson,[1] and the other in Verdun where Richard Williamson, mariner, of Scarborough, and at that time a prisoner of war, married Lucie Pierre, daughter of a local locksmith.[2] The future was to see the descendants from these two marriages brought together by a common interest in shipping. The qualities which the Williamsons undoubtedly possessed as mariners when added to the business acumen which the Harrisons assuredly had as shipowners, proved to be a formidable and a highly successful combination. It was this conjunction which provided the source of initiative and enterprise and so led, through a complex structure of partnerships, to the promotion of a world-wide shipping business. The present firm of T. and J. Harrison of Liverpool is the inheritor of a long tradition of skill in seamanship, wisdom in the use of financial resources and objective service in the management of ships; it is a tradition which is the essence of past experience, not least from that of the lives which sprang from the two marriages in 1812.

James Harrison and his wife Ann had six sons and two daughters.[3] Of the five surviving sons four left the countryside of their upbringing for the warehouses and wharves of Liverpool. The eldest son Richard

1. Lancashire Record Office. L.59 Cockerham. The marriage took place on 22 December 1812; James was aged 31, Ann was 26.
2. Tonnay-Charente MSS., Extrait des Registres des Actes de l'État-Civil, 30 September 1812.
3. Harrison MSS. Harrison genealogy, one son James, died in infancy: the two daughters were Anne and Alice.

(1813–62) was apprenticed to a firm of shipbrokers and, by 1837, was apparently established in that occupation on his own account. Thomas (1815–88) was apprenticed to the shipbroking firm of Samuel Brown and Son in 1830 and became a full partner in the firm of Samuel Brown, Son and Company in 1839[1]; by 1841 the style of this firm had been changed to George Brown and Harrison.[2] Thomas's obvious success undoubtedly persuaded his father to allow his third son James (1821–91) to join his brother in Liverpool where he was apprenticed to the same firm in 1838. James, in turn, became a partner in 1849. Edward Hodgson (1825–1907) the youngest son, was apprenticed to a Liverpool firm in 1840,[3] possibly Wright, Crossley and Co., though there is no actual record of this. It is clear, however, that by 1844 he was acting as a general broker and, in the following year, had become part owner with his brother James and with Richard Williamson in a ship the *Charles Souchay*. The fifth son John (1819–67) remained at home and eventually took over the management of the farm from his father.

This migration of the four Harrison sons to Liverpool was part of a general process of attraction. It had its parallel in other families. The Brocklebanks came from Whitehaven, the Ismays from Maryport, and the Inmans from Silverdale. Such names are more than adequate testimony to the inducements which the growing port of Liverpool offered to young and adventurous spirits who wished to seek their fortunes in the business of shipping. As far as the Harrison brothers were concerned, there was the added incentive that the family farm-lands could neither have provided for, nor could have contained, the prospective ambition of five sons.

The partners Samuel Brown and his son George, had become established in Liverpool by the year 1820 as merchants, shipbrokers and agents.[4] In 1827 the style of their firm was changed from Samuel Brown and Son to Samuel Brown, Son and Company.[5] This change, was simply the outward indication that a new partner, Henry Smith,

1. Liverpool Statutory Registers of Merchant Ships 1839. The entries for this year show that ships in the Charente trade were being consigned to George Brown and Harrison.
2. ibid., 1841: *Gore's Liverpool Directory*, 1841.
3. Harrison MSS., E. H. Harrison's cash book pp. 1-2.
4. *Gore's Liverpool Directory* 1820.
5. ibid., 1827.

merchant of Liverpool had joined the firm.[1] After Samuel's death in 1841, George Brown continued the partnership with Thomas, and later admitted James. It was by virtue of this association with the Browns that the Harrison brothers were brought into contact with the Williamsons. In the absence of any precise family records it has been possible to discover the nature of the early relationship between the Browns, the Harrisons and the Williamsons only through an analysis of the Liverpool and Scarborough Shipping Registers and Bills of Entry. These show that in 1800 Thomas Williamson of Filey owned the ship *Eagle*.[2] This vessel was under the command of Richard Williamson and, in 1804, was captured by the French,[3] Richard and his son of 17 (also named Richard) being taken prisoners and confined in the *depôt* at Verdun[4]. Eight years later, as we have already seen, Richard now aged twenty-five married Lucie Pierre. In the following year their only child Richard Pierre Williamson was born.[5] A year later, the war over, the Williamsons were back in Scarborough and Richard Williamson senior had renewed his former interest in shipowning, whilst his son Richard Williamson junior acted as mate, and eventually as master, of his father's vessels. Their first joint venture was with *Jubilee*, a square sterned Brigantine of 101 tons. This ship, built in 1814, was under the ownership of John Hovington (who was, until 1817, her master) and of Richard Williamson and Cornelius Glaves,[6] a Scarborough farmer. It was through this ship that the Williamson connection with Liverpool began, for in 1820, there is a record of four ships, among them *Jubilee*, having entered Liverpool with cargoes of brandy from Charente.[7] The *Jubilee*'s cargo was consigned to Samuel Brown and Company. Here, then, is the first real evidence of association between the Williamsons and the Browns.

Although the entry in 1820 suggests that the relationship was simply that of master mariner and agent, it was not long before this relationship was strengthened through the financial bonds of co-ownership.

1. ibid., 1830.
2. Scarborough Statutory Registers of Merchant Ships 1800, entry no. 36. *Eagle* was a square sterned Brigantine built at Scarborough 1793.
3. ibid.
4. Tonnay-Charente MSS., Extrait des Registres, loc. cit.
5. Tonnay-Charente MSS. 2 March 1813.
6. Scarborough Statutory Registers of Merchant Ships 1814, entry no. 8.
7. Liverpool Bills of Entry 1820.

In 1823, Samuel and George Brown, the Williamsons, father and son, and Cornelius Glaves joined together in purchasing the *Margaret*.[1] On his father's death in 1826, Richard Williamson junior, who had established himself in Liverpool, joined Henry Smith in buying out the Browns' interest.[2] As we have already seen, Henry Smith became a partner in Samuel Brown and Son sometime during 1827 but Richard Williamson had already had some experience of Smith's business ability before their joint interest in the *Margaret;* in 1825 they had been co-owners in the *Mariote*,[3] a ship which they successfully engaged in the Charente brandy trade and the Oporto wine trade until 1837. Thus, by the middle of the 1820s, the Browns and their partner Henry Smith were concerned either as agents or as co-owners with at least three Williamson ships. This was a sufficiently powerful inducement to attract the Williamsons to the port of Liverpool. Thereafter, it was but a matter of time before this connexion expanded into a fuller partnership between Richard Williamson and the Browns' two young associates Thomas and James Harrison.

II

The somewhat haphazard connexion between the brothers, Thomas and James Harrison in association with Samuel and George Brown on the one hand, and with Richard Williamson on the other, assumes a more precise relationship after 1840. The activities of these men before that date were so inextricably intermingled, either through their joint investment in ships or through their operational and managerial functions, that it is extremely difficult to obtain a clear and concise picture of the growth of their various individual interests. The key to a better understanding of the multifarious pattern of association is to

1. Liverpool Statutory Registers of Merchant Ships 1823, entry no. 51. 18 June 1823.

2. ibid., *Margaret* was re-registered on 2 May 1826 in the names of Henry Smith, shipbroker, Richard Williamson, Thomas Herbert, shipowner and Hannah Williamson, widow. The two latter were executor and executrix of Richard Williamson the elder.

3. ibid., 1825, entry no. 213. 5 September 1825. Richard Williamson held 43 and Henry Smith 21 shares.

be found in their common enterprise to develop the Charente brandy trade with Liverpool. The organization of this trade became more clearly defined after Thomas Harrison had entered into partnership with George Brown in 1839. Henceforth, the inter-connecting threads of enterprise became more closely identified with the firm of Brown and Harrison in Liverpool and in Charente with Richard Williamson the second (who had re-married and settled there in the early 1830s) and his son Richard Pierre Williamson. The difference in function was that Brown and Harrison acted largely in their capacity as managers and ships' husbands, whereas the Williamsons acted as agents and masters of the ships under joint investment.

The build-up of the association between Thomas Harrison and Richard Williamson started in 1836 with joint investment in the Jane[1] and the Tom Tough.[2] There is every indication that this simultaneous investment in vessels in the same trade was no chance speculation, but a deliberate association of resources for the purpose of expanding what had hitherto proved to be a lucrative trade. In the following year, 1837, Harrison and Williamson made a further investment in the Crescent,[3] but Harrison's interest in this vessel was short-lived, his elder brother Richard taking over his share in August of the same year.[4] Thus, with this vessel the Harrisons may be said to have embarked, as a family, on the business of ship-owning. It must be borne in mind, however, that though these investments were made in association, they were individual in character and not made under partnership.

James Harrison joined his brothers as a shipowner in 1842, having been previously employed, since 1839, with Brown and Harrison in the ship-broking side of the business. He took over eleven shares in the Tom Tough[5] in January 1842 and, in July of the same year, jointly with his brother Richard, acquired a share in the Jane[6].

1. Jane was laid down at Shields in 1833 and was of 115 tons gross burthen.
2. Thomas Harrison bought a one-third share in this vessel.
3. Crescent was a 93 ton vessel built at Plymouth. Harrison purchased a one-third interest in her.
4. This investment had a somewhat fluctuating ownership; Richard Harrison sold his interest to Richard Williamson in 1842, but repurchased 16 shares from Williamson in 1858.
5. Liverpool Statutory Register of Merchant Ships. Entry no. 103. 1830. Bill of Sale 18 January 1842.
6. ibid., 1836, entry no. 227. Bill of Sale 29 July 1842.

The final purchase in this period was that of the Nova Scotia-built brig of 160 tons, *Sir Colin Campbell*, in which Thomas Harrison owned 16, Richard 24 and Richard Williamson 24 shares[1]. Thus, between 1836 and 1842, the Harrisons' shipping investments were confined to four small ships[2], all of which were engaged in the Charente brandy trade to Liverpool and, on occasion, in the Lisbon wine trade. In all these ships Richard Williamson was a co-investor with the Harrisons; he was, in fact, the majority owner during the greater part of this time, but by the end of 1842 the Harrison brothers had increased their share of the investment to something less than fifty per cent of the total. In general, however, Williamson can be said to have been the major partner if participation in the trade as a whole is taken into account. He was frequently master of the ships and his wide knowledge of the Charente trade was as much a prime asset as his capital investment.

The structure of the Liverpool-Charente trade was extremely simple. It consisted of coal and limited quantities of Scottish iron products outwards from Liverpool, Whitehaven, Shields and Ardrossan, and homewards from Charente with brandy and occasionally with Portuguese and Spanish wines from Oporto and Cadiz.

The demand for British coal was increasing and there were occasions on which outward voyages were made with coal cargoes to French West Coast ports without any counterbalancing return cargo of brandy. On the whole, arrivals of brandy cargoes in Liverpool were spread throughout the year, but were not so frequent in late winter and early spring.

Some illuminating details about the working of this trade come from the pen of Richard Pierre Williamson, who compiled a notebook from ships' logs and diaries written during two decades of seafaring life. It was from Charente that he took over the command of the brig *Tom Tough*.[3] His notebook makes it clear that while the carriage of coal and brandy were the staples of the trade, other voyages were made

1. ibid., 1839 entry no. 4.
2. There was a fifth ship *Euphemia* bought in 1838 by Thomas Harrison and Richard Williamson. This ship was lost in 1840.
3. Tonnay-Charente MSS., R. P. Williamson, 'Names of Ships I have commanded and ports that I have been at'. (Hereafter cited R. P. Williamson Notebook I). 1 June 1834.

to ports in Western France, Oporto and Cadiz[1] as and when opportunity occurred. Sometimes the Charente ships were sent to the Baltic and there is one entry in 1837 recording Richard Pierre in charge of the *Jane* sailing on a charter voyage to Messina, thence by charter to Leith. From Leith he was despatched by his owners to Aricate in North West Brazil, and from there to Ceara, bringing back cotton and hides. This cargo proved to be profitable and he was thereupon ordered to sail to Pernambuco and return with a similar consignment.[2]

When brandy cargoes were scarce in Charente he would sometimes sail to Swansea in ballast to pick up coal or, alternatively, with cargoes of grain from Charente and Lucon to Liverpool.[3] The relevant fact about these details from Richard Pierre's notebook is that while the Williamsons continued to be mainly engrossed in the trade from Charente, the Harrisons, with a more dominant interest in extending the range of their shipping activities, were seeking to employ their capital on new routes and new trades in more distant parts of the world. After 1842, this divergence of interest became more marked though Richard Pierre continued, as a master of the Harrison ships, to maintain an operating link between the two families.

There is much additional and, very often, interesting information in Richard Pierre's notebook which helps one to assess the courage and the character of the man himself. There is considerable detail about the length of voyages, of seamanship under adverse conditions of wind and tide, of the hazards of lying up in fog and, by implication, of his own skill as a master.[4] There are also references of a more personal nature. After his marriage to Jane Allen of Ormskirk in 1836, his wife accompanied him on board ship. 'Sailed for Whitehaven', he wrote, 'took Mistress with me to commence a sailor's life'.[5] For some years his wife seems to have led a peripatetic existence, but after 1845 she settled near Ormskirk making only occasional voyages with her husband, ending with a trip round the world in the *Admiral Grenfell* in 1857–8.

The reference to *Admiral Grenfell* brings us to the last chapter of

1. Tonnay-Charente MSS., R. P. Williamson Notebook I.
2. ibid., 20 June 1838.
3. ibid., 20 September 1841.
4. ibid., R. P. Williamson, Notebook I., 1839–40, *passim*.
5. ibid., 9 November 1836. They were married on 1 November 1836, Richard Pierre being 23 years of age and his bride 19.

Richard Pierre's seafaring life as well as to a change in the emphasis of Harrisons' ship-owning activities. Richard took over this ship (a large barque) in 1854. He did so in order to accommodate the Harrisons who, having bought her, discovered that the master they had engaged had deserted to another command. The ship had been intended to augment Harrisons' growing trans-oceanic connections: and Richard's first voyage in her was to Pernambuco and Paraiba ('a duce of a place for sand flies') to load cotton and other Brazilian products homewards to Europe. The Crimean War, however, was in process of diverting British shipping tonnage from peace-time trade routes, and Harrisons, in conjunction with many other shipowners, found it highly profitable to charter their vessels to the allied governments for the purpose of carrying war supplies. On her return from Brazil the *Admiral Grenfell* was chartered to the Sardinian government and sailed for the Crimea where, on arrival in Balaclava harbour, she found other Harrison ships unloading war cargoes. Such war-time employment was short-lived and, when charters ceased, the *Admiral Grenfell* sailed for Guatemala and thence to Shanghai. From this port she went to Quinsan where she loaded alum for Hong Kong. Richard records that they left Hong Kong with a cargo of sugar and cask wine and, after a stormy passage reached Shanghai again on 25 July 1857.[1]

After discharging this cargo the ship loaded homewards for Liverpool with a cargo of tea. Her arrival at the Albert Dock on 27 March 1858 marked the end of Richard Pierre's life at sea, apart from a short voyage to Havre where the *Admiral Grenfell*, which had been sold on her return to Liverpool, was handed over to new owners. Thereafter he, his wife and family joined his father and settled in Tonnay Charente.[2]

III

We must now return, if not in time, at least in subject matter, to the

1. ibid., R. P. Williamson, Notebook II 25 July 1857. It was while the ship was off the Barren Isles, on the way to Shanghai that Richard Pierre's wife gave birth to her fifth child, a son, who was appropriately christened Grenfell.
2. ibid., 9 October 1858.

Charente trade. In attempting to assess the primary causes of Harrisons' overseas interests, it cannot be sufficiently emphasized that these interests stemmed from the dichotomy of function between the Williamsons in Charente and the Harrisons in Liverpool. Having established that fact, however, it is equally true that the early development of overseas trade was materially influenced by changes in the pattern and operation of the Charente brandy, and Lisbon and Cadiz wine trades. The change was partly accelerated by technological factors and, consequently, by a sharpening of competition in the structure of the brandy trade itself; for, when, in the 1860s steam power was applied to the Charente ships, there was a quickening in the rivalry between Liverpool, as represented by Harrisons, and London, as represented by the General Steam Navigation Company. The outcome of this struggle had a direct bearing on Harrisons' decision to widen the scope of their shipping activities and to establish services to India, the Gulf, the West Indies, Brazil and Mexico.

The early history of the application of steam power to ships has been reasonably well covered and documented. Similarly the assessment of the economic advantages of steamships over sailing vessels has been treated exhaustively. The low ratio of power to weight and bulk in the early steamships reduced their range and profitability; they were, therefore, only acceptable as an innovation in the short distance and coastal trades. As cargo carriers they could operate successfully only if coaling facilities were available; very often they would not have been able to maintain cargo services at all had it not been for the additional income from the carriage of passengers and mails, the latter being subject to contract and subsidization. Not until the steamship had been given a more powerful and a more economical engine (thus giving greater hold space for cargo rather than fuel) could it compete on favourable terms with the sailing ship over the sea routes of the world.

It was in 1860 that Harrisons made their first experiment with steamships, though there was nothing reckless in this innovation. Their early ventures were tried out in the trade in which they had most experience, namely, the Charente trade. This particular trade was not beyond the proved capacity of the early steamship; the west coast of France was only a few days steaming from the western ports of Britain where, as we have seen, coal cargoes were loaded for carriage to Charente, Lisbon and Cadiz. There was, therefore, no difficulty in obtaining good bunker coal at low rates. Furthermore, the distances steamed were such that coal bunkers would not make inroads on cargo carrying space. In short, the earning space of the ship was not too seriously restricted and, consequently, the voyages could be made with a reasonable certainty of returning a profit.

The decision of the Harrisons to employ steamships in the Charente trade was undoubtedly influenced by two main considerations. In the first place, the signing of the Cobden-Chevalier Treaty and the Gladstonian Budgets of 1860 and 1861, led to a simplification of the tariff structures of France and Britain, and included a *quid pro quo* in the form of reduced duties on French wines and spirits in return for a promise that the British government would not prohibit or tax the export of coal.[1] This was an obvious incentive to expansion in the staples of the Charente trade. In the second place, the fact that the Williamsons, father and son, were now settled in Charente was influential in bringing Harrisons to a decision to develop the trade more energetically. The Williamsons' experience of the port and its traffic over many years, together with their connections by marriage and their commercial links with many of the most powerful members of the Charente business community, were essential elements in the process of promotion and expansion. As part of this process it seemed to be logical that the new steamships should not only maintain the Liverpool-Charente service, but that London should henceforth be included as a regular port of discharge for brandy cargoes. Richard Pierre Williamson had occasionally called in at London during the 1840s and early 1850s without opposition from London-based firms engaged in the trade. When, therefore, Harrisons took possession of their first steam ship, *Cognac*, in December 1860[2] there was every prospect that the Charente-London trade would augment the existing trade and add to the profitability of the venture as a whole. At first, these expectations were realised. The *Cognac* was an undoubted success and, on the basis of this success, Harrisons and Williamsons decided to start a direct line

1. F. E. Hyde, *Mr. Gladstone at the Board of Trade (1934)* p. 219; J. H. Clapham, *An Economic History of Modern Britain; Free Trade and Steel 1850-1886*, (1952), p. 245.

2. Liverpool Statutory Registers of Merchant Ships, 1860, entry no. 258. The *Cognac* was an iron-screw steamer of 376 tons whose two engines developed 70 h.p. She was also schooner-rigged for sail. The ownership in this vessel established a new pattern, Harrisons taking three quarters and Richard Pierre Williamson one quarter.

Jane (1836)

between Charente and London. To do so they acquired, in April 1862, two new steamships, the *Dragon*, an almost new ship bought from a Liverpool shipowner,[1] and the *Charente* built to order in Sunderland.[2] Their London agents were Temperleys, Carter and Darke and their loading brokers in Charente were V. Renault et Cie.

The initial hopes and bright prospects which had prompted the establishment of this new line were, however, short-lived. Harrisons began to meet with opposition from other London shipping firms the most important of which was the General Steam Navigation Company. This latter company had been founded as early as 1824 and had built up a fleet of steamships linking London with the major French ports and engaging in the brandy and wine trades. During the 1840s and 1850s, relations between Harrisons and the General Steam Navigation Company had been amicable, the occasional brandy cargoes taken by Harrisons into London being too small to affect the competitive pattern of the trade. With the advent of rival steamships in the Thames, however, the General Steam Navigation company was forced into measures of retaliation. Harrisons had originally decided to fix a rate of 25s. per ton with 10 per cent primage,[3] a lower rate than General Steam Navigation had been charging. This was not intended as a deliberate provocation though it was represented as such[4] and, in the final event, Harrisons were persuaded to put their ships on the berth at the same rates as their competitors. This was an unfortunate beginning; it aroused the suspicion of the London company and was the prelude to a rate-cutting war.[5] The financial aspect of rate-cutting was a new, and a very unpleasant experience for Harrisons; there was even greater annoyance and damage to follow. Opposition by the General Steam Navigation Company also took the form of putting their vessels on berth for Liverpool, Dublin and Glasgow at comparable rates, thus returning the blow which Harrisons had given them, by attacking the Liverpool firm in their established markets. Harrisons might have been prepared to fight such a battle on two fronts had they been confident of success in their new London-

1. ibid., 1862, entry no. 79. *Dragon* was 252 tons.
2. ibid., 1862, entry no. 84. *Charente* was 450 tons.
3. Tonnay-Charente MSS., Correspondence, T. and J. Harrison to V. Renault et Cie, 30 April 1862.
4. ibid., also memo. from Temperleys, Carter and Darke, 19 June 1862.
5. ibid., Messrs. Martell and Co. to T. and J. Harrison, 23 February 1863.

Charente service; but the London connection was not yet strong enough and when, in 1863, the established shippers Martells and Hennessys refused to give them the preference over the General Steam Navigation Company, the struggle assumed unequal proportions. It had become obvious that the London merchants preferred to maintain business relations with a large joint stock company providing a permanent and reliable service, rather than entrust their cargoes to a smaller company which was attempting, with only three steamers, to serve both the Liverpool and the London trades.[1]

In January 1863, James Harrison, on his way to Italy on holiday, made a detour to Charente for the express purpose of consulting with the principal brandy shippers, in particular, Hennessys and Martells. The ensuing discussions were effective in bringing Harrisons to the decision to abandon the London-Charente trade. In the following month Harrisons wrote to Martells expressing the view that the fluctuations in the trade caused by the intense competition, were damaging to all concerned and that, in consequence, they were prepared to withdraw their regular sailings to London.[2] Notice was sent to the agents of the General Steam Navigation Company, that while they would retain their right to send ships to London, they would not open any further charters to that port from Tonnay-Charente.[3] Furthermore, it was clearly understood by both sides that if Harrisons withdrew from the English Channel route to London, General Steam would withdraw from the Irish Channel route to Liverpool, Glasgow and Dublin.[4]

This was, undoubtedly, a severe setback to Harrisons' hopes of expansion in the Charente brandy trade. They were bitterly disappointed that the most influential shippers had refused to co-operate with them. A somewhat critical, though non-recriminatory re-examination of events revealed the unpalatable fact that their commercial organization was not as well managed as their shipping organization. Richard Pierre Williamson may not have been so energetic as an agent as he had been as a ship's master in promoting

1. ibid., T. and J. Harrison to Messrs. Martell and Co., 18 February 1863.
2. ibid.
3. ibid., T. and J. Harrison to Messrs. C. and A. Hackett and Asender 2 February 1863.
4. ibid., Messrs. C. and A. Hackett to T. and J. Harrison 30 January 1863.

Tom Tough (1829)

the interests of the firm.[1] Whatever may have been the ultimate assessment, it is true that this whole episode marked yet another turning point in the relationship between the Harrisons and the Williamsons and gave impetus to the alternative schemes of expansion involving the search for, and the development of, markets in other parts of the world.

In the short term, however, the trade with Charente and with the Spanish and Portuguese ports had to be maintained and wherever possible increased[2] but, even so, the three new steamships were underemployed. To offset this they were despatched to Spanish and Portuguese ports to bring back cargoes of wine. At the same time Harrisons made determined attempts to strengthen the commercial side of this business, first, by making arrangements to obtain accurate details of wine shipments from Cadiz;[3] secondly, by canvassing support among Liverpool wine merchants in the hope that they would persuade Spanish exporters to load on Harrison ships;[4] and thirdly by promising to institute more or less regular sailings from Cadiz.[5] They also conducted negotiations with Sandbach, Tinne and Co., (considerable exporters of brandy to Demerara) with the object of fixing favourable freight rates which would allow Harrisons' sailing ships to compete with London-based steamship companies in the carriage of brandy from Liverpool to Demerara.[6] Finally, Harrisons made a brief entry into the Mediterranean fruit trade, a somewhat fortuitous, though not entirely unsuccessful interlude in the mid 1860s, in their endeavour to maintain full holds and return a profit on the voyages.[7]

Of the efforts outlined above, the attempt by Harrisons to expand

1. ibid., fragments of letters from Messrs. Martell to Messrs. Lockett dated 17 and 20 January 1863. 'We are peculiarly unfortunately situated in having such a poor agent as Williamson.'

2. Calls at Charente were as follows: eight in 1862, eleven in 1863, twenty in 1865 and, thereafter, with a degree of fluctuation until the peak year of 1873 when twenty five calls were made. By 1884, the trade had fallen off considerably, under a dozen calls a year being normally made.

3. Harrison MSS., J. de Cuvillo et alia, notices concerning wine trade 15 and 17 May 1864.

4. ibid., September 1864.

5. Harrison MSS., Liverpool importers to T. and J. Harrison, 13 November 1863.

6. ibid., Sandbach Tinne and Co. to T. and J. Harrison, 5 April 1872.

7. ibid., G. F. Woodley to T. and J. Harrison, 23 June 1866.

their connections in the Spanish and Portuguese wine trades was the most important. At first, their enterprise met with success, the number of calls at Cadiz rising from one in 1862 to sixteen in 1865.[1] Occasional calls were also made at Cartagena, Malaga, Taragona, Vigo, Villa-real and Pomeron, the ships moving from port to port as cargoes, or the prospect of cargoes, dictated.[2] Unfortunately, however, the initial burst of activity was not maintained. The Cadiz trade declined after 1865 and ended altogether ten years later.[3] The trade with the other ports was never really established and, after a spasmodic increase in the mid-1870s, calls at these ports virtually ceased. The explanation of this unhappy sequence of events is to be found not so much in Harrisons' failure to establish a closely-knit commercial organisation, as in the retaliatory measures imposed by the Spanish government following the Cobden-Chevalier Treaty. Henceforth, Harrisons' main trade with the Iberian Peninsula was *via* Lisbon. There was, however, a change of emphasis; by the latter half of the 1870s Lisbon had become a port of call in Harrisons' growing overseas trade with Latin America rather than a focus for the wine trades along the coasts of Europe.

The turn of these events was not without effect on the technological aspects of the change from sail to steam in the Harrison fleet as a whole. The brothers Harrison did not see eye to eye on the question of the relative merits of steam over sail.[4] Thomas, remembering the advantages to be obtained from stout clipper-type ships, clung persistently to a belief in the potentialities of the sailing ship. His judgement was confirmed by many a successful record; *Admiral Grenfell*, for example, had sailed a distance of 242 miles in one day and the *Lightning* (before she came under Harrison ownership) had logged 463 miles in a single day.[5] James on the other hand, saw the possibility of commercial advantage in the employment of steamships on long overseas voyages. In the end, this latter opinion prevailed though, during the 1860s and 1870s the Harrison fleet was composed of both sailing ships and steamships. The first small steamships engaged in the brandy and wine trades were, perhaps, in a class by themselves. Of approximately 400 tons

1. Harrison MSS., Voyage books, 1862–65.
2. ibid.
3. ibid., 1865–75.
4. Harrison MSS., Memo. by James Harrison 1863.
5. Brian Watson Hughes, *One Hundred Years of Progress* (1953), p. 11. *Lightning* was purchased from the Black Ball Line in 1865.

gross they were admirably suited for the confined harbours, and sometimes the winding river courses, of the European wine ports. The exigencies of the trade, however, demanded constant improvement in the structure and design of the ship. By 1864, the *Charente* had been replaced by the *Gladiator*[1] and, when the *Dragon* was sold in 1866, she was replaced by the *Chrysolite*.[2] These two ships of improved design were not only suitable for the brandy and wine trades, but were also, by reason of greater motive power, capable of making transatlantic voyages to Pernambuco and New Orleans. Conversely, the slightly larger vessels such as the *Alice, Amazon* and *Olinda* which were intended for oceanic trades, were not too large to make the odd voyage to Charente and Spanish ports.

Thus, through the impact of political and economic factors the Harrison fleet was transformed and, as a result, the activities of the two brothers were translated from that of coasting in the narrow seas to the wider horizons of oceanic trades. In this process, the close links which, for so many years, had bound the Williamsons and the Harrisons together were severed. Apart from continuing joint interests in the Charente trade, the direction of investment and the control of policy had now passed into the hands of the Harrison brothers.

IV

Although we have so far described the varied relationships between the Harrison brothers and the Williamsons as partnerships, it must be made clear that this designation is not exact either in practice or in terminology. The individual investment of each brother, though made in association, was not in any strict sense in the form of a partnership. In the early years, their interest in ships was widely spread; in fact, there were few occasions when all the brothers were joint owners in a particular ship. Richard Williamson, on the other hand, was their fellow investor in their first five ships and continued to be so at least until 1845. Thereafter, the pattern of ownership changed and, as the Harrisons' capital increased, the control of the Williamsons

1. Liverpool Statutory Registers of Merchant Ships 1864, entry no. 395.
2. ibid., 1867, entry no. 132.

c

diminished and the partnership in all the ships became more tightly knit as a Harrison family business.

After the death of George Brown and the establishment of the firm of T. and J. Harrison in 1853, the process of concentrating capital into fewer hands, and preferably into those of the family or their close connections, was accentuated. It would, perhaps, be an untrue definition of what happened, to say that this process was part of a conscious policy. Many changes in the pattern of ownership were brought about either through the deaths of former associates, or by the reluctance of shareholders in the earlier sailing ships to re-invest their capital in steamships. The family interest itself was confined during the 1860s, through the death of Richard in 1862 and that of John in 1867, to the three surviving brothers, Thomas, James and Edward Hodgson. From the late 1860s, therefore, a fairly regular pattern of ownership emerges, in which a relatively small group of shareholders owned a consistent number of shares in each ship. An analysis of the entries in the Liverpool Statutory Registers of Merchant Ships confirms this.[1] As one might expect, the chief shareholders were Thomas and James, the former normally holding 22 shares, the latter 20; their younger brother Edward Hodgson usually held 8 shares and Richard Pierre Williamson 6; while for a few years after 1867 James and Edward jointly held shares as trustees under the will of their brother John. Thus before the foundation of the Charente Steam-Ship Company in 1871, practically all the shares in the ships had been concentrated into the hands of four men.

There is, however, a slight exception to the above statement. A new name, that of John William Hughes, begins to appear in the list of shareholders from 1866 onwards. In that year he held, under the title of 'book keeper' two shares in *Fire Queen*[2] and, in the following year, two shares in *Pantheon*.[3] Hughes continued this process of accumulating a relatively small number of shares in successive ships until 1884 when the capital of the Charente Steam-Ship Company was reorganised within the terms of a limited company. Previous to this,

1. Liverpool Statutory Registers of Merchant Ships. Entries for the years 1867-71 inclusive, for all ships in which the Harrison brothers had an interest.

2. ibid., 1866, entry no. 73. *Fire Queen* was built at Middleton, near West Hartlepool in 1864.

3. ibid., 1867, entry no. 81. *Pantheon* was built at Preston in 1867 and was lost on the Bar of the Mississippi River March 1869.

in 1871, Hughes purchased shares to the value of £6,750 being three sixty-fourths of a total capital of £144,000.[1] By July 1874, the loan securing these shares, together with the interest, had been paid off; the dividends on these shares were an undoubted asset in enabling Hughes to complete the purchase.[2] This admission of John William Hughes into the firm was an earnest of the high regard which the brothers Thomas and James Harrison held for him. The small amount of extant correspondence between Hughes and his principals shows that the relationship was increasingly one of equality and, indeed, of affection. The bond between James Harrison and Hughes seems to have been particularly strong. In August 1874 Hughes purchased a further £17,500 worth of shares or three sixty-fourths, of a capital approximating £375,000. The difference in the price of a three sixty-fourths share between 1871 and 1874 indicates the measure by which the capital of the firm had appreciated during these years. It is perhaps interesting to note that these two purchases were made by Hughes from James and Edward Hodgson Harrison in their capacity as trustees under the will of their brother John.

An explanation of the practical method by which John William Hughes increased his financial interest in the Charente Steam-Ship Company affords a further illustration of the confidence which the Harrisons had in his ability. He was allowed to purchase shares under a number of successive agreements whereby deferred payments could be made in amounts of a minimum denomination and within specified periods of time.[3] This same facility was offered to John William's younger brother Thomas who first entered the firm as a paid official but, during the 1870s, acquired shares and ultimately became a partner.[4] Thomas's first purchase of shares amounting to two sixty-fourths, were bought from the executors of the estate of Richard Pierre Williamson who died in 1874. Captain R. R. Williamson and Thomas Williamson, sons of Richard Pierre, retained one share each after their father's death and, through this inheritance, the Williamson connection was maintained.

The generous encouragement given by Thomas and James Harrison

1. Harrison MSS., Memoranda by John William Hughes, 1870-80.
2. ibid.
3. ibid.
4. Harrison MSS., James Harrison to Thomas Hughes, 17 July 1888. Thomas became a partner in 1888.

to the Hughes brothers was more than fully justified by events. By 1879 it had become necessary to establish a more clearly defined policy determining the relationship between the ownership of the vessels, collectively operated within the framework of the Charente Steam-Ship Company, and their management by the firm of Thomas and James Harrison. The correspondence between James Harrison and John William Hughes (1879–81) makes it clear that commissions were being paid by the shareholders to a small group of Harrison Managers and that, included in this group, was John William Hughes.[1] With the virtual retirement of James Harrison after 1880 and the uncertain state of health of his brother Thomas, however, the active control of daily business passed into the hands of younger men of whom Frederick James Harrison and John William Hughes were the two acknowledged leaders. The organisation of the Charente Steam-Ship Company as a limited company in 1884 was the final act in a carefully prepared scheme by which the two founders of the firm could hand on control of their life work to those in whom they had implicit trust and who, by their proven ability, would be reasonably certain of making the most profitable use of the not inconsiderable resources entrusted to them.[2] The control was both simple and effective. The ownership was vested in the hands of subscribers (the holders of the shares in the ships) under the title of the Charente Steam-Ship Company Ltd.; the management of the ships was undertaken by the private company T. and J. Harrison.

Thus, over a period of fifty years, the inter-connected pattern of ownership between the Williamsons and the Browns, between the Browns and the Harrisons and, eventually, between the Harrisons and the Hughes was given shape, direction and purpose. From the relatively simple structure of trade between Liverpool, Charente and other European ports, the shipping activities of these men had grown outwards to embrace the whole world. The coincidence of two

1. Harrison MSS., James Harrison to John William Hughes, 4 December 1879; ibid., 6 January 1880. The Managers were Thomas Harrison and Fenwick Edwards (Thomas's son-in-law), James Harrison and his son Frederick James and John William Hughes.

2. *Memorandum and Articles of Association of the Charente Steam-Ship Company Ltd.* 16 December 1884. The subscribers were Thomas Harrison, T. F. Harrison, Fred. J. Harrison, Heath Harrison, Edward Hodgson Harrison, John W. Hughes, Thomas Hughes, Thomas Williamson and R. R. Williamson.

Fire Queen, bought by Harrisons in 1866

marriages in 1812 and the conjunction of the descendants from these marriages were pre-requisite to a chain of events which had profound economic significance for this, and many other countries. It must now be our purpose, through the development of the narrative, to examine and analyse the consequential sources of power and enterprise which were generated by a few able men linked together by family ties and activated by a common interest.

CHAPTER TWO

The Organization of the Oceanic Trades: New Orleans and Calcutta

I

ON 8 July 1866, Harrisons inaugurated their liner service between Liverpool and New Orleans, the ships on this route operating under the title of the Southern Line.[1] As we have already seen, Harrison ships had, on many previous occasions, made transatlantic crossings to Brazil, the West Indies and Gulf ports. It is probable that frequent calls were made at New Orleans before 1866, but the records do not provide any clear evidence in substantiation apart from a few entries which show that the *City of Lincoln* loaded cotton there in 1848, 1849 and 1850.[2] It is known that *Gladiator* (before her acquisition by Harrisons in 1864) had made several voyages to Mobile, Charleston and Wilmington. Her first voyage to New Orleans, under Harrison management, was made at the end of 1866.[3] Before that date, however, the first ship of the new service, *Fire Queen*, had completed the first round voyage arriving back in Liverpool from New Orleans on 18 September 1866.[4] The decision of the Harrison brothers to start this service was, without doubt, prompted by the urgent need to supply Lancashire cotton mills, following the dislocation of their supplies of raw material both during and after the Civil War.[5]

The trade between Liverpool and New Orleans proved to be highly successful. The firm of Lucas E. Moore and Co., listed in the New Orleans *Directory* of 1877 as Commission Merchants, acted as Harrisons'

1. Harrison MSS., Shipping notice giving details of New Orleans service dated 1867.
2. ibid., Voyage books 1848, 1849, 1850.
3. ibid., 1866-7.
4. ibid., 1866.
5. W. O. Henderson, *The Lancashire Cotton Famine* (1934). •

agents. Within a few years, however, the rapid growth of the trade and the increasing complexity of business operations required the attention of a direct representative from the Head Office. The man chosen for this post was Alfred Le Blanc Smith (who changed his name to Alfred Le Blanc in 1874).[1] Le Blanc was a cousin of Frederick James Harrison and the son of Charles Tunstall Smith, vicar of Wirksworth. After leaving Haileybury he was apprenticed to the cotton and shipping firm of Leech, Harrison and Forwood[2] in 1872. Le Blanc was acknowledged as a man of great ability and industry.[3] Within a very short time after his arrival in New Orleans in 1877, he had successfully established Harrisons' United States office and had become Agent-General of the Southern States. For a few years, however, he worked in collaboration with Harrisons' original agent, Lucas E. Moore. The increasing demand for raw cotton led to a rapid expansion of business not only in New Orleans (where, by 1885, Le Blanc was negotiating for the purchase of land on which to build a wharf for Harrison ships)[4] but also in the rival Texan port of Galveston. Le Blanc, therefore, appointed William Parr and Co., as agents for the Harrison ships using the latter port. Thus began a long-standing association between Harrisons and William Parr and the foundation of a most profitable trade in cotton from Galveston to Liverpool in return for cement from the United Kingdom and the Continent.[5] These developments were entirely to the satisfaction of the Harrisons. Le Blanc had not only shown initiative and foresight in the promotion of their shipping interests, but had proved himself capable of becoming their sole agent. The somewhat attenuated link with Lucas E. Moore and Co. was broken, though not without mutual feelings of regret, in 1888.[6]

Apart from Le Blanc's energy and business acumen he possessed

1. Harrison MSS., Le Blanc correspondence, witnessed document, 20 January 1874.
2. ibid., Indentures dated 30 August 1872.
3. Harrison MSS., Le Blanc correspondence, Leech, Harrison and Forwood to Alfred Le Blanc, 31 July 1877, 'We have a high opinion of your abilities and bear (willing testimony to the zeal, industry and intelligence with which you discharged your) duties . . .'
4. ibid., Frederick J. Harrison to Le Blanc, 3 October 1885, 7 November 1885, 3 April 1886.
5. The loading brokers for the Galveston trade were Geo. Lingham and Co.
6. Harrison MSS., John William Hughes to Le Blanc, 27 October 1888. 'We shall be sorry to sever the connections with Mr. Moore as we entertain a very high regard for him and all our relations have been so uniformly pleasant.'

another rare quality, that of judgement in the choice of men. As we shall shortly see, the carriage of another commodity, namely grain, became second only in importance to that of cotton. The collection and distribution of these primary products from the farm areas to the ports became involved in complicated negotiations with American railroad companies. It was, therefore, necessary to have well qualified men on the spot to deal with railroad freights and shipment facilities. As and when the pressure of events demanded, Le Blanc made the right decisions. In 1907 he established an office in Memphis under the direction of J. H. Mallory,[1] and, in 1910, realizing that a vast amount of cotton and grain was being routed through Dallas, he established an office there and put F. O. Riebe in charge of it.[2] Harrisons' long-standing connection with Mobile had prompted Le Blanc to open an office there in 1910, under the title of Mobile Liners Inc.[3] Though the Harrison interests were given priority the business of this office was open to other shipping lines and it eventually became the largest shipping agency in Mobile. Le Blanc put his own son Stewart Alfred in charge of this new office. This young man had gained experience through previous service with Harrisons in Liverpool, and with his father in New Orleans. These appointments were all-important and successful steps in the organization and growth of the Harrison trades centred upon the Gulf ports.

The competitive structure of the New Orleans and Gulf trades was largely governed by two main factors. As the trade was seasonal it required the exercise of logistical calculation in the provision of shipping space of the right kind at the right time. In the first place, therefore, there was a consequential competition between Harrisons and other shipping companies for the provision of such space at a profitable rate of freight; secondly, the shipping companies themselves had to strike a favourable balance with the powerfully entrenched American railroad interests controlling the flow of supplies to the ports. There is ample evidence to show that Le Blanc not only understood but also took effective action in dealing with the variable nature of this competitive pattern.

1. Harrison MSS., Raymond Martinez file 'Agents of the Harrison Line in other cities of the U.S.A.'

2. ibid.

3. Founded jointly by Le Blanc and M. J. Sanders, New Orleans manager for the Leyland Line.

On his arrival in New Orleans, Alfred Le Blanc's main preoccupation was in stimulating the dispatch of the main cargoes of cotton, grain and tobacco to Liverpool and other European ports and in arranging for incoming shipments of French prunes, Spanish wines and metal products from Britain, to be transhipped from New Orleans up the Mississippi.[1] It is clear from the correspondence with their agents in New Orleans, Deacon, Zerega and Company, that Harrisons were principally interested in carrying direct cargoes. There were occasions however, when Le Blanc wished to accept cargoes on transhipment rates in order to fill up empty space. This made good economic sense, though such cargoes were not always acceptable to the Liverpool office. 'We are careless (sic) about taking through rates' wrote Thomas Hughes 'We much prefer bringing a full cargo for Liverpool. If at any time there should be no other course than to take these goods to fill up, please add to the Liverpool rate. . . .'[2] This letter is of interest not only for the information on commercial practice, but also because it defines the active participation of Thomas Hughes in the business of the firm. As already stated his brother, John William Hughes, had held the position of accountant since the early 1860s and had already acquired a partnership and a substantial financial interest.[3] The influence of these two brothers was henceforth to play a dominant part in the growth and transformation of Harrisons' shipping enterprise.

The economic implications of maintaining full holds and of securing a quick turn-round of ships were equally well understood by the Harrison and Hughes brothers in Liverpool and by Lucas E. Moore and Alfred Le Blanc in New Orleans. 'Some shippers here inform us' wrote Hughes 'that they get greater facilities at the Mississippi Company's wharf at New Orleans than at ours, and, consequently, ship their goods by that line.'[4] On another occasion when there seems to have been a misunderstanding on Moore's part about forward bookings, Frederick James Harrison wrote 'You were all along empowered to

1. Harrison MSS., Thomas Hughes to Deacon, Zerega and Co., 15 Nov. 1878.
2. Harrison MSS., Thomas Hughes to Deacon, Zerega and Co., 9 October 1877. Cotton shipped from the U.S. Gulf moved on railroad-through Bills of Lading, i.e. the railroad freight agents at inland points issued a negotiable document from the railroad point of shipment through to Liverpool. When the cotton covered by that bill of lading reached the seaboard the steamship agent issued what was called a port bill of lading, or a custody bill of lading, both non-negotiable documents.
3. See chapter 1, section IV.
4. Harrison MSS., Thomas Hughes to Deacon, Zerega and Co., 15 November 1878.

act on the arrival of the steamers, and it was a rude shock to us to find out you had kept *Legislator* and *Inventor* so long doing nothing.'[1] He ended this letter with a significant sentence; 'uncertain quantities and unrestricted deliveries appear to us undesirable, and to savour too much of "heads I win, tails you lose".' Bearing in mind that the main commodities in this trade were subject to seasonal variation in supply, it became of the utmost importance to secure additional subsidiary cargoes to keep the ships reasonably well employed during off-peak periods or, alternatively, to make supplementary engagements in new trades altogether.

In this latter connection Moore had conceived the idea in 1884 of sending a Harrison ship to load cargoes of fruit at Belize in British Honduras and at other ports along the Mexican coastline. He made a strong and persuasive case by showing that, within five years, the value of this trade into New Orleans had increased seven-fold. After a due consideration of prospects, Harrisons asked Le Blanc to initiate the trade and sent out *Warrior* in September 1886 to work between Belize and New Orleans.[2] The expectation was that this, and any other ship taking part in the fruit trade, would return a net profit of £4,000 per annum.[3] Unfortunately, the expectation was not realized. Competition from other shipping companies already entrenched in this trade made the venture unprofitable. Speed was an essential element and *Warrior*, a 10-knot vessel was outpaced and outclassed by the keen rivalry of ships which could steam at 12 knots. To have built a new ship capable of steaming at 12 knots would not have cut costs to the level required for profitable working as the experience of other firms in this trade adequately demonstrated. 'With George Irvine's experience before them' wrote Fred Harrison 'I am sure our people would not send out a costly vessel: he gave, or rather his company gave, £38,000 for what was supposed to be a most suitable vessel (the *Barracouta*) with the result that she has never paid a dividend, is now certainly not worth £15,000 and he, I understand, is giving up the business in disgust.'[4] Apart from financial considerations, the risks

1. Harrison MSS., Fred J. Harrison to Lucas E. Moore, 9 October 1886.
2. Harrison MSS., Fred J. Harrison to Le Blanc, 21 May 1886. 27 July 1886, 20 August 1886.
3. ibid., 26 October 1886.
4. Harrison MSS., Fred J. Harrison to Le Blanc, 4 June 1887.

involved by working a ship so far from the home station were a deterrent to the promotion of active business relationships.[1]

This short episode was indicative of a good intention being frustrated in practice by economic circumstances.[2] It also demonstrated how keenly alive Harrisons were to the competitive nature of their business. This competition became more intense in the Gulf trade as a whole with every succeeding year, and both Harrisons and Le Blanc were increasingly involved in the struggle to cut costs, maintain cargoes at remunerative rates and develop worthwhile contacts. In the early 1870s one of Harrisons main rivals was the Liverpool and Mississippi Steamship Company. The managing owners were Messrs. Hains, Mains and Montgomery and their ships were designed especially for the New Orleans trade.[3] By the 1890s the competition from this company had been superseded by a more intense rivalry from opposition ships belonging to Elder Dempsters (under the vigorous management of Alfred Jones) and the West India and Pacific Steamship Company. In general terms, the battle for cargoes was waged on three fronts; the first involved the negotiation of satisfactory contracts with American railroad companies (mainly the Southern Pacific, Texas and Pacific, and the Illinois Central) for the carriage of cotton and grain to the southern ports; the second was in the provision of ships with capacity equal to the demand for 'railway' cotton; and the third was in meeting the eventual competition which arose from a combination of American railroad and shipping interests whose principal object was to divert the bulk carriage of agricultural products from the southern to the northern and eastern ports of the United States.

Alfred Le Blanc was, from the outset, much exercised in the conclusion of satisfactory railroad contracts for the carriage of cotton to New Orleans. One difficult factor in the situation was that the cotton

1. Harrison MSS., Fred J. Harrison to Le Blanc, 4 June 1887. 'It does not look like business' wrote Harrison, 'to fight a keen opposition with an unsuitable tool so far from home'.

2. ibid., 19 October 1887. Harrison's fairness towards Le Blanc can be judged by the following 'We all here regret the result of the venture much more for your sake than our own as we feel you have spared yourself no pain or trouble . . . For ourselves the loss is simply one a businessman who tries anything new perpetually faces.'

3. *Liverpool Telegraph and Daily Shipping & Commercial Gazette.* 11 July 1870, 'These steamers will have large carrying capacity, with a light draught of water, highest class at Lloyds, and will be fitted up with the latest improvements.' They were built by G. R. Clover & Co. of Birkenhead and the first ship was named *St. Louis.*

carried into Galveston matured before that which came down to New Orleans. There was, in consequence, a rivalry between the two ports for the supply and loading of new cotton. In his first enthusiasm, Le Blanc had attempted to estimate the size of the cotton crop and to advise John William Hughes accordingly; 'don't prophecy' replied Hughes, 'we expect roses in June and cotton in September'! It was with a fatherly eye that John William Hughes regarded Le Blanc's efforts to establish contacts with the railroad companies, and there is evidence that Harrisons kept a fairly tight control over railway freight arrangements. As late as 1898 Hughes was writing to Le Blanc in connection with negotiations with the Southern Pacific Railroad 'We are still doubtful about the standard "4 cents per 100 lbs. below Galveston". It leaves us at the mercy of Galveston competition and hardly seems justified by experience. We booked cotton at Galveston last week at 17/64 (less 3/64 for pressing) when you were quoting 7/32.'[1] On a subsequent occasion when the West India Company was prepared to undercut Harrisons, Le Blanc was informed that following a discussion with the directors of that company, Harrisons were not willing to carry Texas and Pacific railroad cotton at a rate less than 40 cents and hoped that agreement might be concluded at around 45 cents.[2] The contract was finally agreed at 42 cents. This keen bargaining not only brought Harrisons to a sharp realisation of the power exercised by the American railroad companies, but also convinced them that they had to maintain in their own hands a control over rate-fixing. 'We quite agree with you' wrote John William Hughes 'that the railroads are becoming more and more masters of the position and that it is essential to work with them'.[3] Harrisons also agreed that if it were possible to obtain maximum rates on each railroad contract and provide sufficient tonnage without detriment to better paying cargo, the trade could be well organized. This expression of the ideal situation was, however, subject to misapprehension and doubt. It was a matter of argument whether the 1899 contract price of 42 cents had been the best rate that could have been negotiated. Furthermore, as between the Texas and Pacific and the Southern

1. Harrison MSS., John William Hughes to Le Blanc, 4 June 1898.
2. ibid., 25 June 1898. 'In my day (i.e. after 1900)' writes John Cowan '27 cents were penury, 30 cents made us more cheerful, at 32 cents we were happy and 35 cents was almost opulence'.
3. ibid., 2 May 1900.

Pacific railroads, there did not seem to be much point in trying to shorten the margin between the rate to Galveston and that to New Orleans. Such a policy had been suggested, and on occasion practised by Le Blanc to the evident dissatisfaction of the Liverpool directors. 'As to the Southern Pacific' concluded Hughes, 'we could not convince ourselves that our interest lay in undercutting the Galveston rate in order to bring cotton to New Orleans which, in the natural course, would have gone to Galveston whence we could have carried it.'[1]

Complementary to Harrisons' relationship with the railroad companies was the important issue of competition between the various shipping companies engaged in the Gulf cotton trade. This competition had been fierce in seasons of short supply, but towards the end of the century, crops had improved and, with a growing demand for raw cotton, the problem had become centred upon the need to allocate cargoes in proportion to lifting capacity. This, in turn, reacted upon the level of freight rates and upon the design and speed of the ships employed on the New Orleans route. In 1897, Le Blanc had been perturbed by the incursion of Elder Dempster and Company, but Harrisons had the situation in hand; their prospective assessment of future competition had already induced them to invest in larger and speedier ships. 'Meet their competition like you would anyone else's' wrote John William Hughes, 'get cargo for the vessels at the best rates you can. . . . We, and W.I. and P.S.S.Co. are preparing for hot competition by ordering new vessels.'[2] The extent of Elder Dempster's interest in the trade can be judged from the figures supplied by John William Hughes. In the cotton season September 1897 to March 1898, Elders carried 161,501 bales for April delivery, of which 129,329 bales came via the Texas and Pacific railroad, 19,908 bales via the Illinois Central and 12,264 bales were spot cotton.[3] By comparison, the West India and Pacific Steamship Company carried 112,483 bales of spot cotton and 136,000 bales of railway cotton, a total of 248,483 bales. Though Harrisons' figures were not complete, preliminary estimates suggested that, as all available ships were fully laden, they and the West India Company could not, in any event, have carried all the

1. ibid.
2. Harrison MSS., John William Hughes to Le Blanc, 20 November 1897.
3. ibid., 26 March 1898.

shipments of Texas and Pacific railroad cotton.[1] The addition of new tonnage in the following season, however, made it possible for these two companies to lift an extra 300,000 bales. In short, the basis of cargo-sharing between the shipping lines had been altered. In taking account of all possible sources of competition Harrisons thereupon instructed Le Blanc to make arrangements with all three railroad companies to load 35,000 bales a month. They estimated that the West India Company would be able to load 100,000 bales monthly and that two White Star steamers (loading as part of the West India Company's fleet for one season only) would lift a further 30,000 bales a month.[2]

The ships which Harrisons used in this trade were *Governor*, *Explorer*, *Legislator* and *Engineer* from 1892 to 1894, and, as the volume of cotton cargoes increased, new ships of larger tonnage such as those of the *Magician* and *Craftsman* class were added to the route. The strength of the competition at this time required ships of relatively large carrying capacity and Harrisons' new construction, laid down at the turn of the century, was more than adequate for the foreseeable needs of the trade. The available evidence suggests that Harrisons and the West India Company had, by 1898, made strenuous endeavours to solve the problem of shipping space. In that year John William Hughes estimated that if 'one-third of this space is occupied by grain, cake, etc., there would remain accommodation for 800,000 bales of actual cotton in three months, rather beyond the requirements (i.e. of space) of the New Orleans-Liverpool market, and may turn our thoughts to Galveston.'[3] There was an obvious need to allocate this shipping capacity to the mutual advantage of both firms. Discussions were held on the basis of a 55 per cent share to the West India Company and 45 per cent to Harrisons.[4] This was an equitable division and more than satisfactory to Harrisons because the operation of this arrangement was not exclusive of both companies' interest in the carriage of West Indian and other local cotton. 'We do not want our vessels stuffed full of railway cotton' wrote Hughes, 'to the exclusion of better paying local cotton'.[5] It would have been extremely profitable had this expression of intent been capable of realization. The amicable relationship

1. ibid.
2. ibid., 14 May 1898.
3. ibid.
4. ibid., 4 June 1898.
5. ibid.

with the West India Company lasted barely more than a season. Other, more powerful competitors, attracted by the profitability of the New Orleans trade, entered the lists and thereby created a new and disturbing situation in the structure and organization of the trade.

In 1873 Frederick Leyland bought the Bibby Line and established his own line of ships with trading connections with the Mediterranean and the north Atlantic ports of the United States. By 1882, this fleet numbered twenty-five ships and, between 1888 and 1896, several new ships were added specifically for the Atlantic trade. After Leyland's death in 1892, the firm continued to expand its transatlantic interests and developed capacity for the carriage of cotton. In 1900 the Leyland Line came under the guidance of John Ellerman who, almost immediately after the acquisition of control, started negotiations for the purchase of the West India and Pacific Steamship Company.[1] 'The change of ownership of the West India Company' wrote John William Hughes 'is a new and disturbing feature.'[2] The new deal introduced an element of uncertainty into the New Orleans trade. 'We are disappointed' continued Hughes in his letter to Le Blanc 'because we had taken some trouble to establish an *entente cordiale* with the West India directors, which was certainly mutually advantageous. We are on very friendly terms with Mr. Walter Glynn, the managing director of the Leyland Line and can doubtless arrange to avoid "open" competition, but we can hardly hope for the close alliance we had with the West India Company.'[3] In the same letter Hughes expressed the further fear that ships belonging to the Atlantic Transport Company (which had hitherto confined its sailings to East Coast ports) might compete with the Harrisons in the Gulf Trade. 'Under these circumstances' concluded Hughes, 'we are more than ever desirous of maintaining our relations with the railroads either with, or without the West India Company or their successors.'[4]

There was a greater shock to come. John Ellerman, having purchased the West India Company for approximately £1,000,000 sold the whole of the Leyland transatlantic interests in 1901 to the International Mercantile Marine, a complex of shipping companies controlled by

1. For the Harrison assessment of these negotiations see Harrison MSS., John William Hughes to Le Blanc, 2 May 1900; also ibid., 1 May 1910.
2. ibid., 2 May 1900.
3. ibid.
4. ibid.

the American railroad magnate, J. Pierpont Morgan. Commenting on this new turn of events, John William Hughes remarked 'the general opinion here is that the purchase is part of a great scheme of American capitalists to control, if not capture, the whole north Atlantic trade and that application will be made to Congress to flag the vessels as the nucleus of an American mercantile fleet.'[1] Thus, within the space of a year, the whole competitive structure of the Harrison trade to and from the Gulf ports had been transformed. The cargo-sharing arrangements with the West India Company had been undermined, and the counterbalancing agreements with the railroads for the orderly supply of cotton and grain to New Orleans and Galveston, had been jeopardized by the likely intervention of a powerful railroad king. The inference was that, by his control of certain railroad systems, Morgan might seek to divert shipments of primary products to east coast ports to fill the ships of his International Mercantile Marine. 'The Morgan combination' wrote Hughes 'would appear to have Boston, Philadelphia, and New York absolutely in their control, and will work them in close connection with the big railroads with a view to monopolising the north Atlantic trade. . . . The new arrangement is to prevent too much produce going to the Gulf ports for ship-ment.'[2]

In fact, the bogey which the Morgan empire had conjured up did not materialize. Harrisons continued their friendly relations with Leylands even though by their purchase of the West India Company they had entered as competitors in the New Orleans trade,[3] and the Illinois Central and Texas and Pacific railroads continued to supply the Harrison ships.[4] In general, however, the increase in competition led to a rising cost structure because, with the additional ships on the route, holds could not be filled to capacity.[5] Harrisons estimated that the loss on the twelve ships working the New Orleans route in 1903 (January to July inclusive) amounted to £5,000 without taking interest on capital into account.[6] Despite this, however, Harrisons continued to carry substantially larger cargoes of cotton than Leylands and, in

1. ibid., 1 May 1901.
2. ibid., 23 April 1902.
3. ibid., 7 March 1903.
4. ibid.
5. ibid., 29 August 1903.
6. ibid., 29 August 1903.

total carrying capacity, maintained a better service than many of the
ships belonging to the International Mercantile Marine.[1] 'So that in
point of extent of traffic' stated John William Hughes to Le Blanc
'New Orleans has done well'.[2] The most disquieting feature of this
competitive struggle was the intensification of seasonal pressure. The
large Harrison ships which had originally been built expressly for the
cotton trade had now, under changed conditions, become too costly
to run in 'the dull season, and so cannot make a regular service all
through the year'.[3] In face of such a realization it would have been
disastrous to have adhered rigidly to a traditional pattern of trade.
In 1902, Harrisons had entered the South African Conference (the
details of which will be referred to in subsequent chapters) and this
new trade provided greater flexibility in the management of their
larger ships; when the Gulf trade was slack some of the New Orleans'
ships could be readily switched to Cape Town. Thus, the increasing
pressure of competition in one trade was successfully offset by expansion
in another.

II

Parallel in development with the service to the Gulf ports during the
1860s, was that of a second major trade to the Far East and, more
particularly, that to the ports in India and Ceylon. The Harrison
brothers had made early contact with India through *Templar* (in which
they held one-quarter share), a ship of 566 tons and designed for long
distance voyages rather than for the specific requirements of the
Charente wine and brandy trades. The ownership of this vessel is,
perhaps, significant in that it is the first recorded instance in which
Harrisons had entered into partnership with persons other than
Richard Williamson. It is probable that *Templar* made several voyages
to India although there is only one authentic reference to her engagement in that trade. She returned from Bombay on 13 October 1847,

1. ibid. The evidence shows that some of the Boston ships and also some of those
belonging to Leylands had to be laid up in this year.
2. ibid.
3. ibid.

D

carrying cotton and pepper.[1] Following the voyage of the *Admiral Grenfell* to China in 1857–8, Harrison ships made an increasing number of voyages to India and the Far East as and when the opportunity for profitable cargoes offered.

Although there was nothing in the nature of a direct service there is evidence from the instructions issued to the Captains of their ships, that Harrisons had given considerable attention as early as 1862 to the possibility of establishing more regular contacts with Indian and other Far Eastern ports.[2] The obvious care which had been taken in drawing up these instructions, together with the great attention to detail, suggests that Harrisons had already acquired experience and not a little practical knowledge of the difficulties of navigating in Indian waters. If the ships went to Calcutta they were to receive consignments through Messrs. Peel Bellaine and Co. (later Peel, Jacobs and Co.); if to Bombay, through Messrs. W. and A. Graham. A specific mandate, however, was given to each captain concerning the stowage of his cargo. 'In loading for England' so ran the instruction 'if light or measurement goods offer at the same rates per customary ton as heavy goods, take no more heavy goods than sufficient to stiffen the vessel.'[3] After giving a weight/measurement table for such commodities as sugar, rice, linseed, poppyseed and tealseed, hides and jute, the statement continued 'By the above scale it will be seen that the ship will make more freight and at a less draft of water, by filling up with jute, hides or other light goods (after taking sufficient deadweight for stiffening) than by taking rice, seeds, etc., which occupy about the same space and weigh so much more. To this point your attention is especially directed, as we find it is often either overlooked or not understood by the agents.'[4] Calls at Bombay, where cotton was the most important cargo, were subject to rather different instructions. 'The most favourable cargo for a vessel to England is about one third deadweight and two thirds light goods, taking care to employ a measurer who is independent of the house shipping the cargo that there may be no bias. Get the cotton stowed away as soon as practicable after being measured, in fact, it is better not to measure it until you

1. Liverpool Bills of Entry, 1847. The name *Templar* with its obvious association with Malta suggested the cross as the emblem for the Harrison house flag.
2. Harrison MSS., Instructions to the Captain of *Botanist* 1 January 1863.
3. ibid.
4. ibid.

are ready to stow it, as it expands afterwards if left. . . .'[1] Precise details
were also given on freights and charters, on accidents and on the
maintenance of efficiency in the working of ships, constituting a
series of precautionary measures designed to reduce voyage costs to a
minimum. Finally, all captains were advised that 'in chartering or
loading for England we always prefer the vessel coming direct to
Liverpool in preference to London even at the sacrifice of about £400
in freight.'[2] The inference that one draws from these quotations
is that the Harrisons had reached a decision (probably in 1861 or 1862)[3]
to engage in, and promote the carrying trade between Liverpool and
India. They had prepared the ground for such a venture very carefully;
their ships not only were of sufficient tonnage to make the long
voyage round the Cape, but their carrying capacity was such that so
lengthy a voyage could be made highly profitable always provided
that they could establish a strong commercial organization in the
Indian ports. As far as the records are available the first ship to explore
the possibilities of this new venture was *Botanist*[4]; she anchored in
Madras Roads on 1 July 1863.[5]

It is, perhaps, relevant to emphasize that this venture into the Indian
trade coincided with the initial change over from sail to steam. After
1865 a more decided voyage pattern between Liverpool and Calcutta
begins to emerge, the sailing ships *Botanist, Geologist, Astronomer,
Naturalist, Philosopher* and *Artist* being primarily concerned in serving
this route.[6] Between 1865 and 1869 about a dozen calls a year were
made at Indian ports, more than half of these being to Calcutta. As
the volume of trade grew the need for larger and speedier ships
became imperative and the decision had to be taken to service the

1. ibid.
2. ibid.
3. *Lloyds Register* 1860-1 gives details of *Anna Dorothea* built at Ardrossan, owned
by W. Barber & Co., Liverpool. This ship sailed from Liverpool to Bombay in 1861
(*Lloyds Register* 1861-2). 'For Freight apply to Thos. & Jas. Harrison.' See *Liverpool
Journal of Commerce*, 2 October 1861.

4. Liverpool Statutory Registers of Merchant Ships 1863, entry no. 66. *Botanist* was
completed in 1863 and was registered on 24 February.

5. Harrison MSS., Voyage account, *Botanist* 1863.

6. Harrison MSS., Voyage accounts 1865-6. *Geologist* sailed to Madras in February
1865 and to Calcutta April 1866; *Astronomer* sailed to Bombay in July 1865 and to
Calcutta September 1866. *Naturalist* sailed to Calcutta in September 1865; *Philosopher*
sailed to Calcutta in July 1866; *Artist* sailed to Calcutta in October 1866.

Indian trade with steamships. Before this decision could be fully implemented, however, the opening of the Suez Canal had provided a new route to India and had changed the economic basis on which shipping companies had for so long calculated their returns from investment in this trade.

Liverpool sailing-ship owners, fearful lest the shorter route to India *via* the Suez Canal would give the steamship an overwhelming competitive advantage, sought reassurance in their ability to carry bulk cargoes over long distances at competitive rates. 'They thought' so ran the argument 'that as outward cargo, such things as railroad iron, salt and coals would probably continue to be sent by sailing ships. They were certainly of the opinion that, although there was a great feeling at present in favour of steam, the saving of expense for heavy cargo would more than compensate for any loss of time as compared with the steam voyages.'[1] The conclusion was that, apart from years of abnormal trade fluctuation, there would be sufficient freight offering for sailing vessels round the Cape 'to afford a fair remuneration to that part of their fleet which might be employed in that trade.'[2]

There was some economic sense in the argument even though, in practice, the logic was eventually undermined by simple arithmetic and widening profit margins. The Liverpool shipowners had been exercised by the rates ruling at the opening of the Canal, and their case had been fully supported by documentary evidence from the Liverpool Chamber of Commerce.[3] The assumption was that a sailing ship carrying approximately 1,000 tons of cargo could make the voyage from Liverpool to Bombay, *via* the Cape of Good Hope, in ninety-five days at an average freight rate of 38s. per ton; whereas, the steamship, though making the voyage through the Canal in less than half the time, could not operate profitably on a freight rate of less than 80s. per ton. Within a month from the opening of the Canal, however, steamship rates had fallen to about 30s. per ton. The Harrison brothers, undaunted by the prognostications of their fellow shipowners, had already convinced themselves that the Suez Canal route was the key to a vast expansion of their business with India and the Far East. In

1. *Liverpool Shipping Telegraph*, 25 January 1870.
2. ibid., see also G. S. Graham 'The Ascendancy of the Sailing Ship, 1850-85'. *Economic History Review*, Vol. IX, No. 1, August 1956, pp. 74-88.
3. *Liverpool Shipping Telegraph*, 31 January 1870.

the first days of January 1870 the *Liverpool Shipping Telegraph* announced that three steamships were loading in Liverpool for India, *via* the Suez Canal. One of these was the Harrison ship *Fire Queen* which sailed on 13 January.[1] She was followed in succession by the steamships *Cordova* and *Alice* in February, *Statesman* in March, *Chrysolite* in April, *Olinda* and *Historian* in May.[2] It would be tedious to continue the catalogue; but the mention of *Historian* throws some relevant light on the economic importance of this new route. On her second outward voyage (30 August 1870) through the Canal to India she called at Colombo on her way to Calcutta. The Colombo newspapers were sufficiently impressed with her performance to record that her actual steaming time from Liverpool had been no more than twenty-seven days, a record time. 'Now that these steamers have proved themselves in every way suited to the voyage between Great Britain and the East' concluded one report 'we may expect to find, not only passengers coming out by them, but others availing themselves of the opportunity to go home by them at a much cheaper rate than by the mail steamers'. In other words, the early phase in establishing contacts and in developing the Indian market had now come to an end. The Harrison ships had, by 1870, become accepted as a reliable comfortable and economic means of transport; it was but a matter of time before a regular service to India was put into operation.

This identification of Harrison interests with India was something more than an initial act of faith in the advantage of a shorter sea route to the Far East. Their strong liberal principles not only approved of, but gave active encouragement to the construction of this new international route. James Harrison had contacts with, and subsequently met de Lesseps[3] and when the Canal was opened, he and his fellow

1. I am greatly indebted to Mr D. A. Farnie of the University of Manchester for corroborative references from the records of the Suez Canal Company. *Fire Queen*, initiating this new service, passed through the Suez Canal in February 1870 her passage being the 27th transit through the Canal. The advertisement quoted from the *Liverpool Shipping Telegraph* was apparently not the first reference to *Fire Queen* sailing on this route. Mr Farnie quotes a previous advertisement dated 27 December 1869.

2. Harrison MSS., Voyage books, 1870.

3. *Journal of Commerce and Shipping Telegraph*, 7 November 1934. 'James Harrison —A man of vision' Quoting a letter from James Harrison's daughter dated November 1933.

shareholders took a personal interest in its administration.[1] John William Hughes became a Director of the Suez Canal Company in 1905. The tradition of such active participation was maintained for a period of fifty-five years, Sir Thomas Harrison Hughes Bt. becoming a Vice-President and, during the Second World War, acting on behalf of the Company as sole British Administrator responsible to the war-time government.[2]

There was, however, an equally compelling economic reason why Harrisons should have given such determined support to the opening of a shorter trade route to India. As both the outward and homeward trades with Calcutta, Colombo and Bombay were reasonably remunerative, and as they were not so narrowly seasonal as the commodity trades with the Gulf ports, a more regular voyage pattern could be arranged. The use of the Canal made it possible to increase the number of voyages each year, thereby securing a greater utilisation of capital resources with the attendant economies arising from the scale of operations. The justification for a quicker turn-round of ships had been based upon a rising trend in both the volume and value of India's imports and exports during the course of the 1860s. The impact of this trend, together with the effectiveness of the new route through the Canal, is clearly shown in the records surviving in Harrisons' voyage books. In 1869 Harrison ships made fourteen calls at Indian and Far Eastern ports; in 1870 this figure exceeded fifty and, in the following year, reached ninety. It was a concatenation of factors which gave stimulus and importance to this trade route. The opening of the Suez Canal coupled with the steamship building boom of the early 1870s constituted only one side of the picture; the changing pattern and growth of India's trade was the other.[3] Though there were short-term fluctuations in Far Eastern Trade during the 1870s, and though these fluctuations were undoubtedly aggravated by an over-supply of tonnage on particular routes, the long term impact of India's economic

1. On 30 November 1883 Harrisons were signatories to the agreement establishing 'the London Programme' for the future development of the Canal. This agreement secured the election of shipowners to the Board of the Canal Company. Ref. D. A. Farnie.

2. Brian Watson Hughes, *One Hundred Years of Progress*, (1953), p. 20. See also Sir Arnold T. Wilson, *The Suez Canal*, (1933), p. 108.

3. S. B. Saul, *Studies in British Overseas Trade 1870-1914*, (1960), Chapter VIII, pp. 188-207.

expansion brought continuous activity to shipping companies engaged in the carrying trade. As is well known, the sailing ship enjoyed a reprieve and, no less than the steamship, increased its business in the bulk trades in primary commodities.[1]

Over the immediate short-term period, however, the fluctuations in the Indian trade during the 1870s had a marked influence on the frequency of the Harrison voyages. In 1872 the number of calls at Indian and Far Eastern ports fell to thirty-eight. There was a substantial recovery to sixty in 1874 and, by 1876, the 1871 total of ninety had again been reached.[2] The measure of this fluctuation in terms of the earning capacity of the ship is, perhaps, less significant when it is remembered that improved engines and boilers reduced coaling costs and eliminated a certain number of calls at Indian ports. To this extent, therefore, the relationship between trading conditions and calls made cannot give a precise definition. Nevertheless, it is relevant to add that, from 1876 to 1884, when the Charente Steam-Ship Company was reorganised as a limited company, there was no year in which less than a dozen Harrison ships passed through the Canal in either direction and that, in 1881, the number was as high as eighteen.[3] Thus, the initial assessment of the potential advantages to be derived from the Canal, was more than justified. The shorter route to India encouraged and developed the use of the steamship at a time when an expanding market required an increase in shipping space. For those shipowners, such as the Harrisons, who seized the opportunities afforded by a new trade route, the economic prospects were propitious. Apart from the early difficulties involved in the adjustment of tonnage to the requirements of trade, Harrisons were enabled, through the establishment of trading contacts, to lay the foundation of a commercial organization which, in turn, was a prerequisite to the employment of the fleet on a major oceanic trade route of the world.

Compared with the Gulf trade, Harrisons' Indian business was relatively simple in structure. The most usual outward cargoes in the

1. G. S. Graham, op. cit., p. 81. This was so despite the fact that, by 1878, there was a marked swing towards steamship building; in this year steamship tonnage built for British owners was double and, in 1879, was nearly five times greater than sail tonnage.

2. Harrison MSS., Voyage books, 1872-6.

3. Information extracted from the records of the Suez Canal Company by D. A. Farnie.

1870s consisted of salt, coal, engineering and railway equipment; whilst the homeward ships brought back to Liverpool and other European ports such commodities as sugar, jute, cotton, rice, oilseeds and wheat.[1] This cargo-pattern changed considerably during the course of the following twenty years when in response to new and insistent demands, such items as tea, cotton textiles and gunnies became staples of the trade. We shall, in a later chapter, deal more fully with the economic implications of this change.[2] For the present, it is sufficient to observe these items of trade within a general context to show that, under normal conditions, the flow of cargoes quickly assumed a measure of stability, both as to content and value, within the framework of new enterprise. In financial terms, the Indian voyages were undoubtedly worthwhile. For the most part costs per voyage were maintained at a remarkably consistent level (on the Calcutta route, for example, they were approximately £7,000); receipts from freights were equally stable, despite fluctuations in the demand for, and the price of, primary products, totalling between £9,000 and £11,000.[3] Thus, the normal profit from an Indian voyage ranged from £2,000 to £4,000 depending upon the particular conditions ruling for any given voyage. In Harrisons' other major trade, that with New Orleans, the margin between voyage costs and receipts was very much lower and, consequently profits per voyage were less. Table I gives the voyage profit on a few representative ships during the years 1879 and 1880. The evidence suggests that, voyage for voyage, the normal expectation of profit from the Calcutta run, at this time, was more than twice that made from ships sailing to New Orleans. Even when these figures are discounted by a factor representing the difference in time taken by the ships on these two routes, the profit from the voyage to India was still the greater.

One subsidiary, though none the less important feature, of the Indian trade has yet to be considered. This was the carriage of coolies from Calcutta to Demerara and the West Indian islands for work on the sugar plantations. The conditions under which the coolies were carried was strictly regulated by law. Such matters as health and welfare, food and cooking facilities, cleanliness and discipline were enforceable

1. Harrison MSS., Voyage books 1871-84.
2. See Chapters IV and VII.
3. Harrison MSS., Voyage accounts 1879-81.

during the course of the voyage. Furthermore, there were additional safeguards in the shape of emigration permits, limitation of contracts to five years and guaranteed return passages. In short, by virtue of this legislation, it was possible for the migrants to find employment overseas and be given suitable transport under a system designed to protect their individual rights and liberties. The Harrisons first started to carry coolies to Demerara in 1870 and continued the service until 1880.

TABLE 1

INDIAN AND GULF TRADES, 1879-80
PROFITS ON SOME REPRESENTATIVE VOYAGES

Year	To Calcutta and Far East		To New Orleans and Gulf Ports	
1879		£		£
	Statesman	902	Warrior	477
	Legislator	4,350	Vanguard	1,039
	Inventor	2,298	Orator	1,575
	Discoverer		Explorer	1,512
	(1st voyage)	3,107	Commander	901
	(2nd voyage)	1,929	Chancellor	155
	Chancellor	1,252	Explorer (2nd voyage)	1,003
			Historian	418
1880				
	Counsellor	3,802	Mediator	1,722
			Author	1,609
			Explorer	2,306
			Historian	1,946

All the ships used were sailing ships and it is, perhaps, of significance to note that the decision by Harrisons to end the coolie trade coincided with their abandonment of the sailing ship as a passenger and cargo carrier. The high regard which they had for the good management of these ships together with their care for the comfort and health of the coolies in transit, were the subject of approbation in many an issue of the local Caribbean press.[1] It was not an easy trade in which to participate, nor were the returns from it particularly remunerative; but the records show that Harrisons conducted it with skill, efficiency and humanity.

1. Harrison Papers, newspaper files, 1870-80.

One organizational problem arising from the voyage pattern of the coolie trade had economic and commercial implications. As originally conceived, it was virtually a triangular trade; bulk cargo being carried outwards from Liverpool to Calcutta, coolies, stores and rice, from Calcutta to Demerara, Trinidad and Guadeloupe and, finally, homeward to Liverpool with whatever cargo might be on offer in Caribbean ports. The third leg of the triangle was very often the most important and, at the same time, the most difficult part of the voyage as a whole, on which to make a profitable calculation. A few of the ships in 1871 and 1872 were able to load cargoes of rum and sugar in Demerara, but more often than not the ships had to sail back to Liverpool in ballast. Under such circumstances the net return on the round voyage was either very small or was, in fact, a loss. The ships were, therefore, sent from Demerara to ports in the United States where cargoes were more plentiful. After 1873, the trade became quadrilateral rather than triangular, regular calls being made at New York or Baltimore from Demerara, by those ships which had been unsuccessful in securing cargoes of West Indian produce.[1] From New York cargoes of cotton, tobacco, hides, wheat, corn, flour, tallow and oil cake were loaded for shipment back to Liverpool.[2] These New York cargoes added between £2,000 and £3,000 to the earning capacity of the ship and thus increased the over-all profitability of the venture.

The coolie trade, with its attendant voyage pattern, was comparatively short-lived and lasted just so long as Harrisons remained faithful to the sailing ship. Their main trade with India, however, had always been conducted by steamships. For a short time during the early 1870s, as we have already seen, these steamships had encountered severe competition, a competition which had been largely caused by an excess of steamship tonnage on the Calcutta route and by certain short-term adverse fluctuations in Indian trade. The Calcutta Conference of 1875 had been conceived as a first step towards the better regulation of the Calcutta trade, and Harrisons, together with other rival steamship owners, had signed the Conference agreement. The nature of the competition and the working of the agreement will be discussed in a subsequent chapter. We need only mention here that,

1. Harrison MSS., Voyage books and supplementary evidence for *Philosopher, Artist, Botanist, Linguist, Senator,* and *King Arthur,* 1871-9.
2. ibid.

as far as Harrisons were concerned, there was a growing need during the 1880s to expand the two-way trade with India in an endeavour to keep their steamship capacity reasonably fully employed. The solution to this problem came in two ways. In 1889 Harrisons acquired the Star Line from Messrs. Rathbone Bros. and Company for £135,000.[1] The importance of this transaction lay not so much in the additional tonnage which had thereby been added to the Harrison fleet (the four Rathbone ships were shortly sold), but in the fact that by taking over the Rathbone interests, Harrisons were given access to the Indian tea trade and berthing rights under Conference agreements. The second important change which undoubtedly stimulated the connection with the Indian market came in 1891. Since the 1860s Harrisons' main agents in Calcutta had been Messrs. Peel, Bellaine and Company (later Peel Jacobs and Company) and this firm had, for upwards of a quarter of a century, acted to the complete satisfaction of the Harrison brothers. In 1890, however, two senior members of staff in the Calcutta office retired. Unfortunately for Harrisons this meant a loss of personnel who, through long experience in handling the Harrison account, had become closely involved in the promotion of all aspects of their Indian trade. Faced with the prospect of new and relatively inexperienced men, and with their own desire to enter new trades (such as tea and gunnies) Harrisons were prompted to appoint new agents. 'What we want is a good man in Calcutta' wrote Frederick James Harrison, 'and on that mainly depends whether your firm retains the agency or not'.[2] After further but abortive negotiations about adequate representation of their interests, Harrisons finally severed their connection with Peel, Jacobs and Company and appointed Messrs. Hoare, Miller and Company to take charge of their steamships as from 1 January 1891.[3] As we shall see, this decision was to have a far-reaching effect on the scope and expansion of Harrisons' shipping services to India.

Great as were the changes brought about through the progressive employment of resources in the New Orleans and Calcutta trades, however, the impact of such change upon Harrisons' managerial

1. Harrison MSS., T. and J. Harrison to Rathbone Bros. & Co., 4 June 1889, see also Minutes C.S.S. Co. for 1890.
2. Harrison MSS., Fred. J. Harrison to F. Peel, 21 May 1890.
3. ibid., Fred. J. Harrison to Alfred Parker, 30 December 1890.

function cannot be rightly assessed on the evidence from these trades alone. These particular extensions of interest were but part of a much wider range of activity in the Caribbean, in Mexico, in Brazil and along the Pacific coast of both North and South America. The acceptance of the steamship had made it possible for new sea routes to be established and effectively maintained. Harrisons were among the first to seek out and exploit the new trades in those parts of the world where, given a strong and well-organized commercial system, potentially large returns could be expected from expanding economies served by efficient and well-regulated overseas communications.

CHAPTER THREE

The Organization of the Oceanic Trades: West Indies, Mexico and Brazil

I

THE third major area of the world where Harrisons sought to employ their resources, through the development of oceanic trades, was in the Caribbean (in its widest connotation) and in Brazil. In tracing the origin of these early ventures across the South Atlantic, we have to go back to Richard Pierre Williamson's voyages in *Jane* and *Admiral Grenfell*. In one sense these transatlantic contacts were but natural extensions of the established trade with the Iberian Peninsula; but, with the growing demand in Europe for cotton, sugar, coffee, tanning materials and other Spanish-American products, and with rising demand from this region for manufactured goods, the anticipation of a profitable two-way trade became a decisive reality. Furthermore, the introduction of the steamship, by ensuring more rapid and regular means of communication, coincided with, and materially helped in the stimulation and satisfaction of these demands. What was, therefore, purely fortuitous in the beginning, turned into a shipping service of some magnitude, linking Liverpool with the economic potentialities of both Spanish and Latin American countries.

From the 1870s onwards Harrisons began to establish shipping routes and, through a network of agencies, to create a commercial organisation capable of serving every major port in the Caribbean. In these early ventures it is possible to distinguish four divisions of trade. The first was outwards, via Colon, to South, Central and Northern Pacific ports; the second to Barbados, Trinidad and ports along the Spanish Main and the Mexican coast; and the third to Kingston, Jamaica and thence to Belize in British Honduras. A fourth trade which was direct and, therefore, separate from those already mentioned was that between Liverpool and ports in Central Brazil. This broad operational division

45

in the pattern of voyages remained virtually unchanged until 1914, though slight variations were made from time to time whenever the need arose, or whenever suitable and profitable cargoes were to be found in other Central American ports. The trade to Colon began in 1875.[1] Between 1876 and 1884 Harrison ships made an average of 12 calls a year at this port, carrying weight and measurement cargo[2] for transhipment *via* the Panama Railroad Company to Panama, where ships of the Pacific Steam Navigation Company and the Panama Railroad Steamship Line on-loaded for carriage to San Francisco and other North Pacific ports. Cargoes for the West Coast of South America were carried by the Compania Sud Americana de Vapores. By the early 1890s, Harrisons were facing stiff, but friendly, competition in this trade from the West India and Pacific Steam Ship Company in both the outward and homeward cargoes, chief among the latter being mahogany, cedar and other timber. In an endeavour to eliminate the effects of this competition a freight agreement between all the steamship companies concerned was negotiated and became effective on 1 March 1902.[3] Under this agreement through bills of lading were issued and through rates of freight quoted from all towns in Great Britain and Continental ports to San Francisco, thus preventing undercutting by establishing equality of rates for all carriers.

It would be tedious to attempt a detailed examination of the complicated shipping services which grew out of expanding commercial relationships in the other Caribbean trades. The main outline is clear. As we have already seen, the contact with Belize had begun in the late 1870s partly as a means of finding employment for the New Orleans' ships during off-season periods. The abandonment of this trade, however, did not entirely sever Harrisons' connections with British Honduras. A limited number of calls at Belize continued to be made during the 1880s from ports in the West Indies. By 1890, these calls had risen to 15[4] a year and a more regular pattern of voyages is discernible thereafter between Kingston, Jamaica and Belize. To a large extent this was a trade in fruit and vegetables, though there was some passenger traffic and, in the early years, a fairly infrequent and

1. Harrison MSS., Voyage books, 1870–90.
2. Harrison papers, Tariff of through freight rates, Liverpool to San Francisco. The list contains over 200 items.
3. ibid., Liverpool to San Francisco, combined services. 1 March 1902.
4. Harrison MSS., Voyages books 1870–90.

non-contractual mail service. A more precise reason for regularity in this trade came in 1897, when a mail contract was negotiated, giving Harrisons the limited sanction of carrying parcels on a poundage basis outwards to Belize under an agreed and, to all intents and purposes, a highly unprofitable scale of fixed charges.[1]

Undoubtedly the most important trade in this whole region was that between Barbados and ports on the Mexican Gulf, Trinidad, Venezuela, Curaçao and Colombia. It is clear from the voyage records that these extensions of the trade with Barbados shortly became divided into two sections; first, that northwards to the Mexican ports of Progresso, Vera Cruz and Tampico[2] and secondly, that to the South Caribbean ports of Trinidad, Puerto Cabello, Curaçao, Savanilla, Barranquilla and Cartagena.[3]

The trade with Mexico was begun in 1876, 14 calls being made by Harrison ships in that year. Between 1877 and 1884, however, an average of one ship per month was despatched. By 1890 the yearly total had reached 19. The Liverpool-Mexican trade was handled on behalf of Harrisons by Richard Bulman and Company, Chapel Street, Liverpool and by Guilliamo Busing and Company in Vera Cruz. The beginning of this trade was largely a result of, and coincidental with, the resurgence of the Mexican economy following the cessation of civil war in that country. The new Mexican Government, desirous of promoting economic recovery and of establishing commercial relation-ships with Europe, inaugurated a shipping policy in 1878 designed to make Mexican ports more readily available to foreign shipping com-panies. On 17 January of that year a contract was signed with the mercantile house of L. C. Garcia and Company for the express purpose of establishing a steamship service between Mexican ports, Havana, and European ports.[4] A government circular was issued explaining the necessity for such a contract, namely, 'in an effort to increase trade by obtaining the lowest possible freight rates on Mexican exports.'[5] Of all the lines which placed Vera Cruz in communication with various European ports, 'that which had the lowest tariff was from Liverpool',

1. Harrison MSS., G.P.O. to Richard Bulman and Co., 26 February 1897.
2. ibid., Voyage books, 1875-90.
3. ibid.
4. Harrison MSS., Richard Bulman correspondence (hereafter cited R.B.). Agree-ment dated 17 January 1878.
5. ibid., Circular dated 12 January 1878.

under the title of the West Indian and Mexican Steamers.[1] These ships were, in fact, those of the Charente Steam-Ship Company.

The importance of this new connexion can be judged first, by relating it to the expansion of Mexican trade as a whole and secondly, by the nature of the service and the varying degrees of control which the Mexican government exercised over it. Between 1886 and 1905 Mexico's main sources of supply were in the United States, the United Kingdom, France and Germany. The annual average value of imports into Mexico were respectively, 1886–90 £1,955,000, £1,438,000, £1,960,000 and £445,000.[2] For the years 1901–5, the corresponding figures were £8,241,000, £1,960,000, £1,417,000 and £1,699,000. The decline in French exports to Mexico was more than matched by a steady increase in exports from the other three countries during this period. If we now take an exactly similar statement of Mexican exports to the fore-mentioned countries, the values for 1886–90 are £3,362,000, £1,235,000, £404,000 and £194,000. By the period 1901–5, however, a great change had taken place, the relevant figures for Mexican exports being £12,502,000, £1,667,000, £393,000 and £863,000. There is little need to emphasize the growing dominance of the United States in Mexico's external trade; as far as the European countries were concerned, the United Kingdom and Germany increased their share of transatlantic trade at the expense of France.

There is no doubt that within the general context of this expanding trade with Mexico, Harrisons, of all British shipping companies so engaged, played a vital rôle. Their ships carried approximately half of the total United Kingdom trade with that country. The contracts with the Mexican Government or its agencies were organized on Harrisons' behalf by Richard Bulman and Company. Such contracts were largely concerned with the carriage of heavy equipment for the construction of railways and harbour works[3] and, for the most part, were undertaken by joint arrangements between Harrisons and the

1. ibid.

2. Mexican trade and navigation returns 1886–90 quoted in the Appendices to the *Royal Commission on Shipping Rings*.

3. R.B. correspondence, 4 December 1895 (Vera Cruz Harbour works); 1896 (cement and bricks for railways and harbour); 18 November 1898, (equipment for Mexican Central Railway Co.); 30 June 1899 (structural iron and machinery for industrial mill at Atlixco).

John William Hughes

West India and Pacific Steamship Company.[1] In addition to the carriage of materials for the construction of railways there were also contracts between the shipping lines and the railroad companies (once they were in operation) for the transhipment of purely railway freight between Mexico and European ports.[2] These cargoes were despatched on through bills of lading *via* the Mexican Inter-Oceanic Railway Company, thus providing a further link in transmission between the Pacific and the Gulf ports. In short, Harrisons not only provided the essentials for a new system of communication within Mexico, but through various traffic agreements with the railroad companies helped to stimulate the flow of railway goods, and thereby assisted in the quickening process of the Mexican economy as a whole.

Apart from what may be termed the public works side of the business, two other aspects of the Harrison service to Mexico have to be mentioned. There was a growing trade in general cargo of merchant goods outwards, in return for copper, sugar, hemp, silver and, after 1900, petroleum products and oilcake. As this general trade developed it became desirable, in order to keep shipping costs at a minimum, to extend services to the Mexican outports by through bills of lading from Liverpool *via* Vera Cruz. In 1896, Richard Bulman and Company negotiated an agreement with R. B. Watson and Company, agents for the Romano Line, for the transhipment of cargoes at Vera Cruz; 'The Romano Line steamers section' wrote Richard Bulman 'is to receive the goods from the (Harrison) steamer's tackle in Vera Cruz harbour and convey them to and land them at the port named in the through bill of lading'.[3] The inauguration of this particular service, however, coincided with an intensification of competition from the Ward Line which had for some time been carrying 'European cargoes *via* New York to Vera Cruz, Tampico and the Mexican outports'.[4] By 1901, however, the Ward Line services had been contracted and a new arrangement was made by Harrisons with the Compania Mexicana de Navegacion whose ships, by that date, were making weekly calls at ports along the Mexican coast.[5] This agreement was highly satis-

1. These contracts were taken over by Frederick Leyland & Co. after 1899.
2. R.B. correspondence, e.g. 17 December 1908 (Tehuantepec National Railway Co.); 19 October 1900—29 November 1913 (The Inter-Oceanic Railway of Mexico).
3. R.B. correspondence, charter party book, folio 29, 7 October 1896.
4. R.B. correspondence, G. Busing and Co. to T. & J. Harrison, 30 April 1897.
5. R.B. correspondence, R. Bulman to R.B. Watson & Co. 12 June 1901.

E

factory especially as it made provision for Harrisons to vary the through rates of freight to the outports whenever it became necessary to combat competition from other shipping companies.

A further differentiation of the service and, in a real sense, determinant of a regular sailing schedule, came with the signing of contracts for the carriage of mails by the Harrison steamships. In 1887, Harrisons, in conjunction with the Hamburg-Amerika Line, were given permission by the Mexican Government to carry mails to Vera Cruz and other Mexican Gulf ports. The ships of the Hamburg-Amerika Line maintained a meticulously regular service from Hamburg *via* Havre to Vera Cruz: whereas the Harrison ships at that time, though frequent in their service, were not bound by any precise timetable. A somewhat unusual plan had to be devised, therefore, in order to meet the exigencies of the Harrison voyage schedule. 'The steamers of the Harrison Line leave Liverpool every four weeks', so stated the contract 'The itinerary of these steamers not being certain, Messrs. G. Busing and Company agree to advise the Secretary of State per telegraph with 8 days anticipation, the date of arrival of each steamer at Vera Cruz, as also sailing, and the ports to be touched at.'[1] A further advice giving eight hours anticipation of the sailing of the mail steamships from Vera Cruz was given to the Post Offices in the Mexican outports. A second, and more specific, mail contract was signed in 1895. On this occasion the agreement was made directly between the Mexican Government and Messrs. G. Busing and Company representing the Charente Steam-Ship Company Ltd.[2] Under the terms of this agreement Harrisons were given a much wider scope for their service, permission being granted for calls at virtually all the most important ports in the Gulf and in the West Indies.[3] In addition, rights were also afforded for an extension of coast-wise trade.[4]

Thus, from an early identification of interests with an expanding economy, Harrisons were able to increase the scope of their shipping activity in the Gulf area, from Curaçao, Savanilla and Cartagena in the South to Tampico and New Orleans in the north. Served by loyal

1. R.B. 88. Contract between Romero Rubio on the part of the Mexican United States Executive, and D. Carlos Martens on the part of G. Busing and Co. of Vera Cruz, 12 February 1887, Clause 3.
2. R.B. 9. The contract was signed 9 July 1895.
3. ibid., Article I.
4. ibid., Article II.

and energetic agents, they had, within the space of twenty years, diversified their services and kept their ships fully employed, notwithstanding the adverse pressure of cyclical fluctuations. In so doing they, in turn, contributed to the general economic and commercial growth of the region as a whole. This was no mean achievement.

II

The trade with Brazil was centred primarily on Pernambuco and, as we have seen, was somewhat more traditionally-based than the trades with the Gulf and with Calcutta. Like Mexico, Brazil was at a particular stage in its economic development and required large quantities of heavy engineering equipment for the establishment of railways, harbour works, sugar mills and flour mills. In return there were lucrative cargoes of hides, cotton, sugar, rubber and other tropical produce. The prospects of a high return on the employment of resources in such a market did not escape the notice of shipowners and manufacturers in this and in other European countries. In particular, the long-standing commercial ties between Liverpool merchants and their correspondents in Brazilian ports gave both assurance and encouragement to those companies which might be interested in starting regular steamship services to South America. Just as the Holt brothers had been pioneers in sending steamships to the China coast,[1] so, too, were the Booth brothers inspired to start a transatlantic steamship service with Central Brazil.[2] A simple, though none-the-less relevant fact, however, was that approximately two years before either Holts or the Booths had sent out their first ships on their prospective and initiatory voyages, the Harrison brothers had inaugurated permanent steamship connections with Pernambuco.[3]

Although Harrison sailing ships had made fairly frequent voyages to Pernambuco and Maranham since 1847,[4] there was no regularity

1. F. E. Hyde, Blue Funnel, (1956) p. 19.
2. A. H. John, op. cit., p. 53.
3. Liverpool Statutory Registers of Merchant Ships and Bills of Entry 1864-66 or Gladiator, Olinda, Amazon, Alice, Chrysolite and Fire Queen.
4. Liverpool Bills of Entry 1846-53. Urgent and Dauntless arrived from Brazil in 1847; Dauntless in 1850; Gem in 1852; Edward Boustead in 1854; Orkney Lass in 1855; Templar which was lost in the Bay of Maranham in 1855, and Edward Boustead in 1859.

or set pattern to these voyages. In 1860, however, Thomas Harrison made a tour of the Central Brazilian ports with the express purpose of assessing the strength of the commercial organisation and of obtaining first hand information about trading prospects.[1] Before 1856, Harrisons' Brazilian trade had been handled by Messrs. McCalmont and Company and, thereafter, jointly by Saunders, Needham and Company and Johnson, Pater and Company. Thomas Harrison, having satisfied himself as to the adequacy of the commercial links, was reasonably convinced that trade with Brazil could be rapidly increased. In 1864, therefore, *Gladiator* sailed as the first ship in a regular steamship service and, together with *Olinda* and *Amazon*, established a consistent trading pattern. The expansion of the venture may be judged from the fact that four calls were made in 1864, fourteen in 1865, fifteen in 1866 and between this latter date and the early eighties there was a systematic despatch of never less than one ship a month.[2] During the 1880s there was a marked increase in trade, the number of calls at Pernambuco being virtually doubled and those to Maceio being put on a monthly schedule.

These early steamships, of something less than 500 tons and powered by engines of 80 h.p., had been designed originally for the Charente trade; but they were equally serviceable for transatlantic crossings and, in particular, to those Brazilian ports where easy navigation was restricted by the natural hazards of sand bars. There was an obvious economic advantage in being able to switch the ships from the one trade to the other, especially when it is remembered that there was an equivalent interchange of service between Charente and the Portuguese wine ports centred on Lisbon. The commercial and racial links between Portugal and Brazil provided a further powerful reason for the engagement of the Harrison ships in South American trade; in fact, on most of the outward voyages to Brazil calls were made at Lisbon for the provision of both passengers and cargoes. In its initial stages, therefore, the Brazil trade might well have been regarded as an extension between Liverpool and Portugal.

During the 1850s and 1860s Alfred Holt had, through a process of continuous experimentation, made it possible for the steamship to be used economically on long oceanic voyages. With an improved hull

1. Söhsten Papers, *Diario de Pernambuco*, 29 February 1860.
2. Liverpool Bills of Entry 1864-82.

design, increased carrying capacity and powered by compound-tandem engines, his ships of approximately 2,000 tons were capable of making the 12,000 mile voyage to China at a low coal consumption rate of $2\frac{1}{4}$ lb. per horse-power per hour.[1] In 1865, Alfred and Charles Booth, in collaboration with the Holt brothers, had worked out the specifications of two ships which they proposed to put into the Brazilian trade. The first ship, *Augustine*, sailed from Liverpool on 15 February and the second ship, *Jerome*, on 15 May 1866.[2] These ships were approximately twice the tonnage of Harrisons' *Gladiator* and *Olinda* and might, in relative terms, have been expected to have returned a greater voyage profit than the Harrison ships. This, however, was not the case. Apart from particular technical problems, the Booth ships, which were about the same size as Holts' *Agamemnon*, had engines with approximately half the horse power of the latter and only a little more power than those of the much smaller ships of the Harrisons. The first voyages of the Booth ships were far from profitable, whereas those of the Harrisons, by reason of a shrewd control of voyage costs and relatively large cargo receipts made a consistently high return on capital employed.[3]

Probably the most important factor determining Harrisons' early success was that they had the service of a better and more carefully prepared commercial organisation than had the Booths in their respective entries into the Brazilian trade. From the available evidence, it is clear that their Pernambuco agents, Saunders Bros. and Company (a branch of the Liverpool firm of Saunders, Needham and Company) were persistent in their efforts to secure full cargoes of sugar and cotton. This satisfactory relationship lasted for a period of twenty years. After 1884, however, the very rapid expansion in Brazilian trade made it necessary for the Pernambuco office to have control of greater financial resources and William Blackburn, manager of the Liverpool office, was sent out to effect a reorganisation. In 1887, having been given power of attorney, he decided, with the full approval of John William Hughes, to liquidate the firm and to establish himself as Harrisons' agent under the title of Blackburn, Needham and Company.[4] The active control of the

1. F. E. Hyde, op. cit., p. 173.
2. A. H. John, op. cit., pp. 53-55.
3. Harrison MSS., Voyage accounts 1864-6 for *Gladiator* and *Olinda*.
4. Söhsten papers, 22 September 1887.

business was placed in the hands of Julius von Söhsten who had been acting as manager for Saunders Bros. and Company.[1] On 22 September 1890 the partnership between William Blackburn and J. D. Needham expired and was not renewed.[2] Blackburn thereupon invited von Söhsten to become a partner on a 60/40 per cent profit-sharing basis, the firm continuing under the same style. Harrisons, in recognition of past services, transferred their sole agency to the newly constituted firm, thus severing their connection with Johnston, Pater and Company, a connection which had, by this time, become somewhat attenuated. Although this decision had been prompted as an act of courtesy to Julius von Söhsten the change in status had widespread implications. Since 1887 the agency had been managed on a power of attorney in favour of William Blackburn, subject to instructions from Thomas and James Harrison. After 1890, however, the power of attorney having been rescinded, von Söhsten was given complete freedom to load Harrison ships on the best possible terms without having to cable for instructions.[3] To have placed their affairs in such energetic hands at a time when trade was increasing was something more than coincidence. Von Söhsten not only stimulated the support of shippers in Pernambuco but extended contacts on Harrisons' behalf in Maceio, Cabedello and Natal. His efforts were so successful that, during the height of the sugar and cotton season, other Harrison ships trading to the West Indies had frequently to be diverted to make sufficient shipping space available for the volume of cargo under contract. Finally, in 1901, upon the withdrawal of the Blackburn interest, Harrisons' agency was transferred to the individual name of Julius von Söhsten.[4] It is also relevant that Booths, after having at first neglected Pernambuco as a port, had now recognized the importance of the von Söhsten service; they transferred their agency to him when he acquired control of the firm.[5]

The implications of these changing relationships in Harrisons'

1. ibid., 17 October 1887.

2. ibid., 22 September 1890.

3. ibid. In 1893 the style of the firm was again altered to Blackburn and Co. and in 1896 the partnership between William Blackburn and Julius von Söhsten was dissolved. (*London Gazette*, 6 June 1896). This did not alter the business relationship except that Blackburn's eldest son Charles came in as junior partner.

4. ibid., 16 July 1901.

5. ibid. The author is greatly indebted to Mr Frederick von Söhsten for extracts from the files of the Pernambuco office.

agencies can only be appreciated if they are set within the narrative of Brazilian trade as a whole. Between 1886 and 1905 the United Kingdom, France, Germany and the United States were the main suppliers of both capital and captial goods to Brazil though, within this period, the pattern of trade changed considerably. Up to 1895 the annual average value (1886–95) of goods imported into Brazil from these countries was rising, the United Kingdom being by far the largest exporter with a total annual average value of £8,991,000. From 1896–1900, however, there was a general decline in the level of Brazilian imports, though the United Kingdom retained its major position, a position that was virtually unchanged until 1905. As regards the imports from the other countries, those from Germany remained relatively stable while those from France fell by approximately forty-three per cent, a loss which was to some extent offset by an increase in the import trade from the United States. These same four countries were also the most important markets for the export of Brazil's primary products. In the same period of twenty years from 1886, the United States imported increasing quantities, rising from an average annual value of £11,181,000 (1886–90) to £16,876,000 (1900–05), though there had been a reasonably sharp fluctuation from a peak of £18,000,000 to £13,000,000 in the intervening years. Exports from Brazil to the United Kingdom did not follow such a wide degree of fluctuation as those to the United States, and rose from £5,384,000 (1886–90) to £6,659,000 (1901–5), while those to Germany showed a more substantial increase (though there was a degree of fluctuation similar to that in the trade with the United States). France was the only country of the four to show a marked decline in this trade. A measure of Harrisons' status can be assessed from the fact that, in the period under review, their ships carried outwards from the United Kingdom to Brazil approximately 10 per cent (by value) and brought homewards about 14 per cent of total cargoes.

As in the case of trade with Mexico, Harrisons had, in their trade with Brazil, linked their fortunes with those of an emergent and an expanding economy. One may infer many other points of similarity. In each separate trade, the provision of shipping space was no guarantee of a successful venture. Without a complementary commercial organization, no ship, however well managed, could be certain of maintaining full holds and, in consequence, of making a maximum return to her owners. By ensuring strong and loyal representation of their interests in Pernambuco (as indeed they had done in New Orleans and Vera Cruz) Harrisons were both wise in the exercise of their managerial function, and prudent in laying the foundation essential to the growth of their enterprise. The effort involved was not without its hazards for, as these various trades expanded and became profitable, other shipping lines, British and European alike, were attracted by the potentially large rewards from such routes. Competition increased as tonnage was switched to the more profitable trades; freight rates fell and friction between shippers, on the one hand, and warfare between rival shipping companies, on the other, were inevitable consequences. In such circumstances those shipping lines having the support of loyal and active agents could usually overcome opposition and arrive at some mutually beneficial form of agreement. The Harrisons were no exception. As competition intensified in the Gulf, West Indian and Brazilian trades, they, with the help of their agents, secured such freight agreements as might enable them to maintain their interests and protect their commercial contacts. In short, the physical organisation of the oceanic trades was paralleled by the intense commercial activity within the now well-known framework of the Conference system.

III

The intensification of competition in these various trades corresponded with the periodic downward movements of trade with individual countries in the Caribbean and South American area. At such times British shipping companies were subject to pressure from European subsidised lines, in particular, from the German Hamburg-Amerika and the French Compagnie Generale Transatlantique. Richard Bulman, always desirous of obtaining an agreed system of regulation, had, from the early 1880s, been conducting a series of negotiations with rival steamship lines with the object of equalising freight rates. In 1880, for example, he was party to a Conference of lines engaged in the West Indian, Gulf and South American trades;[1]

1. R.B. 89, 18 March 1880.

these included, apart from the above mentioned European companies, the West India and Pacific Steamship Company and the Royal Mail Steam Packet Company. Harrisons, on Bulman's representation became members of this Conference.

As a corollary to the increase in the volume of trade, a large number of vessels belonging to lines outside the Conference began to take part in the transatlantic trade. In periods of boom this competition was not serious but when cargoes were scarce (as, for example, during particular years in the 1890s) the competition became more vigorous through the process of rate-cutting. In such circumstances British lines were placed in a disadvantageous position as compared with their foreign subsidised rivals. They were, therefore, forced to seek protection and secure the loyalty of their shippers by means of a deferred rebate system. Such rebates were given by Harrisons in the outward trade to Belize in 1895,[1] and the Conference as a whole introduced rebates in the trades to Savanilla, Barranquilla and Cartagena in 1898[2] and on the outward trade *via* Jamaica to Limon in 1899.[3] These were followed by other similar arrangements in the various sections of the trade, and were applied by individual steamship lines in their respective spheres of influence.

In 1904, the several agreements were brought together under a comprehensive Conference agreement. This new association, known by the title of the Conference of West India, Atlantic Steamship Companies, included not only the lines previously in association, but also the other main carriers. These latter were the Leyland Line, the Dutch Line, Koninklijke West Indische Maildienst, the Italian La Veloce Navigazione Italiana a Vapore and the Spanish Compania Trasatlantica de Barcelona. Thus, all the most important British and European steamship companies trading with the West Indies and the Gulf were brought within the range of a single Conference organisation.[4]

This association established a central secretariat and proclaimed the object of the Conference to be maintenance of harmony in the relations

1. R.B. 21, 8 September 1895.
2. Harrison papers, notice to shippers, 28 February 1898.
3. ibid., 1 January 1899.
4. Harrison Papers, Conference of West India, Atlantic Steamship Companies, 4 February 1904.

of the associated lines 'to avoid all cause of competition between them'.[1] The agreement provided satisfactory bases for the fixing of freight rates while giving flexibility to the conservation of particular interests. 'It is understood' so ran the agreement 'that for outward cargo, each line concerned has the right of fixing rates of freight, transit expenses, commissions etc. . . . for its own proper sphere and those rates are to be strictly observed by others of the Associated Lines, obtaining traffic from that sphere, either directly or indirectly'.[2] One further significant feature was directed towards the suppression of competition from outsiders. 'In the event of any outside competition arising' stated Article 9, 'the parties to this agreement (are) to be at liberty to fight such competition unfettered by the stipulations of this Agreement, but to confer with other members, and to give them every opportunity of joining in the contest'. By such means the principles of *laissez-faire* were safe-guarded even though enshrined within a regulatory *grille*.

The Conference was extended in 1907 by the inclusion of other shipping lines[3] and separate agreements were negotiated controlling the level of freight rates in each of the four sections, *viz:*—Islands, Mexican, General and Cuban. Members of the Conference could belong to one or more sections. Harrisons, in fact, belonged to the first three. In each sectional agreement a 10 per cent deferred rebate was paid to shippers. This whole structure, apart from a few minor amendments, was maintained until the beginning of the Great War when the Hamburg-Amerika Line ceased to be a member. In 1916 all the participating members retired from the Conference and reorganized themselves under a series of new agreements as the Association of West Indies Transatlantic Steamship Company Lines.[4]

In the Brazilian trade Harrisons had encountered increasing competition from British and German lines during the 1890s. The rivalry had been particularly intense in years of short supply and it eventually became necessary to seek agreement on freight rates and shipping capacity. The four chief British lines (Lamport and Holt, Royal Mail, Pacific Steam Navigation and Harrisons) thereupon entered into negotiation with three German lines (Hamburg-Amerika, Norddeutscher

1. ibid., Article 7.
2. ibid., Article 14.
3. These were Det Ostasiatiske Kompagnie, Scrutton Sons and Co., Prentice, Service and Henderson and Booker Bros., McConnell and Co. Ltd.
4. Harrison papers, copy of Agreement (General Section) dated 26 October 1916.

Lloyd and Hamburg-South American Steamship Company) and in 1896 formed the Central Brazilian Conference. Under the terms of this agreement a classified list of freight rates was put into operation together with a deferred rebate of 10 per cent. In short, this trade, in common with those to the Gulf, emerged from an initial stage of unregulated growth and had now become subject (in the relation of shipping space to cargoes) to systematic control.

IV

In tracing the course of the expanding fortunes of the Harrison brothers and their partners, we have been primarily concerned with the analysis of sources and of events which may illuminate, and eventually help to answer, specific questions about their business behaviour. In a strictly commercial sense their origins were humble; their initial capital could not be written into a balance sheet as an asset. It was simply an immeasurable quality, a sound judgement and a spirit of adventure. Thus equipped, their actions were almost wholly innovatory in character. From a complex series of part-ownerships, they extended their financial interest and finally gained control of a shipping line providing services to the major ports of four continents.

Any attempt at an assessment of the managerial potentialities of the founders of the firm of T. and J. Harrison must be determined by a previous consideration of four facts. In the first place, the Harrison brothers themselves were always conscious of the need to bring their diverse financial interests in ships under one logical and, at the same time, relatively simple system of control. This had been achieved first, by taking over the original enterprise (including commercial contacts and administrative methods) of Samuel and George Brown; and secondly, through the gradual weakening of the once dominant Williamson share in the ownership of capital assets. Long before the Charente Steam-Ship Company became a limited company, the partnership had been reduced to a small group of individuals each of whom held a fixed proportion of shares, the Harrison brothers owning a majority interest.

The second important factor is to be found in the dynamic approach which was made to all aspects of their function as decision-takers. The shift in the emphasis of their activity from the European wine and brandy trade to the wider prospect of trans-oceanic trades, their transfer from sail to steam, their active promotion and use of the Suez Canal and their flair for operating in new and expanding trades, were all germane to an understanding of their success. The third factor is, by implication, coincidental with the second. They were well aware of the economics of ship-handling. As we have repeatedly stressed, they were continuously exercised in securing full holds and in making shipping space available by switching ships from one route to another. Admittedly, some of their early ships had been sent out on speculative voyages, but with the coming of the steamship an entirely new policy was adopted. After 1860, they always made extensive and careful preparation before entering upon a new trade. Their interests were always safeguarded and well represented; it was not fortuitous that their agents were men of ability and foresight. Finally, having created a shipping company, a life's work of skill and patient labour, the Harrison brothers were ready to defend and protect it with every just means accessible to them. They were rarely worried by open competition; they were always amenable to agreement. Discrimination, rate wars and unfair competitive practices, however, were rigorously attacked. To the Harrisons, the Conference system seemed to offer a logical and realistic alternative to unregulated chaos. In practice, as we shall see in the following chapter, this acceptance of a principle was not always conducive to harmony. Nevertheless, as far as it has been possible to make an objective appraisal of the records, the evidence is strongly on the side of the Harrisons. They were nothing if not courageous in their business affairs; they were generous to their friends; and their undoubted wisdom, from which their achievement had stemmed, enabled them to earn the respect of what few opponents they had.

Did the Harrison brothers and their successors make full and proper use of their accumulating resources? In modern terminology, did they secure the marginal efficiency of capital in their varied enterprise? To these and other relevant questions the following chapters will attempt an answer.

PART TWO

Expansion, Competition and Financial
Organization, 1885 – 1914

CHAPTER FOUR

Conference Agreements and Freight Rates:
the Indian Trade

I

IN recent years, there has been considerable discussion about the operation of Conference agreements. In general terms, the view is that the Conference system, by virtue of the restrictive practice inherent in the form and content of the agreements, is harmful both to the shipowner and to the shipper alike.[1] A countervailing argument is based on the fact that the need for a Conference system arises from the economics of cargo-liner operations, especially when there is an over-supply of tonnage on a given route.[2] Once a cargo has been taken on board practically all costs become overhead costs, and any extra cost incurred in the carriage of additional cargo is only the cost of loading and discharging that cargo. If, therefore, a shipowner can negotiate a rate of freight above the costs of handling the cargo, the additional freight may be offset against the overheads. It is obvious that a full ship is better than a half empty one. At the same time a rate of freight just sufficient to cover handling costs would not be particularly attractive to shipowners on any route whether the ship could be guaranteed full or only partially full cargoes. From the shipowner's point of view, a Conference agreement is not only a device which enables an efficient and regular service of ships to be put on a

1. S. G. Sturmey, *British Shipping and World Competition*, (1962) pp. 322-58; this view is also variously expressed in Minutes of Evidence, Royal Commission on Shipping Rings; see also A. E. Sanderson, *Control of Ocean Freight Rates in Foreign Trade*, U.S. Dept. of Commerce (1938) and D. Marx Jr., *International Shipping Cartels* (1953).

2. For an excellent commentary on this point, in relation to the supply price of ships the author is indebted to R. O. Goss for the opportunity of reading his paper, 'Economic Criteria for Optimal Ship Designs,' before publication in the *Quarterly Transactions of the Royal Institution of Naval Architects*.

route at an equitable rate which will not only cover costs, but secure depreciation and a return on capital whether or not the ships sail with full holds; it is also a means of securing the undivided support of shippers.[1]

The merchant wishing to use ocean transport, however, does not accept the shipowner's logic. Under conditions of free competition in an open freight market, all rates would be forced down, particularly so whenever there was an oversupply of tonnage. In such circumstances the merchant might benefit at certain times though, if this situation continued, the shipowner would be forced to curtail or withdraw his services when rates became uneconomic; speedy and regular communication would then cease and trade would be seriously impeded. This is the second line of argument used by the shipowner in support of the Conference system.

The majority of the merchants who gave evidence before the Royal Commission on Shipping Rings in 1907 were unable to substantiate the contention that a Conference agreement established a monopoly, though they were able, with varying degrees of success, to create apprehension about the restrictive nature of such agreements. Their criticisms, however, were all too often based upon a misconception of the way in which agreements were operated. The system itself establishes not a monopoly but an oligopoly in which there are varying degrees of competition, open both to the shipowner and to the shipper. In the first place, Conference lines have to withstand competition from tramp steamships in the carriage of bulk cargoes, the severity of this competition usually increasing in direct relationship with the extent of fluctuation in the trade cycle. Secondly, the contentious argument which centred round the 'loyalty' contract between the shipowner and the shipper was not always based on fact. This contract, for example, did not, and still does not, offer a universal coverage as in certain circumstances the shipper can use non-Conference ships, provided he and the Conference shipowner agree upon such a course. Thirdly, the physical differentiation of primary products must always ensure classification and the existence of a variety of freight rates and, therefore, there is the likelihood of competition between Conferences engaged in the carriage of similar commodities from different parts

1. *The Report of the Royal Commission on Shipping Rings* (1909), hereafter cited *R.C.S.R.* This point is stressed time and again in the Minutes of Evidence.

Thomas Hughes

of the world. In this context, the fact that different rates may be charged on cargo of the same type for different voyages of about the same length and duration is no justification for believing that one rate rather than another is excessive. Obviously the more efficient and better equipped ports will be able to offer lower rates than those less well equipped. Thus, in the last resort, the level of freight rates must be fixed by the economic conditions governing the supply, loading and discharge of goods at ports, and the variable expenses on particular routes.[1]

The main controversy in the evidence before the Royal Commission was not so much about the question of the restrictions upon the liberty of action by the shipper, but rather upon the problems concerned with the determination of rates. It is arguable that, though limitations on the restrictive powers of Conference agreements exist, this by itself should not be made a reason for the toleration of restrictive practices in trade and shipping. The existence of service and pooling agreements within Conferences, the methods by which freight rates are determined, the secrecy with which Conferences conduct their operations and the lack of adequate external or public control over their policy decisions are, perhaps, the main reasons why concern was, and still is, expressed. We propose, however, to concentrate more particularly upon the way in which freight rates were determined, because in such determination lay a root cause of the difficulties between shipowners engaged in Conference operations and between shipowners and shippers wishing to use their services.

Given the premise that a shipowner must secure the marginal efficiency of his capital and produce a profit, the first problem arises from the nature of his operation. A typical liner cargo (so ran the argument before the Royal Commission) might consist of a multitude of consignments of widely differing categories of goods; on no two voyages might an identical cargo be carried. Part of the costs of carrying this diverse cargo is identifiable (such, for example, as handling charges) but by far the greater proportion of such costs are unidentifiable. Furthermore, except in times of boom, liners rarely sail with completely full holds, so that the costs (which are largely fixed) have to be allocated in accordance with the average utilization of space. In other words, because there is little precise information on the alloca-

1. Such as, for example, those arising from the taxation policy of the country of shipment which may affect the rates of freight.

tion of costs, the ultimate rate fixed may often be higher than need be for the specific service rendered. In practice, the Conference lines have always agreed upon a wide and varied classification of goods to be carried. Of these items, value is most important in rate-determination, though in some trades, for example, the Calcutta trade, the rates on rough cargoes such as jute and linseed determined the higher rates for more valuable commodities such as tea. In the pre-1914 period it was usual for rates for each class, from each of a number of ports, to be compiled, taking account of the volume of cargo on offer at the port, the facilities available, the balance of the inward and the outward trade and the distance to be steamed with the cargo. Any permanent change in costs was always met by an over-all percentage change in the rates. During the past ninety years, these schedules of rates have been built up as a result of experience, of pressures from merchant associations and by the addition of new items. It is very rare for the lowest rates in the schedules not to exceed the extra costs, incurred by the shipowner in carrying the particular cargoes, on which these rates have been fixed.

The criticism directed against these methods of freight-rate determination covered a variety of points. It was stated that the system was inflexible to the changing needs of trade, particularly with regard to the relative variation in rates from different ports. The rigidity in the rate structure very often persisted despite a growing efficiency in the handling facilities at ports. Secondly, there was inherent in the process of rate-determination a degree of cross subsidization, whereby shipments of high value, and easily loaded cargo, subsidized other shipments of low value difficult of storage. Merchants wishing to export high value cargoes were, therefore, often induced to charter their own ships and so reduced the volume of cargo to the Conference lines. This, in turn, impelled the latter to increase rates on other classes of goods. Although the rates might subsequently fall when the volume of shipping space offered by the Conference lines became adjusted to the loss of cargo, the new rates were invariably above the old subsidised rate. From this it was logical to conclude that as far as the relative positions of large shippers and small shippers were concerned, the small were always placed at a disadvantage. In point of fact, however, the evidence before the Royal Commission was wholly inconclusive on this issue.

Yet another consequence of this procedure arose from inflexibility in the adjustment of rates to meet changing conditions of trade. It was admitted that much depended upon the organisation of the individual Conference. If changes in rate schedules had to await ratification by a full meeting of the Conference, delays might occur and benefits from adjustment might be missed. Furthermore, it was a constant complaint by merchants that as the schedules were regarded as confidential, the shipper had difficulty in obtaining precise information about changes of rates and, consequently, what it might cost him to ship a consignment. On these particular charges the evidence of Sir Donald Currie and that of John William Hughes was enlightening. In the Indian and South African Conferences there were regular weekly meetings by the participants and the schedules of rates were made freely available to the agents and loyal shippers. In these trades the grounds of complaint on these points were, therefore, contrary to fact and practice.

On the question of loyalty contracts, the case was less clear. Conferences claimed, as indeed they still do, that loyalty contracts made possible the running of regular shipping services, offering non-discriminative freight and passenger facilities at stable and foreseeable rates. In return, the agreements specify some kind of tying arrangement between shipper and shipowner. Whether the tie took the form of a deferred rebate system or of a contract or dual rate system, the merchants were equally vociferous in their demands that these loyalty arrangements should be abolished. In the Indian, Far Eastern and South African trades, the operation of a deferred rebate was regarded as a means of keeping rates at an artificially high level and, by limiting the freedom of action of the individual merchant, of imposing restrictions on the normal flow of trade. The fallacy in this argument was exposed by the Commissioners themselves who put the counter-argument that merchants could always freely use the services offered by tramp steamers.

Apart from the purely political motives which have led to the qualification or suppression of loyalty contracts, there are, nevertheless, economic arguments which question their usage. In the first place, the existence of a tying arrangement does not, by itself, prevent a rate war from breaking out.[1] The rate wars which occurred before 1914 were caused more often than not by an over-supply of tonnage either

1. *R.C.S.R.*, Evidence of John William Hughes, Q. 21277 *et seq.*, 26 May 1908.

at particular ports or on particular routes, rather than by absence of tying arrangements. Faced by intense competition the shipowner is on the horns of a dilemma. If a Conference should admit new members freely, competition within the Conference might be intensified to the extent that the Conference itself could be endangered. On the other hand, if new members are not admitted a rate war is more than likely between Conference and non-Conference lines. Deferred rebates and contracts are, therefore, in the nature of palliatives; they do not provide a solution to this problem.

In general, it would appear that the claim by the shipowners that the system promotes a greater stability than is the case under free market conditions is well founded. It is, perhaps, true that liner companies do not profit from booms as tramp shipping is able to do. In theory this advantage is offset by the higher profits earned by liners in times of slump. In practice, however, the offset is limited. In slumps liner rates are usually well maintained but the degree to which cargo liner capacity can be utilized diminishes in greater proportion to that in tramps. The reason for this is that in time of depression tramps are laid up whereas liners continue to operate often at a loss. In periods of boom both liners and tramps are used to capacity. Efficiency in the use of shipping resources, therefore, and the effectiveness of a Conference system, must depend, during periods of trade fluctuation, upon a balanced relationship between liner and tramp tonnage.

Having examined some of the relevant economic arguments which arose from the operation of the Conference system before 1914, we can now proceed to an analysis of the growing strength of the Harrison Line within the framework of the two most important Conferences with which they were associated. The first of these Conferences was in the trade to Calcutta, a trade in which Harrisons had a long-standing experience of both the commercial structure and the operation of ships; the second, that to South Africa (which Harrisons entered in 1902), was much less amenable to the more traditional forms of regulation and, therefore, presents a wider variety of problems for analysis. Taken together, however, the successive agreements in these two trades cover, and give illustration to, the points raised in the pages above. Jointly, they can be regarded as typical of the many other Conference agreements in which Harrisons participated.

II

Unlike some other Liverpool shipowners such as, for example, the Holt brothers, who were at first highly suspicious of, and uncooperative with, the operating conditions laid down by Conference agreements, the Harrisons accepted the need for some system of joint regulation of freight rates. They were participants in the Calcutta Conference of 1875, the first Conference and the one which set the future pattern of collaboration between shipowners and, ultimately, of contractual relationships between shipowners and merchants.[1] Under this Conference, Harrisons were permitted to send a ship to Calcutta every twelve days, making an aggregate of thirty voyages a year.[2] By 1908, when John William Hughes gave evidence before the Royal Commission on Shipping Rings, Harrisons were members of the following Conferences: the Calcutta Conference, Outward and Homeward, the South African Outward, the South African Coastal, the Colombo Homeward, Central Brazil Conferences and the West India Transatlantic Conferences. These virtually covered all the trading operations in which the Harrison Line held a substantial interest and from which the firm drew the bulk of its receipts.

Harrisons' general experience of the working of the Calcutta Conference agreements confirmed the view that, in this particular trade, there was no absolute restriction upon competition either from lines outside the Conference, or between lines within it. For example, John William Hughes held that the operation of a rebate system on Manchester piece-goods (introduced into the Calcutta Conference in 1877) in no way inflicted injury on a merchant who shipped his goods outside the terms of such a system.[3] The merchant could always make use of the Conference ships and of their services for frequent and regular conveyance, with cheap insurance. In such circumstances he was charged the Conference rates, but was not eligible for the rebate. In expressing this, Hughes overlooked the fact that the merchant might have been able to ship his piece-goods to India in non-Conference vessels at lower rates than those prescribed by the Conference.

1. The first China Conference of 1879 was, perhaps, more comprehensive in its loyalty contract provisions.
2. *R.C.S.R.*, Evidence of Sir James L. MacKay, Appendix to Vol. II, 14 April 1908.
3. *R.C.S.R.*, Evidence of J. W. Hughes.

In actual fact, this rarely happened and when, in 1889, the rebate system was extended to all kinds of cargo, there was little substantial organisation of countervailing measures from competing lines outside the Conference. The main reason for this was that the majority of the merchants in this trade required uniform continuous rates, in order to be able to make forward contracts with a certainty that no competitor, by getting cheaper conveyance, could undercut him and depreciate his stock. Merchants shipping to Calcutta might continue to use the services of competing shipping lines at lower rates, but they encountered serious disadvantages in so doing. These disadvantages arose from the simple fact that the lines outside the Conference, by virtue of the nature of their business were not as well organised and, consequently, not as efficient as the Conference lines in maintaining regularity of service. The existence of a freight agreement, to which several shipping lines engaged in the Calcutta trade were signatories, did not create an exclusive society. Between 1881 and 1885 the Clan and Anchor Lines were admitted; as were Messrs. Brocklebank in 1891 and Messrs. Gosman and Smith in 1906.[1] Such admissions, however, while lessening the severity of the competition from outside, helped to intensify a healthy rivalry in the provision of services within the regulations imposed by the agreement. In other words, competition between shipping lines was still a spur to endeavour, but it was not allowed to threaten the economic survival of any one of the Conference members.

In his evidence relating to the organization of the Calcutta trade, John William Hughes emphasized the strength of such internal competition between Conference members.[2] Each line endeavoured to persuade merchants that its own vessels were able to provide a more efficient service than those of other member lines.[3] A shipowner, therefore, was more interested in securing as much cargo as possible within the framework of Conference agreements than in shipping cargo on his own account. Occasionally, however, Harrisons shipped salt to India on their own account because no other line would carry it.[4] In general, the line offering the best service in terms of shipping

1. *R.C.S.R.*, Memorandum submitted by J. W. Hughes, 26 May 1908.
2. ibid.
3. ibid., Minutes of Evidence J. W. Hughes, Q.21297.
4. Harrison MSS., Voyage books 1879-85.

space, speed of delivery and careful handling would attract to itself the greatest amount of cargo. On the other side of the coin, it was the most efficiently organised bodies of merchants which could secure the best terms from the most efficient shipping companies. This was particularly so in one section of the Calcutta trade,[1] namely, in the carriage of tea.

There were two Indian Tea Associations, one in London, the other in Calcutta, both comprised of members elected by Indian producers who were engaged in the tea trade.[2] These Associations were concerned with the production and distribution of Indian tea and, in this context, were in a strong bargaining position in such matters as Conference agreements, freight rates and rebates. In the smaller trading centres in India, where the merchants were not as well organized, this two-way relationship did not exist and, as a result, there were often slight variations in rates compared with those from Calcutta. In general, however, the negotiated agreements between the shipowners and the Tea Associations created the structure of rate-fixing for the trade as a whole, and whatever variations there were outside the main ports of Calcutta and Colombo were of little real significance. Apart from the carriage of tea, a commodity which had its own peculiar shipment problems, Harrisons found that the regulation of their trade to India, under Conference agreements, in no way impeded their relations with the body of merchants which they sought to serve. On the contrary, such agreements provided an orderly basis on which trade could be conducted and, by ensuring regularity in the flow of cargoes, secured higher receipts than would have been the case under a system of unrestricted competition.

III

In its examination of the Calcutta Conference, the Royal Commission received a volume of evidence from merchants charging shipowners with the use of restrictive practices. These practices, it was contended, arose directly from the operation of the agreements and were designed

1. *R.C.S.R.*, Minutes of Evidence by Sir James MacKay, 14 April 1908.
2. *R.C.S.R.* Evidence of Charles Campbell McLeod, 7 May 1907, Q.5776-83.

to maintain freight rates at unnecessarily high levels. Such devices as loyalty contracts, involving the use of rebates, and pooling agreements were cited in support of their arguments.[1] The testimony was strongly presented with a wealth of illustration by the merchant representatives; it was equally strongly contested by the shipowners. Were there any real grounds to justify such an apparent opposition of interests? Were the merchants making anything more than an *ex parte* statement? Were the shipowners taking too obstructive a view in the protection of their profit margins? To say that these questions are still unanswered more than half a century after they were formulated would be to shirk the responsibility of facing the fundamental issues which they raise. At best, the argument must turn on an impartial examination of economic criteria, at worse, on an unnatural opposition between groups with mutually identifiable interests. All that we can hope to do in this present book is to make a critical examination of the Harrison records to see whether, in their relations with merchants in the Indian and other main trades, any of the rival claims can be substantiated.

Before the establishment of the Calcutta Conference, Harrisons were sending ships at fairly regular intervals to Calcutta, and charging varying rates of freight according to the requirements of weight and measurement, to the amount of cargo offering and to the size of parcels.[2] As we have seen, shortly after the opening of the Suez Canal, they began to increase their steamship sailings, carrying weight and measurement cargo outwards, for which concessionary rates were charged to larger shippers. These rates varied with the degree of competition. Within a very short time, however, the increase in steamship tonnage on the Indian route had made general and unregulated procedure unworkable, and it was largely in an attempt to solve the problem of excess capacity that the Calcutta Conference was formed. Under its provisions all ships were to sail at regular intervals whether fully laden or not, and as a corrective to any potential loss which the shipowner might thereby incur, equal rates of freight were fixed from each port without concession to individual shippers.

Competition from vessels outside the Conference, however, still led to fluctuations in rates and this, combined with growing discontent

1. *R.C.S.R.*, See in particular the evidence of Charles Campbell McLeod, Q.5835 *et seq.*, 7 May 1907.
2. *R.C.S.R.*, Evidence of J. W. Hughes, loc. cit.

among the larger shippers who had hitherto received concessions up to eight shillings per ton of freight carried, led to the establishment in 1877 of a rebate system on the most important outward cargo, namely, Manchester piece-goods. This system was extended to all classes of goods in 1889.

In the matter of fixing rates for tea cargoes there were undoubted complications. The Tea Associations fought a strenuous battle during the 1890s to abolish the rebate system. The grounds of argument were that rebates, by tying shippers specifically to Conference vessels, strengthened monopoly powers and kept rates artificially high.[1] This view ignored the fact that rates for tea (which was a 'fine' cargo) depended almost entirely on the level of rates fixed for 'rough' cargoes such as wheat, linseed and jute. In his memorandum to the Royal Commission, Charles Campbell McLeod, a well-known tea grower and exporter, charged the shipping lines with abuses in calculating the rates of freight. He contended that the 'liners used their power to bolster up the freight for rough cargo in order to enhance the rate for tea.'[2] Furthermore, this rate-fixing principle affected tea rates in Colombo. When rough cargo ruled at a certain rate in Calcutta the rates for fine cargo were automatically fixed in Colombo at a higher marginal rate. Thus, the freight rates in Ceylon depended on the level of freight rates in Calcutta.[3] As tea exports formed 48 per cent of Ceylon's total exports, this rate-fixing by differentials outside the control of the Ceylon merchants had a direct influence on the flow of trade.[4]

Attempts to abolish rebates and to simplify this complicated structure were made in 1891 and 1892, but the Tea Association failed to persuade the shipowners to amend existing practice.[5] The merchants thereupon made arrangements with a line outside the Conference, the Indian Mutual, to carry tea at 7s. 6d. per ton over the rate for rough cargo.[6] This agreement in opposition to the Conference, however, was short-lived because the Indian Mutual could neither offer the service nor

1. R.C.S.R., Evidence of Charles Campbell McLeod, 7 May 1907, Q.5806, et seq.
2. ibid., Q.5835. Charles Campbell McLeod was elected by the Indian Tea Association to represent them and to give evidence on their behalf to the Royal Commission.
3. R.C.S.R., Evidence of Edward Rosling, 28 May 1907, Qq. 7424, 7245.
4. ibid., Q. 7445.
5. ibid., Q. 5809.
6. ibid.

the capacity of the Conference ships. Tea piled up on the Calcutta wharves, and those shippers who were not under direct contract to the Indian Mutual Line were forced to return to the Conference ships. In 1896, as an inducement to the remainder of the recalcitrants, the Conference made a new agreement with the tea shippers as a whole. Under this agreement, the principle of the rebate was retained but the shipowners agreed, as a further palliative, to deduct the amount of the rebate at the time the freight was payable in London. This, in effect, meant that the shippers paid a net rate without the rebates being deferred.[1] Tea rates, however, were maintained at a fairly high level despite this new arrangement. The basic cause of this was not so much the economic conditions prevailing in the trade, as the operation of a quasi-monopoly within the Conference itself. This took the form of a Tea Pool in which all Conference lines shared, even though they might or might not have been engaged in the carriage of tea. The Brocklebank and Anchor Lines were included in this latter category. They did not carry tea though they shared in the general receipts from the trade. Thus their function within the Calcutta Conference sprang from the very nature of the competition which such organisations are supposed to inhibit.[2]

Before 1914, the operation of direct steamship services to India was complicated by differences in the volume of the outward and homeward trades. Ships on the outward leg of the voyage to India more often than not sailed with half empty holds, whereas, on the return voyage, they were filled to capacity. In consequence, there was an inequality in the ratio between costs and receipts. In Harrisons' case, for example, average freights earned on the outward voyage amounted to less than £2,000 (a sum which did not cover their costs) whilst those from the homeward voyage amounted to £6,000.[3] It was obviously of economic importance to Harrisons, therefore, to be able to charge a rate on the voyage as a whole, sufficient to cover the cost both outwards and homewards. For this reason, the Liverpool or Manchester merchant might have paid a higher freight, but in return, through the provision of a regular service, he secured a quick delivery of his goods without serious deterioration of their quality.

1. ibid., Q. 5827.
2. See J. F. Gibson, *Brocklebanks 1770-1950*, (1953) II, pp. 6 et seq.
3. R.C.S.R., Evidence of J. W. Hughes, loc. cit.

IV

The complaint that shipping Conferences exercised monopolistic or quasi-monopolistic functions could only be justified if they embraced the shipping and commercial activities of every single company trading on a particular route. In the case of the majority of Conferences established before 1914, however, the agreements were rarely comprehensive in this sense. They were unstable intruments of power for two main reasons; first, because variations in efficiency between members within a Conference failed to eliminate competition and consequently required the creation of internal devices to offset this; secondly, because over shorter periods of time, powerful opposition from firms outside a Conference could always be effectively organised. An illustration of these weaknesses can be given from the working of the Calcutta Conference. Before 1890 the main participants in this Conference were the P. and O., the Harrison Line, The British India Company, the Clan Line, the Anchor Line and the City Line. There had been a degree of competition from lines outside the Conference though this had been somewhat sporadic following the admission of the Clan and Anchor Lines in the 1880s. By 1890 the main strength of the outside competition came from the Brocklebank Line, especially in the carriage of rough cargoes. In an attempt to safeguard their interests the Conference Lines considered making an approach to Brocklebanks to discuss the terms upon which mutual agreement could be reached.[1] These negotiations came to nothing, however, because the Anchor Line had taken a decision to increase their sailings from their annual total of 15 to 26,[2] a decision which upset the existing balance of sailings between the companies. In addition the Anchor Line demanded a large increase of outward cargo.[3] 'We were all much disgusted with this demand being so suddenly sprung upon us at such a time' wrote Thomas Harrison. 'We unanimously declined to entertain it and accepted the notice to quit us.'[4] In such circumstances, there was no point in discussing the entry of Brocklebanks. The Anchor Line did, in fact, leave the Conference and, for a short time, Conference Lines suffered an intensification of competition from both Brocklebank

1. Harrison MSS., T. & J. Harrison to Messrs. Hoare, Miller & Co., 25 September 1891.
2. ibid.   3. ibid.   4. ibid.

and Anchor ships. A rate-cutting war followed.[1] 'We still think here' wrote John William Hughes 'that it would be better to go at once to an irreducible minimum to show Hendersons (Anchor Line) that we are really in earnest. The extra cost would not matter if it shortened the struggle.'[2] Attempts were also made by the Conference Lines to induce the more important shippers, who had loyally supported Brocklebanks and the Anchor Line, to break away and ship in Conference vessels.[3] This inducement took the form of a reduced freight rate and an increased rebate. At the same time negotiations to bring the Anchor Line and Brocklebanks within the Conference were renewed on the basis that Harrisons and the City Line should have thirty sailings each per year, the Anchor Line twenty-two, Brocklebanks fifteen, and Clan Line twenty-four.[4] Little progress was made however and it was not until August 1892 that the real danger of the situation was forcibly borne in upon the contestants. Under the operation of the Tea Pool, some 30 to 40 million lbs. of tea shipped from India were controlled by Clan and British India agents. There was, however, a large amount (some 65 million lbs.) in the hands of 'free' shippers. The firm of Gladstone, Wylie and Company, staunch opponents of the Tea Pool and the rebate and Conference agreements generally, made it clear to their principals, the City Line, that unless more favourable arrangements were made, the City Line might lose much of their cargoes from the 'free' shippers.[5] The danger to the structure of the Conference was immediately recognized. 'If an unfavourable or even a qualified reply comes to the Conference, Smith (City Line) will break away' wrote Harrisons to Hoare, Miller and Company 'and, no doubt, we shall all have to follow suit; we, at any rate, must. His (Smith's) idea is to preserve the Conference and fix tea rates (without rebate) periodically like seed and other rates are arranged. It is doubtful whether P. & O. will consent to this system; in that case, rates will have to be absolutely open.'[6]

Fortunately for the members of the Conference, Smith's fears were allayed and by 2 September 1892 it was reported that the Conference

1. ibid., J. W. Hughes to G. Smith, 5 January 1892.
2. ibid.
3. ibid., T. & J. Harrison to G. Smith, 22 January 1892.
4. ibid., J. W. Hughes to G. Smith, 2 June 1892.
5. ibid., T. & J. Harrison to Hoare, Miller & Co., 5 August 1892.
6. ibid.

vessels were getting support from the tea shippers.[1] Such potential instability, however, increased the need to bring outside competitors into the Conference and there was an intensification of effort to achieve agreement with the Anchor Line and Brocklebanks.[2] By the end of October agreement had been reached about the sailings allocated to each firm and Brocklebanks and the Anchor Line were brought within the Conference. It was, perhaps, significant that as soon as this agreement had been reached, the suggestion was made that a general call should be sent to all agents in Calcutta advising on the possibility of improving rates 'especially those on tea'.

Contrary to the general tenor of the evidence given before the Royal Commission on Shipping Rings, participation in Conference agreements was far from amicable. Whatever may have been the position in the long run, there was, on occasion, violent disagreement about specific products. As we have seen, the Indian shippers were in favour of a discontinuance of the rebate system and, in its place, the establishment of a free freight market. These opinions caused a great deal of stress and strain among members of the Conference. In the India trade, for example, a free market in tea could not very easily be instituted without similar arrangements being applied to other commodities such as salt, linseed, jute and gunny cloth. George Smith of the City Line was generally in favour of the principle of rebates but was 'dreadfully frightened of offending the tea shippers.'[3] It became obvious that a general arrangement involving fixed freight rates and rebates did not always work to the advantage of one firm as against another or, indeed, because of the special trading arrangements, of one port as against another. Thus, while it might be advantageous to the Glasgow lines to have a freer system of freights on tea, the application of such a principle in general terms would have affected adversely the interests of Brocklebanks and Harrisons in the carriage of salt and gunnies.[4] 'In view of the special interests which the two lines have in salt and Liverpool cargo', wrote Harrisons 'a friendly method of working to avoid undue competition is undoubtedly desirable.'[5] They therefore proposed the establishment of a pooling

1. ibid., T. & J. Harrison to Hoare, Miller & Co., 2 September 1892.
2. ibid.
3. Harrison MSS., T. & J. Harrison to Hoare, Miller & Co., 13 January 1893.
4. ibid.
5. ibid.

arrangement for the carriage of salt and gunnies. 'We do not know what the upshot may be' continued Harrisons 'or how far the loyalty of our colleagues (which so far we have no reason to doubt) may stand the strain; but we must be careful to watch that no private arrangements are made by anyone inside or outside the Conference to our disadvantage.'[1]

Smith, however, remained intractable and threatened to withdraw the City Line from the Conference unless his views prevailed.[2] Brocklebanks and the P. and O. believed that the rebate must be retained or that there must be open competition and would hear of no middle course. 'Cayzer (Clan Line) we understand, shares the P. and O. views' complained Harrisons; 'the British India and Anchor appear lukewarm rather "sitting on the fence". If it rested solely with us, we would certainly hold to the rebate system, but not being sole arbiters, as Smith will not agree with us, we would agree with him rather than have no settlement and, abandoning the rebate temporarily at any rate, ask you to fix the tea rates monthly as you do the rates on other goods.'[3] It was foreseen that such an arrangement would involve fluctuations in the rates according to the availability of Conference ships on the berth and outside ships seeking cargoes. In such circumstances the bonds uniting member firms in a Conference agreement were brittle and tenuous. The argument about the operation of a rebate in the Calcutta Conference continued for some years to divide rather than unite opinion. As late as March 1895 letters (sometimes recriminatory in tone) were being sent hither and thither. At that time Harrisons were proposing that the rate for tea should be 5 shillings (or 10 shillings) above the average rate for wheat, linseed and jute.[4] This rate was to carry with it a cash discount on payment of freight of 5 per cent (or 5 shillings) to firms which undertook to ship exclusively by the Conference vessels. It was thought that the discount would maintain the principle of giving some advantage to loyal customers without the objectionable features of a deferred rebate. Although the proposal was supported by British India it was eventually turned down.[5] 'The P. and O. and Clan Lines are strongly in favour of

1. ibid.
2. ibid., T. & J. Harrison to Hoare, Miller & Co., 24 February, 1893.
3. ibid.
4. ibid., T. & J. Harrison to Hoare, Miller & Co., 15 March 1895.
5. ibid.

deferred rebates, partly, no doubt, because the abolition of them at Calcutta might cause a movement in the same direction in other trades, China, Australia etc. The Anchor Line and Brocklebank would like the tea thrown open like jute and other produce.'[1]

Tentative agreement to maintain the principle of the deferred rebate was reached. A fuller concurrence of opinion was achieved later in 1895 when it was proposed to raise rates on the Calcutta route.[2] The Bombay rate, however, was reduced and this, as might have been expected, caused friction with the Calcutta merchants. They retaliated by forming an Association to bring pressure upon shipowners to arrange rates more profitable to themselves.[3] The strength of this Association was demonstrated when some of the Calcutta merchants attempted to make a unilateral arrangement with the Salt Union to establish a minimum price for salt at Calcutta[4] 'to be enforced by bonding salt when the price fixed is not obtainable overside.'[5] Harrisons and Brocklebanks, the two firms mostly concerned with the carriage of salt, refused to discuss the proposal. 'Our idea is to continue selling freely as heretofore at the best price of the day, in the hope that a continuation of low prices may discourage some of our competitors and enable us to obtain a long-deferred reward.'[6]

The Association, however, did not let matters rest. The opening of the Manchester Ship Canal proved to be a complicating factor in the trade relations between Liverpool and India. On the one hand the Ship Canal Company began to put pressure upon Liverpool ship-owners to send their ships up the Canal to Manchester;[7] on the other hand the Calcutta Merchants Association was tempted to deal directly with the Manchester Shippers' Defence Association, a creation of the Canal Company, in the hope that rates on Manchester piece-goods might be lowered. The arguments used were double-edged. The Canal Company sought to win over the shipowner by stating that if ships sailed directly from Manchester the Calcutta merchants would not

1. ibid.
2. ibid., J. W. Hughes to G. Smith, 10 October 1895.
3. ibid.
4. ibid., T. & J. Harrison to Hoare, Miller & Co., 18 October 1895.
5. ibid.
6. ibid.
7. ibid., J. W. Hughes to G. Smith, 2 October 1895; see other refs. e.g. F. E. Hyde, *Blue Funnel* (1956), pp. 105-109.

object to an advance in rates.[1] Implicit in the argument, however, was the threat that if the shipowners did not accede to the request, the Ship Canal Company would create difficulties. The Conference was moved neither by the prospect of higher rates nor by the implied threats and refused to discuss the matter with the Manchester Shippers' Defence Association.[2] 'The Conference has met' wrote Hughes 'and has always been willing to meet its regular supporters as Rallis, Dewhursts and Ashton Hoares can testify; we do not think any great feeling exists in these gentlemen's minds except that engendered by the General Philosophic Manchester Principle that all freight is robbery.'[3]

In fact, the economics of the situation were well understood by Harrisons. The freight earned from Manchester and Liverpool to Calcutta was generally lower than that earned to other places. 'Our *Statesman*, just sailed' wrote Harrison 'would have earned £2,100 more with coals, Cardiff to Colombo, than she is making to Calcutta. . . . The *Ameer*, chartered by the British India Company gets £2,000 more from Middlesborough and London to Calcutta than she would make from Manchester and here.'[4] It was, therefore, extremely difficult, if not impossible, for the Liverpool firms to contemplate sending ships to Manchester at existing freight rates and to have to set against these rates the increased cost of navigating the Canal.

The general picture which can be drawn of the working of the Calcutta Conference during these years is that it was a fairly loosely-knit structure. As the interests of the various members were affected in the relatively advantageous or disadvantageous conditions prevailing, so their loyalty to particular agreements was confirmed or strained to breaking point. As we have seen, dissatisfaction with the actual working of agreements caused some firms to break away; at various times between 1875 and 1900 nearly all the members threatened to do so. Harrisons, themselves, were forced into this position in 1897 because it appeared unlikely that a satisfactory agreement could be arranged on the working of the Calcutta rough purse,[5] i.e. a pooling agreement for the carriage of rough cargoes. Many other instances could be cited of the danger points at which the Conference nearly

1. ibid., T. & J., Harrison to Hoare, Miller & Co., 7 February 1896.
2. ibid.
3. ibid.
4. ibid.
5. ibid., J. W. Hughes to G. Smith, 3 May 1897.

Frederick James Harrison

came to grief.[1] The view that this kind of Conference was purely an association of strength is not borne out by the facts; nor is the equally publicized view that the shipper was always at the mercy of the united body of shipowners. More often than not Conference decisions were influenced by consideration of the economic position of loyal supporters. There is little doubt, however, that, following a rate-cutting war with competitors outside the Conference, the temptation to raise rates once such competition had been eliminated proved to be too strong to be resisted. Logically it was the one method open to Conference members (given the circumstances of the case) to recoup their losses incurred by war. On the whole, the records show that Harrisons were usually unhappy when it became necessary to increase rates on commodities in the Indian trade. They were less sensitive about other trades. Considering the elements of internal strain, considering the personal attributes of the main protagonists, it is surprising that the Calcutta Conference retained its force and its influence. It follows that the economic advantages of such co-operation must have been considerable, and that what was applicable to this Conference was probably equally applicable in the other Conferences to which the Harrisons belonged.

1. In particular over the question of discriminating rates between Middlesborough and South Wales for the carriage of iron. Harrison MSS., J. W. Hughes to G. Smith, 23 May 1900.

CHAPTER FIVE

Competition, Conferences and Freight Rates: the South African Trade

I

I N their trade to India, Harrisons had frequently instructed their ships to make intermediate calls at ports along the east coast of South Africa. Such calls were, in no sense, part of a regular service; they were in response to limited and specified commitments within the general framework of the voyage pattern to India. In May 1902, however, a group of London merchants invited Harrisons to carry cargo outwards to Natal under contract.[1] As this proposal was in no way inconsistent with existing practice, Harrisons readily agreed to the merchants' conditions. They thereupon approached the members of the South African Conference to see whether the establishment of such a direct outward trade would create any conflict of interests. 'After some very little discussion', stated John William Hughes, 'the managers of the Conference admitted that there was this need for tonnage, and said we might be allowed to go, but they made a condition that we should go to (Capetown, East London and Port Elizabeth) . . . They made no difficulty at all about our coming into the trade; they said we should ourselves become members of the Conference'.[2] This invitation to enter the South African and the South African Coastal Conferences was received with some reluctance by John William Hughes and his brother Thomas, as they regarded the conditions of acceptance as a limitation upon their freedom of action.[3] Nevertheless, the terms of entry into the South African trade were finally agreed and, by the end of 1902, Harrisons were engaging not

1. *R.C.S.R.*, Evidence of J. W. Hughes, Q. 21407, 26 May 1908.
2. ibid., Q. 21408.
3. Staveley Taylor MSS., W. Staveley Taylor to a correspondent, 1 September 1902.

only in a new major trade (with the firm of Staveley Taylor as their Liverpool loading brokers), but were also signatories to new Conference agreements.

In practice, the opening of this new trade route did not immediately affect the disposition of Harrison resources. The ships sailed outwards under Conference agreements to South Africa and thence as tramps either to Bombay or Calcutta (and, at times, to Karachi or Rangoon) where they were put on berth under the terms of the Calcutta Conference agreements. This was a convenient procedure and was made possible because the Calcutta Conference was reasonably flexible in structure. By contrast, the regulation of the trade to South Africa was more rigid in application.

In the South African Conference, the relationship between shipowner and merchant had been laid down by what was known as the '1893 Compact'.[1] This Compact had replaced a previous agreement of 1886 under which a 5 per cent rebate had been allowed.[2] Under the Compact of 1893, however, the rebate had been increased to 10 per cent and freight rates had been increased to cover the additional charges incurred. This was a Conference agreement with a difference. Although the shipowners promised to provide a service and pay a rebate there was no corresponding obligation on the part of the merchants.[3] In the absence of a legally enforceable contract, this Compact worked efficiently until 1898 when a fresh agreement was negotiated.

The peculiarity of this trade was that there was no distinction between the merchant owning the goods and the forwarding agent.[4] The person responsible for taking out the Bill of Lading for the shipment of the goods, whether Principal or Agent, was entitled to claim the rebate. The claimant had to declare, however, that he had not been directly or indirectly interested in shipments by 'outside' vessels. A merchant, therefore, whose goods were shipped by a forwarding agent in an 'outside' vessel would lose his claim to rebates. The consignee was thus brought within the framework of Conference stipulations. By the 1898 agreement, however, these stipulations did not

1. R.C.S.R., postscript to memo. submitted in evidence by Sir Donald Currie, 18 February 1908.
2. ibid.
3. ibid.
4. R.C.S.R., Vol. 1, 1090, p. 30.

prevent shippers from claiming a rebate on their other shipments, if compelled under instructions to ship the goods of a client by an opposition steamship.[1] In practice, this agreement led to unnecessary friction between Conference lines and between merchant and shipowner. It also led to discriminatory action against disloyal shippers on a scale not usual in other Conferences.

When Harrisons entered the South Africa Outward Conference in 1902, the other chief participants were the Union Castle Mail Steam Ship Company (Donald Currie & Co.), the Bucknall Line (Sir John Ellerman), Clan Line Steamers (Cayzer, Irvine & Co.), the Natal Direct Line (Bullard, King & Co.), Aberdeen Direct Line (John T. Rennie Son & Co.), the German East African Line and the German Australian Line, the two latter sailing from Continental ports only. In order to increase their strength in this trade and to be able to negotiate on equal terms with the existing firms in the Conference, Harrisons proposed to enter into an agreement with J. R. Ellerman of the Leyland Line to run a joint service of ships to the Cape from Liverpool. This arrangement, apart from one exception, would not affect the competitive pattern within the Conference between the London lines and the Scottish lines. The exception was in the relationship between Harrisons and the Clan Line, a relationship which sprang from a close identity of interests in the Calcutta trade. In their negotiations with the Ellerman Line, therefore, Harrisons felt bound to consider the implications of such an alliance on both their own interests and those of the Clan Line. It was, accordingly, agreed that a private pooling arrangement be established between Ellermans, Harrisons and the Clan Line. This was necessary because the Clan steamships were much smaller than those sailed by the joint Ellerman-Harrison Line.[2] Agreement was reached on 21 April 1902, whereby Ellermans and Harrison should run a twelve-day service of ships to the Cape from Liverpool and that, in return, the pooling agreement with the Clan Line should provide for a recompense to that Line of 5s. per ton on an agreed freight rate of 20s. per ton.[3]

The working of the pool can best be illustrated in the following

1. ibid.
2. Staveley Taylor MSS., J. W. Hughes to J. R. Ellerman, 17 March 1902, 20 March 1902, 21 March 1902, 26 March 1902, 31 March 1902.
3. ibid., J. W. Hughes to J. R. Ellerman, 26 March 1902.

way. The Ellerman-Harrison ships carried an average of 5,800 tons of cargo, whereas the Clan Line ships carried 2,800 tons. Thus, on the basis of the pooling agreement, the result of one voyage would be:—

	Cargo Tons	Rate shillings	Pool shillings	Coal Tons	Direct Receipts £
Clan Ship	2,800	20	10	1,000	1,400
Harrison-Ellerman Ship	5,800	20	10	1,500	2,900

The total receipts for the two ships would be £4,300 and the Clan and Ellerman-Harrison share would be £2,150 each. Ellerman-Harrison would have to pay Clan £750 plus 5 shillings per ton from the pool on 5,800 tons, equalling £1,450, making a total of 2,200. Thus the final share on the voyages of the two ships would be, Clan £3,600, and Ellerman-Harrison £5,500.[1] There was, therefore, a reduction in the absolute receipts from the trade from a proportion of approximately 2:1 to 1:1½ in favour of the Clan Line. This kind of pooling arrangement was secretly negotiated between the two lines and lasted until 1904, when the admission of the Houston Line into the Conference[2] made it a matter of political and legal expediency to discontinue it. It should be added that upon the cessation of the pool, Ellermans and Harrisons paid a *solatium* of £20,000 to the Clan Line.[3]

Entry into the South African trade intensified changes already taking place in the pattern of cargoes shipped by Harrisons. The firm became increasingly occupied with the handling of engineering products of all descriptions. With the development of the South African economy, there was a growing demand for iron and steel imports. In addition to railway equipment of all kinds, the shipping companies were required to find space for machinery of all shapes and sizes. This, in turn, necessitated the re-designing of holds and the equipping of ships with stronger handling gear. It also pre-supposed adequate wharfage facilities

1. ibid., 21 March 1902.
2. ibid., J. W. Hughes to Sir Charles Cayzer, 11 January 1904; Cayzer to Hughes, 23 January 1904.
3. ibid., T. & J. Harrison to Cayzer, Irvine & Co., 7 January 1904.

at the main ports of call. In other words, the general economic growth within developing economies led to an increase in the carriage of capital goods which, in itself, had a direct effect on the promotion of efficiency in the shipping industry.

There was an obvious source of friction in the Conference arrangements for the carriage of heavy cargo to Natal and South Africa. In the shipment of rails, for example, each company was allocated a specific tonnage, and it was usual for the Glasgow and Liverpool lines to ship from Barrow, and for the London lines to ship from Middlesborough. In 1905, however, some of the London lines proposed to ship their allocations by the Clan Line.[1] William Staveley Taylor (of the firm of Staveley Taylor and Company), acting on behalf of the Ellerman-Harrison Line, took exception to this course of action, or to any arrangement being made by the London lines for transferring any part of their proportion to a northern line without mutual consent. He contended that such action would be prejudicial to the Liverpool lines 'unless they got an equal proportion to the Clan Line', he stated '(they) would be driven, in order to get on any equality with them, to take rails from Middlesborough, which, as a rule, did not suit them'.[2] Agreement was subsequently reached, whereby the Clan and Ellerman-Harrison lines should be permitted to purchase an allocation of rails from the London lines, and that these allocations should not count in their private carrying arrangements. The carriage was, in fact, to be debited to the London lines.[3]

II

Another vexed question, that of the effect of contractual agreements between shipowner and merchant on a Conference rating structure, was brought out in the negotiations which led to the entry of the Houston Line into the South African Conference. Before admission, Houstons had entered into contracts with Messrs. Lysaght to carry galvanized iron from Avonmouth to Capetown and Algoa Bay 'at

1. Minutes of South Africa Outward Conference, 4 July 1905.
2. ibid., also 22 August 1905 and 29 August 1905.
3. ibid., 12 September 1905.

rates of 20 shillings per ton to Capetown and Algoa Bay, 25 shillings to East London and Natal and 30 shillings to Delagoa Bay'.[1] These rates were generally lower than those charged by the existing Conference tariff. If Houstons were admitted to the Conference, therefore, there would be an obvious difficulty, in that by honouring their contracts, Houstons would be operating their ships at rates inconsistent with Conference rates for similar classes of goods. Houstons, in fact, were admitted to the South African Conference on 8 January 1904, and, in the following month, a meeting was held for the express purpose of considering the implications of the Houston contracts.

The Conference lines agreed that, in general, the conditions of the contracts should be strictly adhered to, and that no better services should be provided than those which the contracts specified. 'This would mean' so ran the argument, 'that the shippers, having no better service guaranteed, should be compelled to confine their shipments to the Houston steamers, and that those who have contracts for a guaranteed fortnightly service, should make their shipments by Conference steamers only, *via* Capetown, with the right of transhipment to ports beyond'.[2] The objective of this decision was to induce such shippers to put an end to their contracts with Houstons, and to force them to accept Conference facilities. Houstons, however, objected to this particular arrangement on the grounds that it would leave the Conference open to legal action from their shippers, who might consider themselves subject to breach of contract. Consequently, at a second meeting held on the following day (4 February), the Conference decided that, in order to protect loyal shippers, the first class rate (taking Capetown as a basis) should be reduced 2s. 6d. per ton, second class rates 1s. 3d. per ton, the third and fourth class rates remaining in accordance with the existing tariff.[3] It was felt that these reductions would go some way towards offsetting the low rates quoted in the Houston contracts. A further proposal sought to ensure that when disloyal shippers claimed the right to ship by Conference steamships, over and above the service guaranteed by the Houston Line, they

1. ibid., 12 and 13 July 1903.
2. ibid., 3 February 1904.
3. ibid., 4 February 1904.

should be charged ten shillings per ton additional freight on third and fourth classes of goods.

The entry of the Houston Line thus raised fundamental questions of principle which not only led to a revision of the tariff, but also called for an investigation into the rating structure as a whole. Representatives from the Conference met a special committee of merchants to discuss the matter. The exercise in self appraisal by both sides proved to be both stimulating and profitable. This was, at least, a fair example of the way in which shipowners and merchants could co-operate within the framework of a Conference agreement; it was a procedure (fairly common in practice) which belies the contention that the activities of shipowners within a Conference were invariably opposed to the interests of the merchants whom they sought to serve.

One controversial issue which frequently dominated the discussion at meetings of the Conference members, was the relative competitive position of the two German lines within the Conference. As the evidence before the Royal Commission on Shipping Rings made clear, it was very often cheaper to ship goods from Hamburg than from British ports because there was a lower cost structure at that port. Although freight rates from Hamburg to Capetown were in equality with those from British ports, the German merchant had the additional advantage of being able to ship goods from the interior of Germany by State railway on a through rate agreement.[1] Thus the shipping lines in the South African Conference in general, and the British shippers in particular, found themselves in a distinctly unfavourable position compared with German shipowners and merchants. The essence of rate differentiation between British and foreign lines was to be found in the carriage of bulk cargoes, such as, for example, cement. In this type of commodity, the German lines were undoubtedly able to undercut the British rates of freight to Capetown, and other South African coastal ports. They agreed, however, to equalise their rates from Hamburg to Natal and Delagoa Bay. There was, however, a difficulty in the shipment of such cargo from Hamburg to Capetown. The German shipowners feared that if equal rates were applied to this route, their shippers would charter sailing ships and, consequently, their steamships would lose business. They therefore refused to increase

1. R.C.S.R., evidence of Sir Donald Currie, 18 February 1908; ibid., John Byron, 18 February 1908, Q. 15251-3.

the rate from Hamburg to Capetown.[1] This decision by the German lines, not only increased the fears and suspicions in the minds of British shipowners that there were unfair conditions ruling within the Conference rating structure, but gave incentive to the complaints from British shippers that rates from British ports to South Africa were unduly high.

The ability of a Conference to exert pressure on shippers was often greater when tariff classifications were subject to technical considerations. Again, the South African trade provides many examples of such rate determination and, as a consequence, exhibits the true basis of power and of its use by a Conference. This was, perhaps, fully illustrated in the carriage of steel pipes. During the course of 1906, concessions were made by the Conference to ship quantities of steel pipes at a reduced rate in face of growing competition from outside lines;[2] but in October of that year Stewarts and Lloyds approached Bucknalls for the purpose of arranging a future contract on the basis of previously agreed concessionary rates. The Conference, however, argued that reduced rates could no longer be maintained and decided that the weight-rate on tubes up to 6 inches in diameter should be increased by 2s. 6d.[3] William Staveley Taylor, acting on behalf of Harrisons, raised objections to this proposal on the grounds that present rates were favourable enough; 'but the other lines thought an effort might be made to secure a slightly higher rate and this was eventually agreed to'.[4] Stewarts and Lloyds retaliated by demanding a lower rate for tubes with a diameter *larger* than 6 inches, a proposal which the Conference found to be 'rather drastic'.[5] Nevertheless, in an endeavour to meet Stewarts and Lloyds, the Conference decided to make a reduction of 1s. 3d. on the carriage of the larger tubes. When set against the increase of 2s. 6d. in the rate for smaller tubes, this reduction was not particularly generous. It was obvious that these rate changes, particularly the differentiation on the various sizes of tube, would have a discriminatory effect on the trade as a whole. Taylor himself was apprehensive on this point and, in a subsequent meeting with Stewarts

1. Minutes of the South African Outward Conference, 8 December 1905.
2. Minutes of the South African Conference, 19 June 1906.
3. ibid., 9 October 1906.
4. ibid.
5. ibid., 28 November, 1906.

and Lloyds, was left in no doubt as to the serious consequences of such a rate-fixing decision. 'Stewarts and Lloyds are exceedingly dissatisfied with the action of the Conference lines' he wrote in a note appended to the Minutes, 'which will very much restrict their trade in steel tubes to South Africa.'[1]

These particular negotiations concerned with the fixing of rates did not vitally affect Harrisons' major trading interests with South Africa. John William Hughes was, therefore, not greatly exercised by the outcome of the discussions. In such matters he was far more concerned with the impact of contractual obligations between shipper and ship-owner upon the relationships existing between the Conference lines. He was always apprehensive that a powerful shipper might use his influence to create disharmony within the Conference itself. As we have seen, Harrisons, in their negotiations with Ellermans for the establishment of a pooling arrangement, had been meticulous in their insistence on safeguards for the Clan Line, a shipping company with which they had always had friendly agreements. Such finely-balanced considerations were just as much an integral part of a Conference system as the operation of rate-fixing machinery. When, therefore, Stewarts and Lloyds, having failed to achieve an over-all reduction of rates in their 1907 contract, put forward new proposals which, if accepted, would have caused dissention amongst Conference members, John William Hughes became a more active protagonist.

In previous years, Stewarts and Lloyds had always placed their contracts with the Conference through the Bucknall Line. In their preliminary negotiations for a further contract in 1908, however, they approached not the Bucknall Line but the Clan Line, in the anticipation that this latter company would offer more favourable rates.[2] The move was a shrewd one. It had the immediate effect of creating suspicion in the minds of Messrs. Bucknall Bros. and led to recriminatory exchanges.[3] The imminent danger of a split in the Conference was averted only by the prompt action on the part of John William Hughes. At his suggestion the negotiations were transferred from the

1. Minutes of South African Conference, 11 December 1906. Note added by W. Staveley Taylor.
2. Staveley Taylor MSS., Minutes of the South African Conference, 10 December 1907.
3. ibid.

main contestants to a more impartial referee, the Union Castle Line.[1] The proposals for a new contract were given fair scrutiny and, as a result, 'it was unanimously decided that no reductions in the rates should be made'.[2] This whole episode is interesting not so much from the way in which Conference unity could be maintained, but from the fact that it was often a relatively simple matter for a powerful external interest to create disunity, by upsetting the internal balances of mutual interest between the participants. The oft-repeated view[3] that Conferences are impregnable associations in pursuit of purely selfish interests, is much too broad a generalization. In this specific instance, the South African Conference had acted reasonably by adjusting rates in response to demands; but, when these demands were renewed and were accompanied by a manoeuvre designed to undermine the solidarity of the members of the Conference, the somewhat tenuous and fragile nature of such an association was manifest. The fact that the shipping lines in the South African Conference could, and did, re-establish a united front so quickly is testimony, not so much to the strength of its structure, but to the commonsense of its members.

Having made the above point, however, there were occasions when the South African Conference did exercise a very real power. This is, perhaps, best illustrated by an examination of the agreements between the Conference and the South African Government. Under these agreements, the carriage of cargo under contract to this government had to be carried in Conference ships.[4] In 1906, however, the firm of Maclay and McIntyre of Glasgow, a firm outside the Conference, had negotiated the carriage of 5,000 tons of creosoted sleepers to Natal. The suppliers were Messrs. Christie and Company of Ardrossan. This latter company had approached the Conference and had been quoted the agreed contractual rate of 20s. per ton of 40 cubic feet with no primage or rebate if shipped in parcels of not less than 1,000 tons by berth steamships, or 17s. 6d. if shipped in a full cargo.[5] These quotations were not acceptable to Christies and they thereupon

1. Harrison MSS., J. W. Hughes to W. Staveley Taylor, December 1907.
2. Staveley Taylor MSS., Minutes of the South African Conference, 10 December, 1907.
3. R.C.S.R., passim.
4. Staveley Taylor MSS., Minutes of the South African Conference, 4 September 1906. The only exceptions were coal and creosote oil.
5. ibid., 28 August 1906.

negotiated a contract with Maclay and McIntyre for the carriage of the sleepers at a rate of 16s. per ton of 50 cubic feet.[1] As these sleepers were subject to the agreement between the South African Government and the Conference lines, Harrisons pointed out that the proposed contract with Maclay and McIntyre would be a breach of existing agreements.[2] All the other Conference lines supported this view and, after correspondence with the Cape Agent-General, Maclay and McIntyre were forced to abandon their arrangement with Christies. In fact, the sleepers were eventually shipped from Australia.

At first sight it might appear that the Conference had exerted undue pressure against a non-Conference line over the carriage of a relatively small amount of cargo. The matter, however, was not so easily settled. In the following year Messrs. Christie and Company negotiated a further contract with Maclay and McIntyre for the carriage of 75,000 sleepers to Durban. This contract had quoted a c.i.f. price outside the rates laid down by the Conference and the shipment, on such terms, had apparently been accepted by the Natal Government.[3] The Conference once again protested, not merely on the grounds that this was a breach of contract, but that by accepting a c.i.f. price the Natal Government had altered the terms regulating the shipment of cargoes. Strenuous efforts were made by the Conference, first, through the Agent-General, to persuade the Natal Government to rescind the agreement; and secondly, by an attempt to dissuade Christies from engaging freight until the matter with the Natal Government had been resolved. Such efforts, however, were fruitless. On the one hand, Maclay and McIntyre announced that their contract with Christies was irrevocable, on the other, the Agent-General expressed himself powerless to act further in the matter. If this situation had been allowed to go by default, the legal basis of contractual agreements between a Conference and those it sought to serve, must have been placed in jeopardy. Strong representation was, therefore, made to the Natal Government, stressing the point that two contracts had been made for the same cargo, and that, in consequence, if the Christie contract were allowed to stand, an action for damages might ensue. The point was well taken. The Natal Government, despite earlier reports to the contrary, had not in fact

1. ibid., 4 September 1906.
2. ibid.
3. ibid., 23 July 1907.

signed the Christie contract. After some further discussion it honoured its agreement with the Conference by accepting the shipment of the sleepers in Conference vessels. Thus, the power of the Conference against outside competition was sustained. Though, it should be added. that as an inducement to such a settlement, the Conference members agreed to carry future consignments at lower rates. As a result, Clan, Ellerman and Harrison ships accepted delivery of sleepers from Ardrossan at a rate of 17s. 6d. per ton of 50 cubic feet.[1]

One suspects that Conferences could, and sometimes did, exercise pressure against individual groups of merchants; but it is equally true that merchants had it within their power to mitigate such pressure. In the case quoted above, the South African Conference had not only to protect the definition of mutually-agreed contracts from external interference, but had also to provide an efficient service to an overseas Government. The fact that, in the process, there was a degree of conflict does not justify a conclusion that there was any abuse of power. On the contrary, the satisfactory outcome of the negotiations about the carriage of railway sleepers, can only be construed as an attempt by the Conference to maintain its just rights within the law. Furthermore, it provides an excellent example of the degree of flexibility which a Conference could employ in meeting and overcoming a very difficult situation.

The member firms in the South African Conference, however, were not always as united as in the case of the railway sleepers. On the question of tendering for the carriage of coal for the South African railways, it had been usual for contracts to be shared among the participating lines. But in 1906, Houstons and Rennies declined to join in the arrangements then being made for new coal contracts, Houstons reserving to themselves the right to tender privately on their own account.[2] In the same year, a storm blew up over the carriage of flour. In this particular commodity there was keen competition with American shipping lines. The minimum rate from New York to Natal was 27s. 6d. per ton, whereas the economical rate from British ports was 37s. 6d.[3] When, therefore, in 1907 a letter was received from a firm of millers asking for rates on shipments of flour from this country

1. ibid., 20 August 1907.
2. ibid., 5 September 1906.
3. ibid., 3 July 1906.

to various South African ports, the Conference found itself unable to meet the expressed desire that rates could be negotiated on the same basis as those ruling from American ports. The millers added a rider that if such rates could be agreed 'a great deal of business might be done'.[1] The Union Castle and Bucknalls, however, were not disposed to make a reduction in rates. Ellermans and Harrisons, on the other hand, were of the opinion that as the United Kingdom rates were considerably in excess of the American rates 'they would absolutely prohibit business being done from this country'.[2] If the contrary view prevailed, Ellermans and Harrisons declared that they would take every means in their power (even that of giving evidence before the Royal Commission on Shipping Rings, then in session) to make known their opposition to what they considered to be 'inequitable action of certain of the Conference lines, in granting, in normal times, preferential rates from America in comparison with those charged from this country.'[3] This body-blow had the desired effect and agreement was eventually reached, notwithstanding protests from Houstons and Bucknalls, to reduce British rates to the American level.[4] Such an incident is a refreshing reminder that the powers of a Conference were not invariably employed against outsiders; they could, on occasion, be used to discipline its own members.

III

It is arguable whether shipping conferences give shipowners a decided financial advantage. If Harrisons gained such an advantage from their membership of the Calcutta and South African Conferences, it was because the provision of regular services and speedy ships together with the technical requirements of particular carrying trades, imposed upon them the necessity for constant vigilance in the building and design of their ships. It was only by maintaining an up-to-date fleet that they could uphold their competitive position within the Conference

1. ibid., 29 October 1907.
2. ibid.
3. ibid.
4. ibid., 5 November 1907.

system and, insofar as this was achieved, they were able to minimise operating costs and keep voyage profits at a consistently high level.

If we begin by examining their voyage profits during the period from 1885 to 1914, it is obvious that a well-defined pattern claims attention. From 1885 to 1889, Harrisons' voyage profits increased from £42,000 to £224,000 then fell back to an average of £142,000 in the two following years. In the second period from 1892 to 1900, there was a comparable rate of growth, though with a different order of magnitude i.e. from £72,000 to £422,000, the year 1895 being the only exception when there was a fall to £97,000. Thereafter, from 1901 to 1909 (with the exception of 1908 which was a relatively poor year) profits ranged from £195,000 to £241,000. From 1910 to 1913 there was a very rapid increase, consistent with the earnings of other Liverpool shipping companies; in the Harrisons' case from £311,000 to £733,000. These figures follow very closely the pattern of annual shipping earnings for the country as a whole.

Comparing Harrisons' voyage profits with the fluctuations in freight rates, there is again a fair degree of correlation. Between 1885 and 1889 both inward and outward freight rates followed a rising trend and this was consistent with the rise in the Harrison earnings; from 1890 to 1899, however, there was a fairly sharp decline in the level of rates, the outward rates falling rather more than the inward. The Harrison receipts, having fallen in 1890, showed a fairly steady increase and a greater degree of correlation with the inward rates. After 1900 there was a marked decline and a persistent depression of inward rates until 1909. Outward rates, on the other hand, remained remarkably steady during the same period. After 1902, Harrisons' earnings were not as sensitive to a depression of inward rates as those of many other companies, because in some of their trades (such as, for example, that with South Africa) the major part of their receipts came from the carriage of outward cargo. After 1909 both inward and outward rates moved steadily upwards and this fact, no doubt, accounted for the general rise in shipping incomes including those of the Harrison Line.

Set against the still wider background of fluctuations in the terms of trade, Harrisons' earnings show some degree of inverse correlation in the fact that between 1885 and 1891 terms of trade were unfavourable while earnings were rising; from 1896 to 1914, however, there is a direct relationship between earnings and consistently favourable terms of trade. The explanation of this change is that, in the former period, Harrisons' earnings were made up from a greater proportion of inward cargoes and, in the years after 1900, from a greater proportion of outward cargoes. In other words, Harrisons' earnings can be related to a reasonably predictable inelasticity of demand for primary products in the earlier period, and an even greater inelasticity of demand for manufactured goods in the latter.

If we are to establish with any degree of accuracy the measure of benefit derived from participation in a Conference system, it is obvious that, as Harrisons' activities were generally consistent with economic trends, proof, or otherwise, can only be sought by considering those few years in which these activities were out of line with the general trend. Such years were 1891 and 1892 when Harrisons' earnings fell from £143,000 to £72,000, a fall of much greater intensity than that recorded for shipping earnings as a whole. This was caused by an intensification of outside competition from the Brocklebank and Anchor Lines in the outward trade to Calcutta, and in the inward trade from the rivalry with the Indian Mutual Line.[1] The competition in the outward trade was, however, eliminated by October 1892 when the Brocklebank and Anchor Lines were brought into the Conference.[2] The short, but sharp, struggle with the Indian Mutual Line, though inflicting damage while it lasted, was eventually resolved because the Conference lines, by virtue of their superior service, were able to win back the loyalty of the tea shippers. Whereas the Indian Mutual was offering a cut-throat rate of 7s. 6d. per ton, the Harrisons were able to charge an average of 21s. 6d. per ton even at times of the most intense competition. As a result, Harrisons' earnings resumed an upward trend. The effectiveness of Conference agreements thus enabled Harrisons to offset competition and increase net earnings to a level far in excess of the general trend. In the absence of a Conference system, Harrisons' earnings from free market rates alone, would have been nearly 20 per cent lower than those actually earned.[3]

In the South African trade, the effectiveness of outside opposition on the level of Conference rates is not so easily measured. This is

1. See above pp. 73-75.
2. See above pp. 76-77.
3. Harrison MSS., personal memoranda of John William Hughes, 1891-4.

William Staveley Taylor

because Harrisons were far more interested, during the early years of the present century, in outward cargoes. In 1903–4, however, the Houston Line engaged in a rate-cutting war with the Conference lines. Over short periods of time, outward rates were cut by 10 per cent on specific classes of goods and homeward rates by as much as 25 per cent.[1] Harrisons' earnings showed no diminution in aggregate, though average earnings per voyage tended to decrease throughout 1903, the explanation being that an increasing number of voyages was made each year after 1901. The Houston Line joined the Conference in 1904 and rates were immediately restored to the 1902 levels. Again, the effect of this opposition was qualified by the power of the Conference in the strength of its countervailing methods. Membership of the Conference, therefore, was advantageous in that it provided a cushion against a too violent fluctuation in rates during times of intense competition. It is true that Harrisons' earnings were maintained (and even increased in 1904) during the period of opposition from the Houston Line. The evidence suggests that they had to work their ships harder in order to obtain a more favourable cost ratio. Without Conference backing, however, rates would have fallen more sharply, so persistent was the Houston opposition. In actual fact the Conference so blunted the effectiveness of this competition that Harrisons' earnings continued on a rising trend in contradistinction to a slightly falling trend for shipping earnings as a whole. In such circumstances one can, perhaps, understand the inner meaning of John William Hughes's statement to the Royal Commissioners that 'no one objects more strongly to fluctuating rates than the regular shipper, who is enabled by a uniform, continuous rate to make forward contracts with a certainty that no competitor, by getting cheaper conveyance, can undercut him or depreciate his stock.'[2] Hughes was far too shrewd an observer to attempt an appraisal of the consequential advantages to the shipowner.

1. R.C.S.R., South African Conference, Appendix VII, iv. p. 59.
2. R.C.S.R., Statement by J. W. Hughes, 26 May 1908.

H

CHAPTER SIX

Finance and Policy 1885 - 1914

I

IN the years before 1914 the Harrisons were not particularly distinguished (as were some of their contemporaries) in the promotion of technical innovations designed to increase the tempo of overseas trade. Alfred and Philip Holt so improved the design of the steamship that it became possible to open up a vast market in the Far East; Alfred and Charles Booth using ships to Holts' specification did much the same for South America; Alfred Jones, by virtue of his remarkable foresight and business acumen, secured for his shipping companies a dominant position in the economies of West African countries; John Samuel Swire was a master and initiator of practice designed to eliminate competition among rival shipping companies. The Harrisons and their partners had no such pioneering aspirations. Their particular skill lay in adapting and developing the work of others in their endeavour to promote a reasonably well diversified business activity. They were undoubtedly successful, though such an unqualified assertion is not, by itself, of much value in understanding the basic motives shaping the policies which ultimately achieved success.

To what purpose did the Harrisons direct their energies? How did they use their resources? Did they make the best possible use of those resources? Was their entrepreneurship such that they were able to meet and overcome difficult economic situations inhibitive to a consistent and orderly growth of the firm? These, and many other questions have to be asked if we are to attempt a more realistic assessment of their achievements. Unfortunately, the answers to these questions require a precision which it is not always possible to obtain from an analysis of the source material. Nevertheless, the information of a financial nature which we have, is capable of providing varying degrees and levels of measurement so that, by a process of comparative analysis, one can arrive at a near approximation of the truth. In other words, by making an appraisal of their policy and by testing it against the measure of financial gain or loss, we may hope to define, in more precise terms, the quality of the Harrisons' managerial skill.

As we have already seen, the firm of Thomas and James Harrison owned and managed the Charente Steam-Ship Company. This latter company was incorporated as a limited company on 16 December 1884 with a nominal capital of £512,000, divided into 512 shares of £1,000 each fully paid up.[1] There were originally thirty-two subscribers to the shares, though the majority holding was vested in Thomas Harrison, T. F. Harrison, Frederick J. Harrison, Heath Harrison, Edward H. Harrison, John William Hughes, Thomas Hughes, Thomas Williamson, and Richard R. Williamson. Although each of these subscribers had only one share, their interest in the firm was more adequately represented by their share of ownership in the vessels (twenty-two in number) which had been transferred from T. and J. Harrison to the Charente Steam-Ship Company Ltd. This pattern of share-holding was not based, as in the years before 1884, on investment in separate ships; it was now calculated in accordance with the value of the assets of the firm as a whole. Despite this change, however, ownership was still maintained in the hands of the Harrisons, the Hughes, the Williamsons and their close friends and control was, therefore, limited to a small and closely-knit family group. By 1908 a further alteration in the distribution of the shares had taken place, the majority, by this date, being held by five members of the Harrison family, five members of the Hughes family and one Williamson.[2] This capital structure lasted without alteration until 29 December 1950, when it was subdivided into 512,000 shares of £1 each. The capital was then increased by bonus issue to £2,560,000, divided into 2,560,000 shares of £1 each.[3]

The Memorandum of Association states that the objects for which the Company was established were to take over the steamships from T. and J. Harrison 'with their separate accounts, general accounts, insurance accounts, benevolent funds and other accounts as they may stand in the books of Thomas and James Harrison on 31 December 1884; also all policies of insurance, contracts for repairs . . . charters

1. *Memorandum and Articles of Association of the Charente Steam-Ship Company*, p. iv.
2. Harrisons MSS., Minute C.S.S.Co., 22 February 1908.
3. Memo. and Articles of Association, op. cit., p. iv.

entered into and not completed; and with the said steamers to convey passengers, goods, merchandise, mails, troops and treasure, whether belonging to members of the Company or others, to and from such places as the Managers . . . may determine.'[1]

These objects were specific and, one would have thought, required a reasonably detailed form of book-keeping. There are no general accounts for the Company as a whole before 1885, though, as we have seen, the partners kept certain voyage and personal accounts. After 1885, however, John William Hughes instituted a more formal documentation consisting of a general statement of accounts with the briefest possible explanation of the included items.

To begin with, only a short resumé of the accounts was given at the Annual General Meeting. This statement contained the balance brought forward from the previous year, the net profits from the voyages, and sale of any ships in the previous year. The offsetting items were simply the dividends and the cost of ships which had been added to the line. In the 1890s, however, Frederick Harrison and John William Hughes assumed greater responsibility for the accounts and devised a more efficient system of book-keeping.[2] As a result, the Balance Sheet was made more comprehensive and the Income and Expenditure Accounts much more indicative of the various activities of the firm.

The most important sources of information relevant to changes in policy can be gathered from the Insurance Account and from the Suspense Account. This latter account was changed in 1899 into the Reserve Account. These accounts, together with the Accident, Provident and Stevedore Accounts were credited from, or debited against the General Account. Thus, a number of 'box' accounts were designed to operate for specific purposes. In 1899, Chalmers, Wade and Company were appointed the first auditors of the Company and, thereafter, the accounts as a whole conform to a regular pattern.

In the first place, an indication of the growth of the firm between 1898 and 1914 can be gained from Table 1 (a). The fleet, which in 1884 had been assessed at 40,000 tons, had been virtually trebled in size by 1899 and more than doubled again by 1914, representing an over-all seven-fold increase in tonnage in the space of thirty years. This rate of growth compared favourably with other Liverpool steamship

1. ibid., p. iii.
2. Harrison MSS., Memorandum by John William Hughes, 1890-8.

TABLE 1 (a)
HARRISON FLEET
1884–1914

Year	Gross tons	Year	Gross tons
1884	40,000	1906	197,966
1898	111,766	1907	203,848
1899	127,527	1908	213,475
1900	138,867	1909	220,057
1901	149,083	1910	227,290
1902	169,027	1911[1]	266,974
1903	179,160	1912	284,082
1904	185,999	1913	300,208
1905	189,653	1914	297,133

companies.[2] In general terms, the Harrisons had followed a reasonably consistent policy in building up their fleet by ordering two new ships a year during the 1890s and three new ships a year from 1900 to 1910.

Such consistency in the pattern of ordering ships, however, may not have given Harrisons the full advantage of fluctuations in ship-building costs (the Holts, by comparison, placed orders generally when costs were low) but it enabled them, because they were not inhibited by a rigid cost policy, to increase the tonnage and capacity of their new ships in accordance with the estimated requirements of particular trades. For example, the average size of ship in the Harrison fleet during the 1880s was 3,500 G.R. tons; in the 1890s the size had increased to 5500 G.R. tons, a figure exceeded in the case of *Craftsman* (1897) and *Workman* (1897) each of 6,200 G.R. tons; *Politician* (1898) and *Collegian* (1899) each 7,200 G.R. tons; *Custodian* (1899) and *Mechanician* (1899) each of 9,200 G.R. tons.[3] The cost of these larger vessels increased out of proportion to the tonnage. This was partly because of increasing

1. This figure includes the purchase of the Rennie fleet. For the method used in compiling the figures of gross tonnage see Appendix I.
2. One notable exception to this statement is the Ocean Steam-Ship Company, which had a twenty-fold increase in tonnage during the same period. See F. E. Hyde, *Blue Funnel* (1957), p. 170.
3. Minutes C.S.S.Co., 24 February 1897; 23 February 1898; 24 February 1899; 21 February 1900.

ship-building costs and partly because they incorporated the latest improvements in both design and equipment. In 1893 the cost to Harrisons of a 5,000 ton ship was approximately £53,000; by 1900 a 9,000 ton vessel cost on average £100,000.[1] In fact, *Patrician*, a ship of 7,500 tons laid down in 1899, cost as much as £113,000.[2] Thereafter, until 1914, Harrisons built three classes of ship; the first class consisted of ships of approximately 10,000 tons deadweight, the second of ships of 7,600 and the third of ships of 6,000.[3] The large Class I ships were employed on the Calcutta and New Orleans routes; Class II ships ran mainly to Mexican, Caribbean, South African and North Pacific ports; Class III ships were used in the Brazil, Caribbean and Mexican trades, chiefly to those ports in Brazil where it was necessary to have shallow draught vessels. There was, however, no hard and fast division in the employment of any particular ship, except insofar as limitations imposed by port facilities and cargoes to be handled, dictated their use.*Wayfarer*, *Custodian* and *Mechanician* used for the carriage of cotton, did not cease to be employed out of season, their cargoes from the Gulf in June and July being timber, lumber, staves, grain, molasses, cotton-seed oil and meal. At other times of the year these vessels were used on the Calcutta and South African routes.

This policy of building ships to the needs of particular trades, though logical when considered against the background of Harrisons' total carrying trade, was not, when compared with the shipbuilding costs of other Liverpool companies, strictly economic in its use of capital resources. Table 2 compares the shipbuilding costs of the Harrison fleet with those of other Liverpool shipping companies. From this it is clear that, in the thirty years between 1885 and 1914, Harrisons' shipbuilding costs show a reasonable degree of correlation with those of other companies. There are, however, deviations from the average for particular groups of years within the period as a whole. Between 1885 and 1890 Harrisons were undoubtedly placing their orders at prices well below the Liverpool average; from 1893 to 1897, the Harrison orders were still being placed on advantageous terms, but the margin between their costs and those for other companies had considerably narrowed. From 1899 to 1907 when Harrisons were

1. Minutes C.S.S.Co., 21 February 1900.
2. ibid., 27 February 1901.
3. ibid., *passim* 1900-14; also from information supplied by J. Cowan.

TABLE 2
SHIPBUILDING COSTS

Year	Harrison Line New ships; average cost per gross ton	Harrison Index 1907=100	Average Cost of New ships for other companies[1] 1907=100
	£		
1870	25.5	230	220
1885	10.2	92	121
1886	11.5	103	110
1887	12.0	108	125
1888	13.1	118	130
1889	15.0	135	148
1890	15.2	137	138
1891	13.2	119	115
1892	10.7	96	112
1893	10.4	93	97
1894	10.1	91	98
1895	10.4	93	99
1896	10.0	90	96
1897	10.9	98	106
1898	11.4	102	122
1899	14.7	132	132
1900	15.2	137	135
1901	12.9	116	126
1902	12.2	109	110
1903	11.1	100	108
1904	12.0	108	95
1905	13.1	118	99
1906	—	—	104
1907	11.1	100	100
1908	—	—	90
1909	11.1	100	92
1910	11.5	103	91
1911	12.3	110	102
1912	15.1	136	130
1913	15.2	137	133

1. Compiled from the records of the Ocean Steam Ship Company, China Mutual, Shire, Castle and Glen Lines; also from statistical material concerning costs of new ships from the records of John Swire & Sons and from the Liverpool Steamship Owners' Association.

engaged in building their three classes of ships, their costs fluctuated only slightly above and below the average. After 1908 their costs were approximately 10 per cent above that average. In other words, Harrisons lost much of their initial competitive cost advantage and, by the end of the period, were paying more for their ships than the majority of their rivals. This does not imply that, by so doing, Harrisons were getting less value for their money; on the contrary, the Managers were convinced that the additional charges were more than offset by the provision of superior equipment.

TABLE 3
NET ANNUAL PROFITS FROM VOYAGES, 1885–1914

Year	£	Year	£
1885	42,027	1900	422,875
1886	52,909	1901	224,904
1887	79,276	1902	195,912
1888	164,106	1903	200,619
1889	224,991	1904	208,779
1890	141,483	1905	213,243
1891	143,448	1906	189,627
1892	72,013	1907	241,351
1893	95,015	1908	165,018
1894	118,050	1909	206,482
1895	97,864	1910	311,376
1896	140,949	1911	393,418
1897	170,414	1912	668,379
1898	267,614	1913	733,808
1899	241,469	1914	581,656

If we now proceed to an examination of the use of these ships, it is necessary to relate annual voyage profits to gross tonnage employed. In Table 3 annual voyage profits are shown as a net figure after working payments and other minor charges have been deducted. These figures have been used in conjunction with those in Table 1 (a) to produce Table 4, i.e. net annual profit per gross ton of shipping employed between 1898 and 1914. While not claiming that the figures in this latter table are absolutely reliable as a measure of Harrisons' activity, they nevertheless enable us, with some degree of accuracy, to offset fluctuations caused by changes in the aggregate size of the fleet from one year to another and changes in the pattern of the voyages. It is, perhaps, significant that between 1902 and 1907, earnings per gross ton remained remarkably stable, fluctuating within the comparatively narrow range £0.9 to £1.2. This indicates that despite uncertain conditions in some of their trades during this period, Harrisons were achieving flexibility in the use of their three classes of ship and were thereby maintaining an over-all level of earnings. On the other hand, when trading conditions began to improve (as they did after 1910) they were able, by a more specific direction of particular tonnages to particular markets, to reap an immediate advantage from such an

TABLE 4

VOYAGE PROFIT PER GROSS TON 1898–1914

Year	Average profit per gross ton in £	Year	Average profit per gross ton in £
1898	2·4	1907	1·2
1899	1·9	1908	0·7
1900	3·0	1909	0·9
1901	1·5	1910	1·3
1902	1·1	1911	1·4
1903	1·1	1912	2·3
1904	1·2	1913	2·4
1905	1·1	1914	1·9
1906	0·9		

improvement in trading conditions. To this extent, it may be said that, within the limits imposed upon them by changes in the level and the pattern of trade, they were making the best possible use of their capital resources.

The various methods which were used to finance a consistent rate of expansion in the size of the fleet, flowed directly from Harrisons' achievements in sustaining the profitability of their enterprise. Most of the ships were paid for from the General Account, an account which was largely related to voyage profits. This Account was normally sufficiently in credit to enable them to support a steady policy of ordering two ships a year up to 1901 and three ships a year thereafter. Exceptions to this general pattern in building up the fleet, however, occurred from time to time when outside purchases were made or when deliveries were delayed. On such occasions they supplemented the purchase of new ships out of the sales of old ships and by disbursements from the Insurance Account. This happened in 1889 when the Star Line was bought from Rathbone Brothers and Company. Harrisons paid £135,000 for the ships and goodwill of the Star Line. In addition their contractual agreements for two new ships and part-payment on two further ships had to be met, amounting to a further £131,000. Two of the Rathbone ships were sold almost immediately after purchase, and the receipts from these sales, together with those from the sale of *Sculptor* and *Orator*, helped to relieve the strain on the General Account. Even so, there was a deficit on the transaction as a whole, a deficit which was covered by a transfer of £24,000 from the Insurance Account. Funds in the Insurance Account were used for the purchase of ships as and when the credit in the General Account was not sufficient to cover all commitments. This happened in the years 1892, 1894, 1895, 1902, 1903, 1908, and 1911.[1] In this latter year Harrisons purchased the fleet of Messrs. Rennie of London. This fleet consisted of seven ships, six being paid for from the General Account and one from the Insurance Account.[2] In short, the use of the General and Insurance Accounts in this way meant that Harrisons not only covered the insurance of the fleet themselves, but could write off the fleet and all additions to it as soon as purchased.

The Insurance Account was, in fact, used for a variety of purposes. Its original aim was undoubtedly to act as cover against accident to, and loss of, ships due to marine risks. Thus, like many other Liverpool shipowners, Harrisons created their own fund for the insurance of their ships, a practice which was maintained until 1939, with the exception of the war years from 1914–18. This account was replenished each year from voyage profits, such transfers taking the form of premiums. These premiums were frequently a substantial proportion

1. Minutes C.S.S.Co., 26 February 1902. The largest amount for a single ship, paid from the Insurance Account, was £107,374 for *Yeoman*.

2. Minutes C.S.S.Co., 28 February 1912. The ships and their purchase prices were as follows: *Intaba* £72,073; *Inkosi* £38,199; *Inkonka* £29,921; *Insizwa* £19,552; *Ingeli* £14,005; *Inyati* £10,059, and *Inanda* £45,341. Harrisons retained the services of Messrs. Rennie and Co. as loading brokers in London and as head agents in South Africa. See *The House of Rennie: One Hundred Years of Shipping, 1849–1949* (1949), p. 29.

of the voyage profits and, accordingly, in periods when liabilities were small, balances of some magnitude were built up. As we have seen, these balances were occasionally used to purchase new ships. As a cover against accident and loss, the Account was generally adequate. That this was so, was due very largely to the fact that there were successions of years in which the fleet was involved in no serious loss or accident. There were occasions, however, when more than one disaster occurred in the same year. For example, in 1904 *Yeoman* was lost and *Inventor* was in collision with, and sank, *Goolistan* off Oporto. These misfortunes cost the Insurance Account £91,000.[1] In the following year two collisions cost the fund £26,500. In 1912 the Company's ships sustained three serious accidents; *Workman* went ashore near Rio and was a total loss; *Student* was stranded outside Parahiba and could only be refloated after jettisoning the cargo; *Counsellor* sank the steamer *Canidale* in the Bay of Biscay and was ordered to pay two thirds of the loss.[2] The total estimated loss to the Company amounted to £73,000 and this amount, added to other minor claims, exhausted the credit balance of the fund brought forward from 1911, as well as the income from premiums for 1912. As a result, a debit of £10,626 had to be carried forward in the Insurance Account to 1913. In fact, the actual loss exceeded the estimates by £3,917. Against the background of some twenty-eight years in which the Insurance Account had always been in credit, this deficit cannot be regarded as serious. In 1913, however, a further series of losses occurred involving the Company in liabilities of £25,000. This, again, was not serious when viewed against the record, but a year of deficit raised the possibility that the policy of self-insurance might have to be reconsidered. Fortunately, such a review was not necessary. The income from premiums, less ordinary claims in 1913, amounted to £65,322 and the Account finished the year, despite the heavy claims against it, with a credit balance of £22,447.[3]

One other major disbursement from the Insurance Account calls for attention. In years when claims were small, sizeable balances were accumulated and from these the Company was able to pay bonus dividends. Such dividends were paid in 1887 (£10,200), in 1906

1. Minutes C.S.S. Co., Insurance Account, 26 January 1905.
2. ibid., 26 February 1913.
3. ibid., 26 February 1914.

(£38,400), in 1907 (£51,200), in 1908 (£30,700) and in 1910 (£40,960).[1] The payment in 1908 is of some interest because this particular year was one of depression in trade. The bonus dividend in this year, therefore, was a reflection, not so much of the trading results, as of the general financial stability of the whole organisation. In general, the flexibility which the Managers achieved in their use of this Account, indicates that they regarded it as an additional reserve.

An examination of the accounts as a whole for the years 1898-1914,[2] reveals a number of interesting facts. In the first place the Harrison partners put their resources to consistent and profitable use. Secondly, despite a steady annual increase in the size of the fleet, and despite changes in the pattern and source of trade (for example, by entry into the South African trade), the average annual voyage profit per gross ton of shipping employed, remained depressed between 1901 and 1911. This was due almost entirely to uncertain and adverse economic conditions in those countries which Harrisons served. It is more than likely that had the Managers not succeeded in their efforts to improve the quality and efficiency of their ships or, as will be seen later, to reduce voyage costs, profits from voyages in absolute terms would have suffered a more violent fluctuation during these difficult years. Thirdly, the effectiveness of Conference agreements in the maintenance of earning capacity during this period cannot be ignored. The strength of Harrisons' position was based upon managerial skill which, in turn, gave them a competitive advantage over some of the other Conference lines.

It is clear, therefore, that in the over-all management of their affairs, Harrisons were able to minimize declining trends in levels of activity. From this, certain financial consequences followed. By maintaining consistent flows of cash through their various accounts, they retained a simple, but effective, flexibility in the use of their resources, and, in years of difficulty, had resilience and sufficient strength to sustain the Company without undue loss of momentum. In this context it is, perhaps, significant that they made very little use of their reserve investments (which were, in fact, mainly fleet replacement funds) as an active weapon of policy. Investments were allowed to increase as and when conditions were propitious, the interest from these invest-

1. See Appendix II.
2. See Appendix II.

ments being used as income. Thus the Company's actual resources, at any given time, were always in excess of actual needs. A more careful analysis of the accounts might, therefore, bring to light additional facts which might establish a more accurate picture of real strength and weakness. Such an analysis we now propose to make.

II

The accounts of the Charente Steam-Ship Company, compared with those of many other shipping companies, are reasonably consistent in form and, therefore, capable of varying degrees of analysis. Unfortunately, though individual accounts have been preserved in the annual reports between 1885 and 1899, there was no requirement to present a full Balance Sheet. Such statements appear only after this latter date under the provisions of the Companies Act. It has been necessary, therefore, as pre-requisite to an understanding of the growth of Harrisons' enterprise, to reconstruct a series of balance sheets for the years 1885-99.[1] The major element in such an assessment, namely, the annual valuation of the fleet, has been estimated by taking the initial £512,000 and adding to that sum the annual net additions of tonnage at the gross purchase price for each additional vessel. It must be emphasized that no allowance has been made for depreciation. Such an omission, it is realized, does not conform with the conventions of the accountant. Some further explanation is, therefore, needed on this point.

It is possible in attempting to estimate the value of a Company's employed capital, to choose from a number of procedures. These may be related to cost, or to a current valuation, or to a present valuation of the Company's future prospects. Accountancy practice uses *cost* (i.e. purchase price) as the basis of valuation. Long-term (or 'fixed') assets are then normally depreciated, in one of a variety of accepted ways, by an annual amount which, it is anticipated, will reduce this cost to nil during the lifetime of the asset. In calculating the return on capital employed, 'profit after charging depreciation' is compared with 'capital employed after charging depreciation'. In

1. See Appendix II.

the case of the Harrison accounts, the Company's procedure was to write off vessels when they were purchased out of general profits or out of the Insurance Fund; in consequence, they charged no depreciation against income, but they carried forward, in respect of the fleet, only the purchase price of the original vessels acquired in 1884. The effect of this is three-fold. First, both income and capital employed are larger in absolute terms than they would be if depreciation were written off. Secondly, changes in the return on capital employed follow the same pattern as when depreciation is charged, but the fluctuations are to some extent evened out. Thirdly, the relationship of income to carrying capacity is more closely shown if depreciation is omitted.

The analysis which we have made of the Harrison accounts has, as its essential objective, the measurement of change in the pattern of earnings over a period of time. If the deduction of a depreciation figure, based on an assumed pattern of reduction in the value of the fleet (composed of £ of many different years), from the voyage profits (expressed in £ of a particular year) is introduced, it is possible that a spurious appearance of precision may be given to the calculations. The omission of any figure for depreciation does not materially alter the pattern of earnings over the period 1885–1914; but it must be made clear that in this assessment, however, the assumption is made that a vessel retains a technical capacity for work until it is scrapped. This would seem to be no less realistic than the assumption that vessels depreciate annually according to some preconceived ratio.[1]

Having established the procedure, we can now examine the Harrison accounts in greater detail.[2] In order to determine end-year figures of employed capital we must add to the annual valuation of the fleet the annual value of investments at cost (as market value is not given), and working capital (estimated as a net figure from current assets and current liabilities). The details of these particular items are comprised in the nominal share capital, the credit balances of the Suspense/Reserve Fund, the General Account, the Insurance Account and the Accident Fund. These totals give us the balance sheet equity. To this must be

1. It should be added that to calculate the return for depreciation one must (1) deduct 5 per cent of the fleet cost from the voyage profits of the particular year, (2) halve the fleet cost to give a depreciated value, and (3) compare these two figures to find the percentage return.

2. See Appendix III.

added the difference between the estimated value of the fleet and that of £512,000 which is always shown as a nominal figure. This difference is referred to in Appendix III as 'Ploughed back in vessels'.

After 1900, the Balance Sheets of the firm can be given rather more informative reconstruction because more data are available. As a consequence, it is possible to determine more precisely the breakdown of current assets and current liabilities. The items on the assets side are balances due by the Managers subject to realisation by them of sundry debts and credits in connection with open accounts; the Mexican Mail Service; and, during 1906 and 1907, £50,000 worth of Mersey Docks and Harbour Board bonds. Some indication of the financial strength of the Company can be gained from the fact that, in 1908, current assets included loans of £107,000 to unspecified borrowers, £81,000 in 1909 to Messrs. Ashton, Tod and Noble and £50,000 to the Bank of Liverpool. By 1913, the special deposit with the Bank of Liverpool stood at £300,000 and that with Ashton, Tod and Noble at £96,000. On the current liabilities side there are three main items, excess of receipts over expenditure on open voyage accounts, creditors, and bills payable by Managers. The first of these items was self-adjusting from one year to another and is, therefore, not significant as a guide to any series of fluctuations.

Thus, from this reconstruction of Balance Sheets, it is possible to assess the end-year totals of employed capital in the Company. From £512,000 in 1884, this amount had virtually doubled by 1893 and had trebled by 1899. Between 1900 and 1905 the rate of increase was subject to fluctuation, but after 1905 there was a more regular rate of increase until 1910. By 1914, employed capital stood at £4,143,430, an eightfold increase since 1884. Compared with other large Liverpool steamship companies (Ocean Steam-Ship Company, for example, had employed capital of £3,900,000 in 1914), the Charente Steam-Ship Company had followed a steady, consistent and satisfactory rate of growth. The growth had been steady, inasmuch as the Managers had not only maintained and improved the fleet, but had widened the scope of the services as and when circumstances had been favourable; growth had been consistent, having kept pace with an increasingly diversified pattern of trade with India and the Far East, South and East Africa, the United States and the Caribbean. In financial terms, the growth had also been satisfactory, as the books of the company testify; but could this degree of satisfaction be measured in economic terms? Could it be expressed in terms of utilization of resources or in varying levels of efficiency?

III

In 1906, John William Hughes prepared a short memorandum on the various costs of running ships, making allowance for size, speed and cargo handled.[1] Such costs included fuel, food, wages and salaries of crew, port charges, canal dues and office overheads. Based on one thousand-ton cargoes of tea, linseed, cotton and steel rails, the figures are not readily comparable and must be used as orders of magnitude rather than precise or comprehensive costs. Using the same basis as John William Hughes, we have compiled the following table to include figures for the additional years 1910 and 1914 indicating costs per ton-mile for the various classes of Harrison ships.

TABLE 5

COSTS PER TON-MILE IN PENCE

Year	3,500 tons G.R.	5,500 tons G.R.	8,500 tons G.R.
1885	0·0616	—	—
1890	0·0570	—	—
1895	0·0510	0·0501	—
1900	0·0486	0·0486	0·0372
1905	0·0440	0·0420	0·0360
1910	0·0450	0·0407	0·0290
1914	0·0412	0·0392	0·0260

From this table it is clear that there was a continuous improvement in the cost structure of all classes of ship sailed by the company, and, by implication, a steady rise in levels of efficiency. In particular, the level of costs for the larger ships suggests that there were economies of scale in operation which the smaller ships did not enjoy to the same extent. In general, the costs of working the Harrison fleet were

1. Harrison MSS., Insert in Voyage Books for 1906.

relatively high when compared with other shipping companies. John Swire's estimates of costs for the P. and O. and Blue Funnel Line[1] were considerably lower than those given by John William Hughes for the Harrison ships. Nevertheless, the latter company had a more widely diversified carrying trade and a more costly service to ports in Central America than had either the Holts or the P. and O. to ports in the Far East.

It will be remembered that Harrisons made no allowance for depreciation; they were, in fact, working to what economists call the marginal cost principle. Under such conditions, therefore, a more reliable guide to efficiency in the utilization of resources might be gained from their returns on employed capital, offsetting such figures by reference to general fluctuations in trade. Table 6 endeavours to show the pattern of return on capital employed in the firm from 1885 to 1914. It will be seen that gross income from all sources (i.e. net income from voyages, from insurance premiums, reserve investments— the total in column 2 *before* dividends had been paid to shareholders) followed very closely the cyclical pattern of trade; increasing returns from 1886 to 1889, generally depressed returns from 1890 to 1896; a period of prosperity from 1897 to 1900. From 1901 to 1906 returns were again depressed with the culminating year of general trade decline in 1908. Thereafter there was continuous improvement and, after 1909, increasing momentum until 1914.

There are two significant facts which emerge from this examination. In the first place, the year 1889 was a peak year, as indeed it was for nearly every other British shipping company. It was in this year that Harrisons purchased the Rathbone fleet and gained admission to the Calcutta tea trade. This trade, as we have seen, was highly lucrative, a trade inelastic to fluctuations in levels of income. It might, therefore, have been expected that the reasonably high and stable returns from the carriage of tea might have helped to offset cyclical trends in other Harrison trades. This, however, does not appear to have been the case as the return on employed capital (as indicated in Table 6) followed very closely the pattern of the trade cycle. In the second place, the returns on employed capital during the comparatively lean years from 1901 to 1909, while remaining relatively constant were not apparently influenced to any significant extent by reductions in the cost of operat-

1. F. E. Hyde, *Blue Funnel*; (1957) pp. 64-65.

ing the ships. This is even more surprising when it is remembered that in 1902 Harrisons entered a completely new trade, namely that with South Africa. One cannot escape the conclusion that the skill of the Harrison management, in providing new classes of ships of improved design and in seeking new outlets for the employment of these ships,

TABLE 6

Year	Employed Capital in £000	Gross Income from all sources in £000	Percentage return on employed capital
1884	512·0	—	—
1885	595·0	133·0	22·3
1886	590·0	72·0	12·2
1887	621·0	101·0	16·2
1888	693·0	189·0	27·2
1889	836·0	260·0	31·1
1890	862·0	167·0	19·2
1891	956·0	175·0	18·3
1892	1,024·0	97.0	9·4
1893	1,044·0	123·0	11·8
1894	1,106·0	148·0	13·3
1895	1,171·0	124·0	10·6
1896	1,248·0	166·0	13·2
1897	1,309·0	203·0	15·5
1898	1,419·0	301·0	21·2
1899	1,590·0	278·0	17·1
1900	1,841·0	454·0	24·6
1901	1,992·0	283·0	14·2
1902	2,179·0	262·0	12·0
1903	2,340 0	260·0	11·1
1904	2,407·0	276·0	11·5
1´05	2,466·0	282·0	11·4
1906	2,582·0	266·0	10·3
1907	2,682·0	317·0	11·8
1908	2,781·0	225·0	8·1
1909	2,856·0	274·0	9·6
1910	2,965·0	368·0	12·4
1911	3,310·0	448·0	13·5
1912	3,608·0	734·0	20·4
1913	3,932·0	821·0	20·8
1914	4,144·0	689·0	16·6

was sufficient only to ensure stability under highly adverse conditions of trade. On the other hand, when trade improved (as it did after 1910), the Managers were in a strong position to utilize their resources with advantage. They expanded the potentialities of their connections with the African market through the initiation of a new service with East Africa in 1910[1], and by the purchase of the Rennie fleet in 1911. In this latter year they also expanded their interest in the western hemisphere by the inauguration of a service to Northern Pacific ports.

One or two further comments may be justified. When it is remembered that Harrisons were purchasing their ships on essentially favourable terms between 1885 and 1900, there are grounds for believing that this fact, coupled with their anticipations based upon the relatively prosperous years of 1888 and 1889, led the Managers to embark upon a policy of over-capitalization. In the years after 1902 the same criticism may also apply, though the position was then less serious as decisions of major policy had been taken, giving greater flexibility in the operation of the fleet and, accordingly, a more efficient service in the carriage of a wider variety of merchandise to and from a larger number of ports. The fact that ships were costing more after 1900 increases the figures for the valuation of the fleet and, to that extent, tends to diminish the percentage of income from all sources as a return on employed capital.

In purely theoretical terms, the Harrison Managers were succeeding in their efforts to achieve marginal costs in the running of their ships, but because of adverse external factors they were much less successful in their endeavours to secure marginal revenue. Given more favourable trading conditions during these years, it is possible that they might have reached a position in which it could be said that they had maximized their profit. In practice, however, the shipowner operating cargo liners in Conference trades must be guided by the economic circumstances in which he has to work. Against such a consideration it must be admitted that the Harrison management was effective in maintaining and, after 1910, increasing returns by a realistic utilization of resources.

1. See below Chapter 7, p. 126.

IV

Having arrived at certain conclusions by a purely historical analysis of the source material, we now propose to check these conclusions by the application of a simplified form of economic analysis. There are two principal questions which one can ask of the data relating to earnings and investment for the period 1890–1914, extracted from the Harrison records and made the basis of argument in the foregoing pages. First, can we discern in this record of business operations the use of any distinct policy or body of principles? Secondly, did the Managers' success, or lack of it, in the event, suggest that such principles, skilfully applied, were, in fact, used to guide the firm safely? The determinants of these questions rest, in theoretical terms, on the concept of the marginal efficiency of capital.

The neatest and most incisive way of applying this concept is by the discounting of expected profits to the moment of decision and comparing their discounted total with the (similarly discounted) total of expected outlays for construction. In this conception there is one supreme fact: profits are a wild surmise, and are not, like a borrower's schedule of promised repayments, sums of money of stated size and payable by a certain date by a substantial mortgagor. Expectations of profit can mean no more than having in mind a range of possibilities from large gain to, perhaps, large loss.[1]

To interpret these ideas in the practical terms of the Harrison ships, we must start at a point in time when the Managers were considering whether or not to make a certain investment in new ships. If we then take the cost of a ship of a given size we can (always assuming that the information is available) compare the discounted actual earnings with the discounted anticipated earnings, the rate of interest for the purpose being taken as that ruling, at that precise time, on the Company's investments in other enterprises. As the life of a ship (barring accidents or complete loss) has a definite term it is thus possible to estimate the

1. This range of possibilities has somehow to be reduced to one or two numbers, and this is a virtually untouched problem of investment-decision. See A. J. Merrett and Allen Sykes, *The Finance and Analysis of Capital Projects*, (1963). The author is greatly indebted to his colleague, Professor G. L. S. Shackle, for advice and help in the preparation of this section of the chapter. Professor Shackle's long list of distinguished contributions in this field include his books, *Uncertainty and Business Decisions*, (1957), *Expectation in Economics*, (1949) and *Decision Order and Time* (1958).

complete earning capacity of a given outlay of capital. To judge whether or not the Managers were right in their decision to invest capital in new ships, we can compare the aggregate earnings (discounted) during the life of the ship with the anticipated earnings (discounted) for the same period. If the former figure should exceed the latter it is reasonably safe to assume that the investment was justified and that, bearing in mind the nature of the firm's business, its capital was more profitably employed in ships than in some other form of investment.

Historical evidence confirms that John William Hughes, a man of considerable mathematical ability, had worked out in actuarial terms the investment potential of given quantities of the firm's capital.[1] Through his foresight the Managers had a fairly shrewd idea of what a ship of a given tonnage might be expected to earn within a given range of possibilities. In other words, the Harrisons were in possession of, and using data which enabled them to apply an early, though admittedly rudimentary, technique for estimating the marginal efficiency of their capital. This fact, to a limited extent, answers the first of the questions posed; by making a specific examination of their actual decisions, with all the advantages of hindsight, we may also find an answer to the second question.

In 1893, the Harrison Managers, after considering the commercial prospects of the trades in which they were engaged,[2] decided to lay down two ships of different specification from those hitherto ordered. This new type of ship was of 7,000 tons gross (approximately 9,000 tons deadweight) and, at current prices, cost £70,000.[3] As the net rate of return on the Company's investments averaged 2.8 per cent, it was anticipated that the earning capacity of the new ships, discounted at a rate of 4 per cent, would not only meet the expected demand more efficiently, but that the outlay of capital was justified on a more than reasonably sure expectation of profitability. Such a ship, given normal trading conditions, could earn a net annual income of £7,000 and would have a life of something over twenty years. At a discount rate of 4 per cent the Managers concluded that the

1. Harrison MSS., from information compiled by J. W. Hughes in a series of note-books for each successive year from 1890-1906.
2. Harrison MSS., Memorandum on future prospects, 29 December 1893.
3. Minutes, C.S.S.Co., 10th A.G.M. 13 February 1894.

capital would be covered in under thirteen years and that, accordingly, it was more profitable to continue to invest resources in ships rather than in other forms of investment.

Table 7 attempts to show whether or not these expectations were realized. If it is accepted that on the one hand, the Managers had not perfect foresight and that, on the other, we have advantage of hindsight, these figures can be used to confirm or disprove some of the conclusions already stated and, more particularly, to heighten certain facts relating to the entrepreneurial function. The actual earnings (discounted) from this class of ship (e.g. *Historian*) shown in the first column, demonstrate that the Managers' expectations were more than fully justified in the immediate short term. Between 1895 and 1900, actual earnings were greater than anticipated; from 1901 to 1905, the forecast was just about accurate; from 1906 to 1910 conditions were such that expectations were not fulfilled; but thereafter, until 1914 (the end of twenty years), expectations were not only fully met, but exceeded the general trend of the forecast. This is only to be expected, for no group of managers, however skilled, however shrewd, however prescient, could make, or be expected to make, any worthwhile prognostication for the last five years of a twenty-year forecast. They were, however, justified in their assumption that the construction cost of the ship would be covered in less than thirteen years: it was, in fact, covered in ten.

Perhaps the most significant section of this table is that relating to the years from 1906 to 1910. Not only were the expectations of 1894 unfulfilled, but the general decline in levels of trade, made any investment decisions, during these years, almost incapable of prediction; certainly any decision to lay down a 7,000 ton ship in 1906 would have been determined by a rather different set of factors from those ruling in 1894. The Managers could not have anticipated a net annual return of £7,000 from the use of the ship. By that time, too, the rate of interest was appreciably more than 4 per cent; the Company was, in fact, receiving just over 5 per cent on its investments. It was, therefore, fortunate that the Harrison managers, having laid down thirteen ships of this class between 1896 and 1902 were not called upon (apart from *Yeoman*) to replace them during the difficult years from 1906 to 1910.

In any exercise designed to assess marginal efficiency of capital, it is preferable to have a series of comparative statements and, in a later

TABLE 7
HARRISONS' EARNINGS 1895-1914

Year	Actual earnings (Discounted) £	Anticipated earnings (Discounted) £
1895	5,284	6,722
1896	6,486	6,441
1897	7,244	6,230
1898	9,680	6,028
1899	8,593	5,744
1900	13,208	5,530
	50,495	36,695
1901	6,403	5,322
1902	5,315	5,117
1903	4,776	4,908
1904	4,432	4,768
1905	4,452	4,552
	25,378	24,667
1906	3,795	4,474
1907	4,502	4,209
1908	2,444	4,065
1909	3,326	3,859
1910	5,008	3,718
	19,075	20,265
1911	5,010	3,575
1912	7,762	3,438
1913	7,110	3,294
1914	5,855	3,153
	25,737	13,460
Total for 20 years	120,685	95,087

chapter, we shall repeat this procedure. The evidence from Table 7 can only be regarded as supplementary, in that it substantiates the conclusions arrived at in the earlier sections of this chapter. The Managers had developed a fairly workable set of rules to aid them in their function as decision-takers. With growing experience, these rules became more sophisticated and more precise in application. As a result, one can assert that their policies, founded on wise financial premises, guided the Company safely through periods of difficulty and secured a reasonably high return on the use of its resources, consistent with prevailing economic conditions.

PART THREE

Management and the Allocation of Resources
1914 - 39

John Cowan

CHAPTER SEVEN

Decline and Growth in the Trades
1914 - 29

I

THE fact that shipping companies such as, for example, the Charente Steam-Ship Company and the Ocean Steam Ship Company could become self-financing organizations, was a consequence just as much of the Managers' belief in the effectiveness of reserve funds, as of their skill in the use of their resources. The essential elements in the strength of Victorian and Edwardian capitalism were precisely these two attributes for, without prudence in securing capital and without skill in applying it productively, the cyclical pressures apparent in our pre-war commercial system, might have had more violent and destructive tendencies. This view does not overlook or invalidate the argument that over-caution in the use of financial resources may have been, in itself, a contributory factor to instability. Compared with the pre-war period, however, the immediate post-war years presented the Managers with new conditions of trade, involving changes in traditional patterns, and affecting the fundamental emphases in the structure of Liverpool's commercial activity. Furthermore, when set against the increasing fluctuations of world trade as a whole during the years from 1920 to 1939, the established methods of capital utilization were neither appropriate nor profitable. In the face of an uncertain future, decision-taking became infinitely more difficult, and progressive growth within firms well nigh impossible to achieve. It is, therefore, of interest to mark the relative success or failure of the Harrison Line in a period of fluctuation and depression. To what extent was short-term prosperity real? What was the magnitude of the firm's progress and growth, and how far were the pressures of external events met, and successively overcome, by the shrewdness of the Managers and the strength of their policies?

Despite the very heavy losses of ships by enemy action during the war, the fleet was reasonably well maintained partly by the delivery of new ships and partly through the purchase of ships from other companies.[1] The depletion of tonnage was, therefore, not as great as it might otherwise have been and the company ended the war with a fleet of some 49,000 tons less than in 1914, a loss of approximately 16 per cent.

By comparison with the twenty years before 1914, when there was a consistent rate of growth in the size of the Harrison fleet, the twenty years after 1919 show a very different picture. There was a rise in tonnage from 1919 to 1921—a rise undoubtedly influenced by the short post-war boom. Between 1922 and 1931 the fleet never fell below 252,000 tons (in 1923) and rose to as much as 285,000 tons (in 1929). The full effects of the depression were apparent in the figures for 1932 and 1933. In the latter year, tonnage had been reduced to 222,000 tons, a figure lower than that in 1919. Thereafter a fairly rapid recovery increased the size of the fleet so that by 1937 total tonnage was 294,000, a figure higher than that in 1929.[2]

It is obvious that this pattern of fluctuation stemmed from uncertainty on the part of the Managers in embarking on new capital projects against a background of unstable and fluctuating commercial prospects. It was no longer possible, as in the pre-war period, to base decisions on long-term considerations; the Managers were, in fact, now subject to pressures beyond their control, arising from the rapid instabilities of demand for ocean-going transport and from the incursion of United States subsidized tonnage. The following table giving average net receipts per voyage indicates the measure of the Managers' difficulty.

These figures show that, in average terms, the ships earned more than £2,000 per voyage in only seven years of the twenty under consideration. If we discount 1920 as being still subject to post-war influence and 1939 as a year disturbed by the outbreak of the second World War, there were only five years of working under freely operating economic conditions which returned a reasonable rate of remuneration on capital employed. Throughout the whole period there must have been many

1. Harrison MSS., C.S.S.Co., 25 June 1919, 12 ships were purchased from Messrs. Rankin, Gilmour and Co. in 1917, but two were lost before delivery.
2. Harrison MSS., C.S.S.Co., Minutes of A.G.M., 1919 to 1939.

voyages which were run at a loss. This was so, despite determined efforts by the Managers to offset and combat widespread fluctuations in trade, by technical improvements designed to increase efficiency in running of the ships,[1] and the introduction of new routes and services.

TABLE 8

Year	Average net receipts per voyage in £000	Year	Average net receipts per voyage in £000
1920	21·3	1930	0·9
1921	6·0	1931	0·5
1922	2·0	1932	1·1
1923	2·1	1933	1·4
1924	1·9	1934	1·4
1925	1·7	1935	1·8
1926	1·9	1936	2·1
1927	2·0	1937	4·0
1928	1·6	1938	3·2
1929	1·7	1939	2·2

II

We have already referred to the attempts by the Managers to embark on new trades in the years before 1914. Two of these new trades have some degree of importance in that they provided stimulus to the Company's overall trading position in the difficult years of the 1920s and must, therefore, be considered with other measures taken in this period to promote the well-being of the firm.

One incidental factor in the growth of Harrisons' trade was the establishment in 1910 of their London office.[2] The decision to have a London base was taken initially to look after the firm's interests in the Calcutta trade. London was the port at which the Harrison ships discharged their cargoes of tea; it was also the centre where equipment and stores for the Indian railways could be 'booked', substantial

1. See Chapter 8 for details of these technical innovations.
2. Harrison MSS., Minutes C.S.S.Co., 23 February 1911.

tonnages of which were carried outwards by Harrison ships. Further-more, the Calcutta and South African Conference lines met weekly in London, deciding what rates of freight to quote and, if and when, their tenders were accepted, allocating individual items of cargo amongst themselves. It was obviously advantageous for the Harrisons to have a London connection and Frank Ward accordingly left Liverpool to take up duty in the London office as the partner in charge.[1] The effectiveness of this decision was manifest during the years of war, but was even more relevant to the establishment of a number of London-based routes in 1911 and the immediate post-war period.

With the growth of the economies of the Sudan and East African territories (Kenya and Uganda) during the first decade of this century, demand for British exports began to increase. As cotton-producing countries, they needed markets for raw cotton and Lancashire was a main area for the sale of their product. Before 1910, the only ship-owning company from the United Kingdom, serving the East Coast of Africa *via* Suez, was the British India Company, whose ships sailed from the British East coast ports. It appeared to Frank Ward[2] that there was an opportunity for starting a steamship service from Glasgow and Liverpool to East Africa *via* Suez, carrying British exports of Manchester fine goods, machinery and other engineering products, and returning with cargoes of cotton and other primary commodities. The neighbouring territory of German East Africa (Tanganyika) was virtually closed to any shipping apart from two German lines, the German East Africa line and the Woermann Line. Frank Ward came to an agreement with the German lines (which had been carrying cargo from British East Africa for the United Kingdom, such cargoes being transhipped from the Continent) for Harrisons to engage in this trade. Harrisons then approached their Conference partners in the west coast United Kingdom-South African trade (Clan and Hall lines) with an offer to start a joint service operated by the three com-panies. This offer was accepted and it was agreed that Harrisons should manage the day-to-day working of the service. *Traveller* was the first Harrison ship to sail under this agreement, leaving Liverpool in June

1. Harrison Papers, from information supplied by P. S. Wilson; Frank Ward had the assistance in London, from 1910-11, of Geoffrey Hughes and F. A. Baddeley, and from 1912 J. M. Cowan; Eric Carter Braine entered this office in 1928.
2. Harrison MSS., information supplied by J. M. Cowan.

1910 and passing *via* the Suez Canal to Port Sudan and British East African ports, and returning with cargo for Dunkirk and Liverpool. This joint service, which has continued to the present day, was of significance in the inter-war years, when the export trade in American cotton began to decline in favour of other lower cost cottons of the Sudan, East Africa, Iran, Turkey and Brazil.[1]

Another trade which had relevance in the post-war period was also started in the year of expansion, 1910. This trade was that between the United Kingdom and North Pacific ports, and developed from previous contacts with the firm of Balfour, Williamson and Company.[2] This firm chartered sailing ships to carry their cargoes from the United Kingdom and Europe *via* Cape Horn to the North Pacific, and loaded homewards with grain and canned goods. Following their world tour in 1910 in which, among other things, new routes were prospected, T. Harrison Hughes (later Sir Harrison Hughes, Bt.) and Charles Williamson came to an agreement that, in place of the sailing ships, Harrisons should start a monthly service of steamships from Antwerp, London, Glasgow, Liverpool and South Wales *via* Magellan to the North Pacific ports of the United States and Canada. These ships were to carry structural material, cement, fine goods and tinplate on the outward voyage and load back to London and Liverpool with canned salmon, canned fruits, dried fruit and grain. On the outward voyage, calls were to be made at Santos to load Brazilian coffee for discharge at San Francisco. With the opening of the Panama Canal the service was conducted by way of the Caribbean and was so continued until the incursion of subsidized United States' tonnage made the trade unremunerative.[3] After 1923, vessels which the Company had been despatching with outward cargoes to the West Indies, having discharged at Cristobal, proceeded light through the Panama Canal and found their homeward cargoes from the North Pacific ports. This trade continued to struggle on until 1929 despite the unequal competitive conditions imposed by the United States' Shipping Board.

1. Harrison MSS., documents supplied by P. S. Wilson. Harrisons also managed two coasters *Mafia* and *Pemba* in this trade. These coasters served Beira the main outlet for Rhodesia, and Chinde the main outlet for Nyasaland.
2. Harrison MSS., evidence relating to this trade is to be found in Minutes C.S.S.Co., and from Conference notices, 1920-39.
3. Harrison MSS., C.S.S.Co., 40th A.G.M., 15 April 1924.

In this latter year the Balfour, Guthrie agency was discontinued.[1] In 1930, at the request of the American firm of Norton, Lilly and Company, an attempt was made to renew the service jointly with the United States Isthmian Line. This further venture, however, was short-lived. Britain's departure from the gold standard in 1931 seriously affected costs of cargo operations; expenses incurred in United States' ports had to be paid in dollars, while freights remained unchanged in sterling. Such increased costs made the voyages unprofitable and the service was finally discontinued in 1933.[2]

The West Indian connection based on London had been built up in a variety of ways. The main thread of the Harrison interest in this trade is unravelled from the commercial associations of the long established firm of Henry Langridge and Company. This firm owned and operated sailing vessels which traded regularly between London and the West Indies. The shipping space in these vessels was offered to old established West Indian merchant houses in London, and if the requirements from these houses fell short of full cargoes, Langridges themselves would fill the holds with parcels of such basic commodities as bricks, lime and cement, shipped out and on consignment.[3] Langridges also operated a joint service with Messrs. Scruttons, Son and Company, themselves owners of sailing vessels engaged in the West Indian trade. With the advent of the steamship Langridges gradually relinquished their ship-owning activities in favour of a shareholding partnership with Scruttons. This association continued until 1920 when Harrisons made the double purchase of the Scruttons' fleet sailing from London and the fleet of Prentice, Service and Henderson (the Crown Line) sailing from Glasgow to the West Indies.[4] Although, as we have seen, Harrisons had opened their own London office some years previously, they decided on initiating their new service to the West Indies, to appoint as their loading brokers in London, Langridges for the Islands' trade and William Smith and Company for that to Demerara, thereby replacing Scruttons who had previously operated in

1. Harrison MSS., C.S.S.Co., 47th A.G.M., 22 April 1931.

2. Harrison MSS., from information supplied by J. M. Cowan. An attempt was made in 1931 to widen the scope of the outward trade by the appointment of Messrs. Henry Gowan & Co. of Belfast to secure cargoes in Northern Ireland.

3. Harrison MSS., H. A. Rapson (Langridge & Co.) to W. M. Graham, (T. & J. Harrison), 9 November 1959.

4. ibid.

this capacity. At a somewhat later date Harrisons appointed Langridges as their London agents for their services based on Liverpool to the Caribbean.[1] These purchases not only enabled Harrisons to start a service from London outwards to the West Indies, but also secured for them a trade homewards from the West Indian islands and British Guiana.[2] This trade was further strengthened in 1933 by the purchase of the Leyland Line, an acquisition which added seven ships, each of approximately 5,500 tons G.R., to the West Indian fleet.[3]

One highly-advertised and reasonably remunerative aspect of the West Indian service was in the carriage of passengers. The ships used for this purpose came originally from the London-South Africa service; they were *Intaba*, built by Rennies and *Ingoma* built by Harrisons. On their transfer to the West Indian service they retained their Zulu names. These ships were replaced by *Inanda* in 1925 and *Inkosi* built by Swan Hunters in 1937. The sailing schedule was a four-weekly one from London, the first call being either Antigua or St. Kitts, after which there were regular calls at Barbados, Granada, Trinidad and Demerara. Though ancillary to the main line trades, this West Indian passenger service was of importance during the difficult years of depression, helping to maintain earnings from sources less liable to fluctuations in demand than the carriage of bulk cargo. In general, the development of these subsidiary trades may well have helped to keep a substantial proportion of Harrison tonnage in operation, at times when other cargo liner companies had the major part of their fleets laid up.

III

If we now turn to an analysis of the main trades, such as those concerned with the carriage of manufactured and semi-manufactured goods outwards, and the return of bulk cargoes of primary products, we can obtain a general, though reasonably accurate, idea of the extent of the

1. ibid.
2. Harrison MSS., Minutes C.S.S.Co., 37th A.G.M., 13 April 1921.
3. *Fairplay*, 23 November 1933, p. 336. The ships were built between 1921 and 1928.

K

decline in these trades during the inter-war years, and the effectiveness of the recently established subsidiary trades in maintaining the level of Harrisons' earning capacity.

Post-war prospects in the Gulf trade, which was primarily concerned with the shipment of raw cotton to Liverpool, seemed to be highly favourable because of the anticipated demand for textiles. The Harrisons' New Orleans connection had consequently been supplemented in 1920 by the inauguration of a direct service between Houston and Liverpool, a link made possible by the deepening of the shallow channel between Houston and Galveston Bay.[1] These expectations were, however, not realized. The years 1922 and 1923 were those in which the Managers had to report that 'the American cotton trade has largely disappeared'.[2] The shipping business from the United States and, in particular, that from the Gulf was in great measure ruined by fluctuations in supply and demand, and by the operations of the United States' Shipping Board.[3] There was a slight revival in this trade in 1924, 1925 and 1926, though in the latter year, good cargoes outwards were discounted by the incursions of the Shipping Board into the raw cotton carrying trade homewards.[4] It was not until 1928 that seasonal fluctuations caused an improvement in homeward cargoes, an improvement which continued into 1929, though in the latter part of this year it had to be reported that 'the Gulf trade was in a condition which we have not seen in the history of the Company. The active cotton season this year lasted for six weeks instead of six months and such cotton as came was largely shipped in vessels of the United States' Shipping Board'.[5]

This gloomy picture was, to some extent, relieved by varying degrees of increased activity in the subsidiary cotton trades with East Africa, Brazil and the West Indies. This was apparent in 1923, 1925, and 1926. In 1927 the relatively good homeward cargoes of cotton from East Africa were affected 'by competition which is strong both from this country and from the Continent'.[6] In 1929, however, improved

1. Harrison MSS., from documents supplied by P. S. Wilson; also *Marine News*, July 1920.
2. Harrison MSS., Minutes C.S.S.Co., 39th A.G.M., 25 April 1923.
3. ibid., 40th A.G.M., 15 April 1924.
4. ibid., 43rd A.G.M., 12 April 1927.
5. ibid., 46th A.G.M., 16 April 1930.
6. ibid., 44th A.G.M., 18 April 1928.

conditions in Harrisons' earnings from the cotton trade were 'almost entirely due to unprecedented activity in the Pernambuco trade'.[1] This new factor in the situation was caused by the competitive position of Brazilian cotton; Lancashire cotton mills found that they could buy cotton there at a cheaper price than in the U.S.A.[2] 'We managed to supply a number of extra steamers' reported Harrisons 'with successful results'.[3]

In the two main trades with India and South Africa there were diverse influences at work affecting earnings during the years from 1919 to 1929. The fundamental change occurred in the Company's carrying trade with Calcutta and was a reflection of India's decline as a dominant factor in the United Kingdom's pattern of overseas trade balances. The total earnings from Harrisons' Indian voyages at times fell by as much as 50 per cent of pre-1914 figures, and rarely rose above 60 per cent in the 1920's. Strikes at home and political unrest in India in 1921 were unwelcome auguries for future prospects and the Managers rightly assumed that 'not much relief is contemplated for some time to come'.[4] Conditions were further complicated in 1924 by an extension of the Indian tariff and by 1925 there was general agreement that 'the very changed conditions in India have not been, or are likely to be, conducive to an expansion of business in this direction'.[5] This assessment of the future was correct. Indian business continued in a state of depression for the next ten years. Economic considerations apart, Lancashire's trade with India declined because of the boycott of British goods organized in 1930 by the Indian National Congress. The measure of the decline in trade can be estimated from the figures of the export of cotton piece-goods; in 1913 (a record year) the United Kingdom exported 3,000 million yards of cotton cloth to India valued at £35,000,000. In 1938 India imported less than 300 million square yards valued at £4,500,000. There were also fluctuations, though not nearly so marked as in cotton textiles, in the shipment of tea. While the demand for tea was relatively inelastic, there were changes in the qualities required by the market. In times of depression the demand

1. ibid., 46th A.G.M., 16 April 1930.
2. ibid.
3. ibid.
4. ibid., 38th A.G.M., 16 May 1922.
5. ibid., 41st A.G.M., 16 April 1925.

for cheaper blends of tea increased and this altered the structure of the tea market as a whole. Harrisons found that the cargoes of more highly-priced teas contracted and they experienced growing competition from opposition lines in the cheaper tea trades. The effect of these changes in Indian trade on British shipping services was disastrous and Harrisons, no less than other shipping companies carrying to India, were faced with a serious diminution of earning capacity.

The one really prosperous feature of Harrisons' Indian trade during these years was in the carriage of gunny bags. This cargo had been of considerable importance before 1914. The gunnies were brought back to Liverpool where they were transhipped to Cuba and the West Indies for use on the sugar plantations, to the River Plate and South American ports for the use of flour mills and coffee plantations; the gunnies required for the baling of cotton at New Orleans were, however, oncarried in Harrisons' ships. In 1906,[1] Harrisons, in conjunction with the Clan and Ellerman lines started a service to carry gunny bags from Calcutta to the River Plate. They were later joined by Messrs. Andrew Weir who had previously been in opposition to them. During the 1920s the gunny trade remained reasonably flexible and provided scope for the employment of ships at times when other trades were depressed. The Harrison vessels on the Calcutta-River Plate route would return to the United Kingdom with either a tramp cargo of grain, or with cargoes, loaded on berth terms on Messrs. Lamport and Holt's berth in ports on the East coast of South America.[2]

By contrast with the depressed state of the Gulf and Indian trades, that with South Africa was relatively prosperous. There was an increase in both outward and homeward cargoes in 1923 and 1924, and this improvement was maintained in 1925; 'a refreshing and notable feature has been some excellent outward cargoes to South and East Africa'[3] so ran the Managers Report for 1925. The continuance of the relative strength of this prosperity attracted other shipping companies to this route. In 1927, for example, the Managers admitted, in somewhat rueful terms 'South and East Africa have both been better, but the position here has been seriously complicated by opposi-

1. Harrison MSS., from documents supplied by J. M. Cowan relating to trades before 1914.

2. Harrison MSS., from documents supplied by P. S. Wilson relating to the trades after 1920.

3. Harrison MSS., Minutes C.S.S.Co., 42nd A.G.M., 22 April 1926.

tion which is strong both from this country and the continent'.[1] Their apprehensions concerning opposition in the South African trade were heightened when set against the background of their shipping operations in the world as a whole. In general, despite an increase in outward cargoes, those homewards were unusually small. 'All through 1927 (we have witnessed) the curious phenomenon of scarcity of homeward cargoes from all directions in which we trade outwards. It has been very difficult to get return freight at all'.[2] Unfortunately the opposition in the South African trade was followed by a rate-cutting war, and this had further repercussions on the level of Harrisons' total earnings. The war continued into 1928 and reduced earnings from the South African trade considerably, despite the reasonably good volume of cargo handled. By the end of the year, however, agreement had been reached with the opposition lines and a more optimistic prospect in the South African trade was forecast.

The anticipations of 1928 proved to be well founded for, in 1929 the trade, now relieved of undue competition, increased steadily. To some extent this latter year marked a watershed in the history of the Company. The older and more traditional trades which had been started in the years before 1924 had been maintained with difficulty or had been in process of decline throughout the 1920s. There had been, however, some compensating factors. 'In previous years' wrote the Managers 'owing to the way in which our activities have been divided all over the world, it has been generally found that whereas vessels were doing badly in one direction, they were doing reasonably well in another; but in 1930 trade everywhere was deplorable'.[3] With the unsettled state of trade during the 1920s the general problem had been to preserve interests which had been acquired in the main markets served by Harrisons. This had been achieved with varying degrees of success, 'with a minimum of outward sailings and without laying the routes open to the incursions of vigilant competition.'[4] This retrospective view of a changing world was made before the full impact of the economic blizzard in 1931 and 1932 had transformed the traditional pattern of the Company's overseas relationships, and had

1. ibid., 44th A.G.M., 18 April 1928.
2. ibid.
3. ibid., 47th A.G.M., 22 April 1931.
4. ibid.

created a more dynamic approach to the use and earning capacity of the fleet.

IV

The Managers' references to opposition in the South African trade, and to the minimization of competition on other routes, lead naturally to an enquiry into the nature and effectiveness of Conference agreements during the period from 1914 to 1929. As we have seen, the majority of trades in which Harrisons were engaged were subject to some form of agreement. These agreements were renewed, strengthened or modified from time to time in conformity with changing circumstances. On the whole, these agreements worked satisfactorily, giving shippers and shipowners alike relatively stable conditions in the freight market in years of uncertain trading prospects. The old controversies about the merits of a rebate system, as opposed to a flat reduction in freight rates on the carriage of specified commodities, continued throughout the 1920s; so too, did the argument about differential rates for the same commodity from ports equidistant from the terminal point of discharge. However much Harrisons might have been affected by the outcome of such discussions, they operated their agreements consistently and as a matter of policy. In so doing, they minimized risks arising from the pressure of external competition and secured for the Company a reasonably high return on capital.

The difficulties inherent in the granting of rebates had particular relevance in the trade with South Africa. In 1911, the South African government had passed the Post Office Act which, apart from the provisions relating to the carriage of mail, attacked the principle of a rebate system. In effect, this Act prevented the Governor-General from entering into any ocean mail contract with any shipping company which offered rebates 'upon condition of the exclusive shipment of goods by vessels of particular lines'.[1] As a result of this legislation it became necessary for the Union Castle line (a member of the South African Conference) to discontinue the deferred rebate system because

1. *Post Office Administration and Shipping Combinations Discouragement Act*, (1911) para. 11, p. 10.

it held the mail contract. Subsequently, all the other lines in the South African Conference were forced to follow suit. Deferred rebates were replaced by the Agreement system.[1]

Although Harrisons were signatories to these new proposals they were not particularly happy at the prospect of having to put them into operation. They preferred to work a deferred rebate system but were reluctantly forced to admit that 'if the majority of the shippers in a trade wanted the Agreement, the shipowners would find it difficult to resist them.'[2] They feared that it might be difficult to make the Agreement apply to all merchants generally, whereas the rebate system was automatic. In the event, these fears were not entirely unjustified. Following the cessation of hostilities there was a boom in rates caused by the shortage of ships in relation to quantities of cargo to be handled. By 1922, however, shipbuilding capacity had increased and the shortage of tonnage had been relieved.[3] Outward rates of freight to South Africa, however, did not fluctuate greatly. The reason for this is fairly simple to explain. The freight charged on a piece of machinery or copper tube pipes bears a very small proportion to the total cost of the article. All other things being equal, therefore, freight rates on such cargoes were only marginally affected by changes in demand. On the other hand, rates of freight on homeward cargoes of some primary products fell sharply. This led to an intensification of competition for the carriage of the higher freighted commodities such as metals. In an effort to offset declining receipts from cargoes of bulk products, Harrisons worked out a fairly precise plan for the shipment of high freighted copper from Beira with unlimited cargoes of sisal from East Africa, i.e. close deadweight combined with bulky measurement.[4]

Apart from the various measures taken by the Conference lines, both jointly and separately, to meet changing conditions of trade, there was a growing complexity in the competitive structure of the South African trade as a whole. This was caused partly by the rate-cutting activities of certain tramp companies and partly by changes in the

1. *Report of the Imperial Shipping Committee*, Appendix IV, p. 51.
2. ibid., Appendix II, p. 48; also correspondence with R. D. Holt, 22 March 1922.
3. D. L. McLachlan, 'The Conference System since 1919', *Business History*, Volume IV, No. 1, December 1961, pp. 54-63.
4. Harrison papers, memoranda on the South African trade supplied by J. M. Cowan.

membership of the Conference itself. We shall devote some attention to the effects of competition from tramps in a subsequent section of this chapter. The changes in the membership of the Conference were the result of external pressures. The two German lines, Woermann and D.O.A.L., which had been automatically evicted from the South African Conference during the war, were re-admitted. This, to some extent, helped to redress the balance in Conference membership, as between British and European interests; there remained, however, the external competition from a comparative newcomer into the trade, the Dutch Holland-Afrika Line. This latter company had seized the opportunity of starting a South African service at a time when the Germans had no tonnage. This incursion caused a short-lived, but nevertheless annoying, fluctuation in freight rates. Eventually, the Holland-Afrika Line was admitted to the Conference.

These efforts to secure harmony were largely dictated by growing uncertainty about trading conditions. There were many other attempts by outside lines to break into the South African market (notably that by the Blue Star Line), but the strength of the Conference itself remained during the 1920s and the 1930s as a powerful instrument of control. Nevertheless, the experience of the immediate post-war years coupled with the threat of future competition made Harrisons and some of the old established members of the Conference Agreement apprehensive of further limitations on their rights of negotiation.[1]

Of the many other agreements to which Harrisons were signatories, perhaps that concerned with the Calcutta trade was the most prolific of controversy. Throughout the whole of the 1920s, the Managers had to meet a variety of complaints on the working of the deferred rebate system. In general, the long-established suspicion that ship-owners were operating a rebate system with the corollary of high freights and high profits at the merchants' expense, died hard. This particular bogey which had bedevilled so much of the evidence before the Royal Commission on Shipping Rings was again resurrected in the early 1920s. The complaint that freights were unduly high was based on certain comparisons: first, with the freights charged from continental ports for the same destination and the same commodities; secondly, with the rates charged for the same commodity in other

1. Harrison MSS., Minutes C.S.S.Co., 18 April 1928.

competing trades (e.g. linseed from Argentina);[1] thirdly, that as compared with the Bombay-United Kingdom rates, those from Calcutta were disproportionately high.[2] The point was clearly made that the lower freighted trades from Argentina and Bombay were not subject to the payment of a deferred rebate.

The basis on which these comparisons had been made, however, was open to valid criticism. The argument ignored the adverse effects, on Indian trade as a whole, of the violent fluctuations in the sterling value of the rupee. Furthermore, the Argentine linseed trade, which was said to have given so great a competitive advantage through the incidence of high freight rates from Calcutta, was not a cargo liner trade. The bulk of Argentine linseed was carried in tramp steamers and the rates on these steamers were adjusted according to their outward employment which, at that time, consisted mainly in the carriage of coal from South Wales. The grounds for complaint, therefore, were not soundly based. In a strictly comparable situation, the Calcutta merchants would have had to rely on tramp tonnage, and freight rates would have been higher than those under the Conference Agreement as such ships would generally have had to steam outwards to Calcutta in ballast.[3]

As far as Harrisons were concerned, these arguments, based as they were on traditional modes of thought, were a little unreal. They were more deeply concerned with the changing pattern of Indian trade and with the effect of these changes on the level of their earnings, rather than with controversy about apparent inequalities in freight rates. One has only to read the Managers' Reports for successive years during the 1920s to confirm this. In 1924 it was stated 'Indian business is in an unsettled condition which is aggravated by a tendency towards protection on the part of India'.[4] In the following year there was a brief, but pertinent reference, to the fact that 'the very changed conditions in India have not been, nor are likely to be, conducive to an expansion of business'.[5] Further comments were made in 1927 to the loss of revenue in this trade and, in 1928, there is the significant entry

1. *Report of the Imperial Shipping Committee*, para. 16, p. 13.
2. ibid.
3. ibid., Appendix II, p. 42.
4. Harrison MSS., Minutes C.S.S.Co., 16 April 1925.
5. ibid., 22 April 1926.

'Indian trade shows a further decline. Since India has become a wheat importing country instead of a wheat exporting country, this state of affairs seems inevitable.'[1] These quotations reflect a fundamental and continuing process in the deployment of the Company's resources. Whereas, before 1914, the receipts from the Indian trade had accounted for approximately 45 per cent of Harrisons' total receipts, this percentage had fallen to 31 in 1929 and to 20.8 by 1938. This rapid decline was, perhaps, a presage of Harrisons' complete withdrawal from the Indian trade in the 1950s.

Beset by increasing pressures of a political and economic character, Harrisons' attitude towards Conference agreements in general underwent a subtle change. While strongly supporting such agreements as a means of stabilizing the freight market, they were now convinced that there would henceforth be very little advantage in negotiating freight agreements in accordance with traditional, or accepted, patterns of behaviour. Their widening interests in new markets, the increasingly complex nature of competition in all their trades and the growing dominance of cyclical fluctuations, altered the whole character of rate-fixing operations. These operations had now become much less general in context and more specific to the needs of the trade. In other words, rate-fixing, as exercised by the Conferences, had become a highly competitive operation. As part of a wider process of decision-taking it had also assumed a greater economic function in the Managers' entrepreneurial responsibilities.

V

There was, however, one aspect of the growing threat to earning capacity during the 1920s which caused the Managers great concern. This was the involvement of Conference lines in a rate-cutting war with tramp steamers. 'South and East Africa have both been better,' stated the Managers Report for 1927 'but the position here has been seriously complicated by opposition which is strong both from this country and the Continent'.[2] Behind this laconic reference lay the

1. ibid., 24 April 1929.
2. Harrison MSS., Minutes C.S.S.Co., 18 April 1928.

reality of a bitter struggle in the South African trade, which began in May 1927 and lasted without intermission for more than a year. The opposition in question came from the tramp steamers of the Thomas Line,[1] under the ownership of Sir Robert Thomas, Bt. The fight began when Sir Robert announced that he intended to run his ships from Newport and Antwerp to Capetown, Durban and Delagoa Bay. These ships were to operate under the title the British and Continental South African Line, and it was proposed that they should carry cargoes at rates far below those quoted by the Conference.[2] The prospect of a head-on clash with the Conference lines aroused much controversy and not a little anxiety in shipping circles. There was some doubt as to the financial strength of the Thomas interests and, as a writer in *Fairplay* remarked, 'it is a question of the length of purses.' The conclusion was that 'Sir Robert Thomas has taken on a giant's job when he attacks the preserves of the Union-Castle, Ellerman-Bucknall, Harrison, Clan and other lines. In this particular case, too, the position is aggravated by the fact that the merchants admit that the rates hitherto charged by the Conference lines are fair in every way. Therefore the disturbance which will result from a fight can benefit but few and may do injury to many.'[3]

The Conference took up the challenge. One month before the first Thomas ship was due to sail, a new Conference circular was published announcing an all round reduction of rates, the reductions on some classes of goods (such as galvanized iron and steel sheets) amounting to 80 per cent.[4] This, however, did not deter Sir Robert Thomas from his original intention. Four of his ships were put on to the route and he was reasonably successful in attracting the support of merchants in South Africa. By October 1927 the opposition ships were carrying cargoes of manufactured goods outwards and returning with cargoes of wool. The Conference, thereupon, reduced rates on the carriage of wool by 15 per cent.[5] As a counter to this reduction Sir Robert Thomas claimed that the Conference lines were, in effect, offering a hidden rebate and that this was contrary to the provisions of the

1. *Fairplay*, 12 May 1927. This line was owned by the William Thomas Shipping Company and managed by R. J. Thomas and Co. Ltd. of Holyhead.
2. ibid., 5 May 1927.
3. ibid.
4. ibid.
5. Harrison papers, Conference Circulars, October–December 1927.

Mail Contract of 1912.[1] He further stated that he was 'prepared to quote freights as low as the Conference lines, however low they may go'.[2] This was an idle threat. By the beginning of December the Conference had cut the wool rate by a further 62.5 per cent,[3] a reduction which the Conference lines were better able to sustain because their cargoes were highly diversified in character.

The competitive strength of the Conference had a threefold impact upon the course of this rate-cutting war. In the first place it increased the ratio of costs to receipts and this became especially serious when Sir Robert Thomas, in order to meet his commitments to the wool merchants, had to charter additional tonnage.[4] In the second place the violent downward movement in freight rates increased rather than diminished the difficulties of the wool merchants themselves. The merchants who were under contract to Thomas now found that they were having to pay higher rates than those merchants who had remained loyal to the Conference lines. 'Meanwhile' wrote a correspondent from Durban 'not only the wool trade, but the commercial world generally is weary of the freight war, which, they state, results in unstable freights and unsettled sailings.'[5] Thirdly, as Sir Robert Thomas's financial position became more precarious, he was induced, in an effort to save the situation, to tender for the South African Mail Contract. This contract, as we have seen, had been held by the Union Castle Line for many years and was due for renewal in the Spring of 1928. Sir Robert, in support of his bid, offered to carry both mails and produce at favourable rates for the producer, with the added bait to the South African Government of a modified system of control. This offer, however, was not accepted and by the end of March 1928 the contract had been renewed with the Union Castle Line, coupled with a freight agreement to last for ten years, subject only to certain provisos as to its termination.[6] The significance of this freight agreement was that its provisions were applicable, not only to goods carried by the Union Castle Line, but also to those carried by the ships of other lines in the Conference.

1. *Fairplay*, 20 October 1927.
2. ibid.
3. Harrison papers, Conference Circulars, 1 December, 1927.
4. *Fairplay*, 5 January 1928.
5. ibid., 5 January 1928.
6. ibid., 8 March 1928.

Although there was a brief continuation of the rate-cutting war in the shipment of wool, this freight agreement virtually destroyed the opposition from Sir Robert Thomas's ships. By the end of 1928, it had become apparent that the British and Continental South African Line could not compete with the specially equipped Conference fleets. The accounts of the William Thomas Shipping Co. for the year ending 31 March 1928 show that, after providing for interest on debentures and loans (and without setting aside anything for depreciation) there was a loss on the year's working of nearly £50,000.[1] This compared with a profit of £38,000 in the previous fifteen months. This essay on the part of Sir Robert Thomas therefore, was a costly, disastrous and foolhardy attempt to fight a Conference agreement. For his company the final phase of the struggle took place in the Bankruptcy Court in 1930.[2] On the reverse side of the picture, the losses sustained by the Conference lines and the South African merchants were severe, though unequal in their incidence. The wool exporters required regularity of service to maintain a reasonably stable flow, consistent with changes in demand in the United Kingdom market. By such a service they were able to keep prices at a remunerative level and regulate the value of their stocks. The incursion of opposition lines, and the consequent support of these lines by a section of the wool exporters, however small that section might be in proportion to the total, upset the balance of the flow and thus the amount of wool on offer in the United Kingdom market. Such conditions tended towards over-supply in relation to demand. Low prices were, therefore, a natural corollary of low freight rates. Furthermore, in addition to the losses sustained on shipment, the wool exporter had to write down the value of his stock, thereby increasing his aggregate loss. The conclusion of the rate-cutting war in 1928 brought relief to the shipowner and merchant alike, and gave the latter a more lively appreciation of the benefits of operating within the framework of a Conference agreement.[3]

The experience of the shipowners in this unhappy episode was also not without its salutory lesson. Some of the Conference lines were less

1. ibid., 4 April 1929. If depreciation had been allowed the loss would have been £75,000.
2. ibid., 3 April 1930. The South African venture was a contributory cause, the firm having become involved in a similar fight in the River Plate trade.
3. ibid.

badly hit than others. Those with the most modern ships, and especially those ships equipped to meet the requirements of perishable cargoes, were able to switch from the carriage of wool to the relatively more profitable cargoes of fruit and meat. In this way they maintained full holds and secured profitable voyage patterns. Harrisons were less fortunate. They had, as we shall see, made some effort during the 1920s to modernize their fleet; but the improvements which had been effected were not sufficiently comprehensive to allow for sudden changes in cargo requirements. For example, by comparison with the Union Castle fleet, to which motor vessels had been introduced, the earning capacity of the Harrison ships on the South African route in 1927 and 1928 was determined more by the prevalence of stable freight rates in traditional commodities than by more lucrative rates on new cargoes requiring specialized handling. In other words, a serious decline in the freight rates on wool tended to have a disproportionate effect on the earnings of the Harrison ships as compared with those of the Union Castle. In aggregate, it was estimated that the freight war with the British and Continental Shipping Company caused a fall in Harrisons' earnings of approximately £20,000, whereas that for the Union Castle Line was less than half that sum.[1]

If, in conclusion, we look at the achievement of the Harrison Managers during the decade of the 1920s, it is possible to emphasise certain salient points. Despite political unrest and economic uncertainty in India which led to a decline in this traditional trade, Harrisons were able to maintain the level of their activities in the Carribean and (apart from 1927) in the trade with South Africa. Adverse conditions on other established routes were offset by successful incursions into new trades. As a result, earnings and costs were kept stable because the fleet was kept in relatively constant employment. To this end the various Conference agreements were conducive to regularity in the flow of cargoes and, ultimately to the maintenance of earning capacity.[2] The one case affecting Harrisons in which a Conference agreement was challenged, and a rate-cutting war led to a disruption in trade, proved to be a costly episode for both shipowners and shippers. Nevertheless, the incidence of economic dislocation during the period was not with-

1. Holt MSS., R. D. Holt, Memorandum on Shipping for 1928 and future prospects, 30 December 1928.
2. See Appendix II for figures of voyage profits.

out its effect on the levels of capital employed. Following the post-war boom, Harrisons, in common with many other shipping companies, had to lay up ships. By a series of wise decisions, however, the Managers turned such times of adversity to advantage. They scrapped or sold their oldest ships and replaced them with new ones. The reflection of this policy is to be seen in the annual totals of capital employed.[1] In short, the Managers had shown that by energetic action based upon a realistic assessment of events they were able not only to safeguard the financial structure of the Company, but were competent in their preparation for the more difficult and testing years of the following decade.

1. See Appendix III for annual figures of Capital employed.

Sir Thomas Harrison Hughes

John Watson Hughes

CHAPTER EIGHT

Decision-taking in Years of Fluctuation and Depression, 1924 - 39

I

THE years from 1920 to 1939 were, as we have seen, a difficult period for most shipping companies, not least of all for the Harrisons. Nevertheless, the Managers had shown initiative in seizing every opportunity to maintain earnings and diversify trading prospects. This had involved the taking of decisions based upon a fairly broad range of data relating to voyage and route patterns. As the depression deepened, however, competition became intense and decisions were governed by more precise calculations of cost margins, and by comparative analyses of returns on specific forms of investment. Although the determination of policy continued to be guided by important economic factors, the assessment of current evidence tended to be overshadowed much more by the grim struggle to survive than by any precise calculation aimed at a maximization of profit.

The first major decision embodying change in the policy of the Company was concerned with the adequate supply of shipping space for the needs of post-war trade. The severe losses sustained during the war had not been fully replaced, despite the purchase of the Rankin-Gilmour fleet in 1917,[1] and the total of Harrison ships, which had numbered fifty-seven in 1914, had been reduced to thirty-nine by the end of 1918. To the problem of replenishing shipping space was added that of cost. Before the war Harrisons rarely paid more than £100,000 for a ship with a delivery date of something under eighteen months;

---

1. Harrison MSS., Minutes C.S.S.Co., 26 June 1918. 12 ships were purchased at an approximate average price of £160,000 per vessel. Most of these ships had been built since 1911 and two in 1917. The arrangements for this purchase was one of the last acts of John William Hughes who died on 20 November 1917.

after 1918, however, there was a short period of rapidly rising prices when new cargo liners of approximately 7,500 tons G.R. could not be built for much less than £300,000 and delivery dates, partly because of lack of capacity for civilian orders and partly because of strikes among shipyard workers, were extended over periods of two to three years.

Even though the Managers could, and did, exercise considerable foresight in assessing future trading prospects, the anticipation of securing a profitable return from the investment of large blocks of capital in new ships, was highly uncertain. It was as much for this, as for other reasons, that the decision was, therefore, taken in 1920 to purchase the combined fleets of Scruttons and of Prentice, Service and Henderson. Apart from the obvious advantage which this acquisition had in enabling Harrisons to enter new trades,[1] the working life of these ships was of much shorter duration than those in the Rankin-Gilmour fleet. Of the Prentice, Service and Henderson vessels three, *Crown of Cordova*, *Crown of Navarre* and *Crown of Granada*, had been built in 1901–2 and three of the Scrutton ships were built before 1909. The fairly high proportion of old ships in this tonnage, therefore, made it necessary for several of these ships to be sold off within a few years of their purchase. Nevertheless, this rapid build-up of tonnage enabled Harrisons to overcome the difficulties of the post-war boom and to increase their fleet to a total of fifty-eight ships, a figure somewhat in excess of the number owned in the previous peak year of 1914. The resumption of normal shipping services (now freed entirely from Government control and war-time restrictions) was hindered by incessant labour disputes in most of the major ports of the world. 'The effect of these disturbances' stated the Managers Report for 1920, 'is reflected more particularly in the length of time required to complete voyages in comparison to the pre-war standard'.[2] It was accepted that one-fifth more vessels were required to maintain services at the pre-war frequency.[3] The net result of this was that ports became congested and the flow of trade was impeded.[4]

These difficulties were exacerbated by the heavy shipbuilding

1. See Chapter VII, pp. 125–9.
2. Harrison MSS., Minutes C.S.S.Co., 13 April 1921.
3. ibid.
4. For the economic effects of this congestion see D. H. Aldcroft, 'Port Congestion and the Shipping Boom of 1919–20', *Business History* Vol. III, No. 2. (June 1961).

programme in the years following the end of hostilities. In Great Britain alone there were three million tons on the stocks at the end of 1919, and nearly eight million tons in the world as a whole; by mid 1920 the world's supply of steam and motor tonnage was 14.2 per cent higher than in 1914. Included in this increase was the tonnage built on British Government order (sold to private shipowners from the summer of 1919) and, after August 1920, the Government sales of German prize tonnage.[1] On the other hand the hope of making use of this rapidly increasing shipping space was not likely to be realized; the volume of world trade in 1920 was still 17 per cent lower than in 1913 and the economic prospects for improvement were not encouraging.[2] Against this background, the Harrison Managers were forced to make a realistic appraisal of their future shipbuilding policy. By the end of 1921, Harrisons had several vessels laid up and were still taking delivery of new vessels which had been on order since 1918. Two of these new vessels, *Huntsman* and *Diplomat* (approximately 8,200 tons G.R.), each cost just short of £400,000.[3] It was obvious that, in the conditions of uncertainty then prevailing, no adequate return could be expected from so large an investment. The problem for the Managers to solve, therefore, was that of achieving a proper balance between the retirement of old ships and their replacement by new ones on the most favourable cost terms. In the pursuance of these objectives a more definite policy began to take shape. The following table illustrates this.

TABLE 9

Year	Number of new vessels added	Number of vessels retired
1922	—	5
1923	3	4
1924	4	—
1925	3	7
1926	2	2
1927	5	3
1928	1	2
1929	2	1
1930	—	2

1. C. E. Fayle, *The War and the Shipping Industry* (1927), pp. 381, *et seq.*
2. S. G. Sturmey, *British Shipping and World Competition* (1962), p. 65.
3. Harrison MSS., Minutes C.S.S.Co., 16 May 1922.

This pattern suggests that, despite the deadening effect of a deteriorating and uncertain world economic situation, the Managers did what they could to maintain their fleet and keep it as efficient as possible. In fact, the desire to maintain efficiency became paramount and was achieved, partly by design and partly through the pressure of circumstance.

By contrast with the 1920s the decade of the 1930s witnessed an accentuation of the uncertainties attendant upon dislocations of trade. The year 1930 was the beginning of three disastrous trading years for the Company. In that and the following year fifteen ships were laid up 'while the remaining vessels of the fleet were engaged in the various trades on a reduced basis of sailings, in most of them, on a skeleton basis, just sufficient to preserve our interests in the particular trade'.[1] It was further noted that the outstanding features of the general situation were aggravated by the constant and increasing subsidization of unnecessary tonnage by foreign governments and the 'bolstering up by banks at home of vessels which had much better disappear'.[2] This was an opinion which the Managers were prepared to substantiate. In 1932 they sold ten vessels at break-up prices. This, however, did not entirely solve Harrisons' problem of excess and obsolete capacity for although their fleet was reduced from fifty-one to forty-one ships, three were still laid up.[3]

Though the effects of this depression were far more serious than those experienced during the various slumps in the 1920s, the Managers continued their policy of scrapping and building as opportunity offered. With the gradual improvement in trade after 1934, however, there was a return to the purchase of ships from other lines. The addition of the ships of the Leyland Line in this latter year was a case in point. Seven vessels, totalling approximately 45,000 tons G.R., were added to the fleet to take part in the growing West Indian service.[4] A further purchase of four oil-burning ships belonging to the Prince Line was made in 1935.[5] They were newly built and together added approximately 31,000 tons G.R. to the Harrison fleet. The outlay of £178,000 was more than justified, first, by the fact that it was necessary, at this

1. ibid., 48th A.G.M., 27 April 1932.
2. ibid.
3. ibid., 49th A.G.M., 26 April 1933.
4. *Fairplay*, 23 November 1933; *Manchester Guardian Commercial*, 25 August 1934.
5. Harrison MSS., Minutes C.S.S.Co., 52nd A.G.M., 29 April 1936.

precise time, for Harrisons to have speed in their outward trade to
South Africa in order to compete more successfully with ships of the
Clan Line; and secondly, that this acquisition had involved no
construction or experimental costs. Had the Managers laid down
these ships themselves the capital cost would have been well over half
a million pounds.[1]

Within the physical context of efficient working tonnage, therefore,
the Managers had worked out a viable formula designed to offset the
worst effects of depression. Having diversified their trades, and having
based many of the new trades on London rather than on Liverpool,
they had to exercise their judgement on the best ways and means of
providing profitable services on both old and new routes. The decision
to scrap or sell old ships had to be weighed against the capital cost
and potential earning capacity of new construction. In principle, this
crystallized into a policy of buying ships from other companies when
factor costs were high and when there was an upturn in the trade
cycle; and of laying down ships themselves in periods of more stable
prices. Side by side with this went the equally important consideration
concerned with the relative advantages of investing the Company's
surplus capital in ventures yielding a higher rate of return than that
from its employment in shipping. In the last resort, the Managers'
decisions, and the policy which evolved from these decisions, had the
single objective of sustaining the financial strength of the Company
throughout periods of uncertain and adverse conditions of trade.

II

The second group of decisions of basic importance to any shipping
line involved the Harrison Managers in a constant and vigilant watch
over the technical efficiency of the fleet.[2] One persistent problem was
that of innovation in the design and motive power of the ships. The

1. In 1935 the average cost for ships laid down was £23 per gross ton.
2. The author is grateful to J. R. Harris for the preparation of the technical data
in this section and also to P. S. Wilson, J. M. Cowan and J. H. Beazley (the present
superintendent engineer of Harrisons) for extracting information about the details
of tonnage, power of engines, and other specifications of vessels, from the pocket
'Black Books' kept by successive superintendent engineers since the 1890s.

Managers could have installed oil-firing or could have emulated Scandinavian tramp shipowners by turning to diesel propulsion. Nevertheless, during the whole inter-war period, they continued to own and build a fleet which consisted overwhelmingly of single-screw three-island vessels, coal fired and powered by triple-expansion engines. The only exceptions to this general pattern were a few larger and faster vessels with double-reduction geared turbines built before 1921 (*Dramatist, Huntsman, Diplomat*) and the West Indian passenger vessel *Inanda* of 1925, which was given a quadruple-expansion engine for greater speed. It is, therefore, of relevance to enquire into the reasons for this apparent conservatism on the part of the Managers. Their ship-building policy was undoubtedly framed to suit what they conceived to be the best interests of the line, and it may therefore, be pertinent to consider some of the broader issues of that policy.

In attempting to secure the highest possible return on capital, Harrisons had continuously under review the reduction of operating costs to a minimum. In this context, the relative advantage of the triple-expansion engine and coal-fired boilers had to be put against the performance of diesels. Innovation which might have led to savings of a specific kind, but which adversely affected costs or reliability, was of little interest to the Managers. Nor were they interested in improvements for the sake of technical change; the guiding principle was that any innovation must improve their expectation of profit over the whole range of trades in which the Company was involved. Insofar as triple-expansion coal burners were still proving suitable for a variety of uses in a complex voyage pattern, any new motive power would have had to ensure a substantial increase in commercial advantage to make its adoption worthwhile. In fact, as early as 1919 the very high price of coal had induced the Managers to fit oil-burning apparatus in twelve of their ships. *Actor* and *Governor* were two of the ships in which oil was used, and it was reported that it 'proved exceedingly satisfactory from a mechanical point of view' but that 'its value from the economical standpoint is doubtful on account of the very high price of oil'.[1] This latter consideration was an over-riding one and the experiment was short-lived; two years later the Minutes contained the

1. Harrison MSS., Minutes C.S.S.Co., 28 April 1920.

significant statement 'all the steamers are burning coal.'[1] A similar consideration was given to the introduction of diesel engines. Edward Danger and other partners made extensive enquiries into the comparative costs of coal-burning and diesel motive power. Owing to the diverse nature of the Harrison service, however, the problem was extremely complex in assessment and resistant to solution. 'Although the question of propulsion by diesel engines has been constantly under review during the year' it was stated in 1925 'we have not yet concluded that this class of steamer is useful in any of the trades in which the company's vessels are employed'.[2]

There were many reasons for this reluctance to introduce a new form of motive power. In the first place, the diesel engine itself was not without its technical problems. Few British marine engineers built their own diesels, though there was a considerable amount of building of foreign types under licence. Their first cost was higher than that of the triple-expansion engine; the fuel consumption was higher and the grade of oil more refined than that generally used by diesels after the second World War. Secondly, the evidence showed that there was a greater amount of deterioration in the diesel than in triple-expansion engines. In Harrisons' experience, these latter engines lasted throughout a ship's working life with very little loss of efficiency and had a high degree of reliability. Breakdowns at sea were almost unknown among the Harrison ships. To a company with such a complex of liner trades even a few defective engines would assuredly have caused a widespread dislocation in service and consequent loss in revenue. Thus, while many other lines found the diesel to be cheaper in its operating costs, Harrisons, because of the distinctive nature of their business, still found it more economical to use coal.

A fundamental determinant was the ready access which the Harrison ships had to supplies of cheap coal. Their main base was in Liverpool in the Brunswick group of the South Docks, and arrangements there suited them well. Incoming vessels usually discharged in the Toxteth Dock, where there were double storage sheds which facilitated the quick handling of cotton cargoes. They were then hauled through the Harrington to the Herculaneum Dock to load Haydock and South Yorkshire coal which, throughout the inter-war years, was supplied

1. ibid., 16 May 1922.
2. Harrison MSS., Minutes C.S.S.Co., 16 April 1925.

to Harrisons on favourable contract terms.[1] The South African ships loaded at Birkenhead where they had access to Brymbo coal at the same rates. Apart from supplies of cheap coal on the Mersey, however, there were comparable facilities on their trade routes in other parts of the world. In Calcutta they obtained cheap coal which, though of lower quality, worked out economically in steaming costs as compared with British coal, because the Harrison ships were specially designed to burn a variety of grades. There was also cheap coal available in Natal for the ships on the South African route, while ships sailing to Central American ports, because of the lighter outward cargoes, could dispense with other forms of ballast and carry as much as 2,000 tons of Herculaneum coal to serve their needs on the homeward leg of the voyage. In fact, the vessels of the *Rancher* class (begun in 1927) very often came home on the coal stowed in their sides and alleyways. By this means, bunker space in No. 3 Hold was used for the outward voyage and was cleared for the stowage of cargo homewards.

Within the general framework of management, these cost advantages were undoubtedly decisive in maintaining ship-building policy on traditional lines. This does not imply, however, that there were no innovations either in design or in technical detail during the inter-war years. The Managers maintained a constant watch on the performance of their ships in relation to the needs of the service and, whenever it was necessary, they would introduce modifications and improvements. It was customary at the partners' daily meetings for the state of the vessels to be kept under review. When a decision had been taken to build a new ship, and a builder had been selected, the Superintendent-Engineer would draw up a set of close specifications bearing in mind directions, not only of a technical nature, but those which were essential to the design, for achieving the best commercial results. Harrisons did not seek advice from outside firms of technical consultants; they could rely on the experience and skill of their own engineers, all of whom had been hand-picked from their sea-going officers and had subsequently received training in all relevant departments. As soon as the contract had been drawn up, one of the assistant

1. There was also the added advantage of proximity to the repair shops of R. and J. Evans (in which Harrisons took an interest in 1924) on the Liverpool side, and Fawcett, Preston and Co. on the Birkenhead side of the Mersey.

engineers would take up residence at the shipyard and would check every stage of the construction.

This procedure had obvious benefits, as it embodied continuous action from the point of decision-taking throughout all the intermediate stages to the completion of the generative process. Innovations and improvements thus resulted from an acceptance of evolutionary change rather than from a sudden break with existing practice. One important feature introduced during these years was the heavy-duty derrick. This was increased in size from a 40 ton lift in the 1920s to a 70 ton lift by 1939. Today, with a vastly increased capacity, this derrick has become a speciality of the line. Another equally important feature of Harrison ships at this time, was the provision of adequate deck space for the carriage of heavy deck cargo. As we have seen, the firing of the ships was skilfully adapted to the type of coal which was used; this was particularly so with the cheaper grades of Calcutta coal, the ships being fitted with high funnels (frequently topped with a 'bonnet') and using a natural draught. In addition, the furnace design and engine-room organization for the ships on the Calcutta route were suitably arranged to accommodate the needs of larger Indian crews.[1] There was, however, one innovation which had a short-lived and limited success. In 1928, the Managers experimented with the use of pulverized fuel in *Musician*.[2] It was anticipated that this method of firing would reduce both coaling time and trimming and handling costs. The process involved the taking in of small coal (i.e. slack or duff), pulverising it on board and blowing it into the boiler furnaces. In principle, the idea was a good one and, in the following year the new *Recorder* was 'entirely fitted for pulverised fuel'.[3] In practice, however, the savings from this process were outweighed by other larger diseconomies. The noise and dust generated in operation was excessive. There was also the really fundamental disadvantage that only a few international ports could supply suitable small coal in sufficient quantity; even in Liverpool time was lost because of the shortage of berths for this service. Thus, the flexibility of routing a vessel using pulverized coal was limited. This fact was implicit in the Managers report for

1. The increased complement gave continuity of working and allowed more time to be spent on the maintenance of the vessels.
2. Harrison MSS., Minutes C.S.S.Co., 24 April 1929.
3. ibid., 16 April 1930.

1931 when they stated 'the powdered coal experiment has proved that if a vessel fitted with the appropriate machinery can be run between two given points regularly, a considerable saving might be effected.'[1] The obvious limitations to a more general application of this type of firing shortly afterwards brought the experiment to an end.

In contradistinction to this somewhat uncertain innovation must be set the undoubted success of the decision to introduce double-ended 'Scotch' boilers. Harrisons pioneered this development in 1921 and the evidence suggests that it brought a considerable reduction to over-all running costs. Compared with the older type, the new 'Scotch' boilers required less engine-room space and this, in turn, allowed correspondingly larger spaces for the handling and stowage of cargo. In short, the earning capacity of the ship was thereby increased.

These various efforts, directed towards constant improvement, were continued during the 1930s. Apart from the depression years 1930, 1931, and 1932, there were times when notable and important advances were made in the technical efficiency of the fleet. A careful balance was maintained between the purchase of ships and the laying-down of new tonnage. In the former case the acquisition of the Prince Line vessels was undoubtedly a wise and, as events proved, a successful decision. The four ships of this line had been originally built for the Furness Withy service on the North Atlantic. They were powered by oil-burning turbines and were capable of speeds approaching 14 knots. Unfortunately for their owners, their heavy fuel costs made them uneconomical to run, especially during the years of acute depression. They were later put on to the North Pacific route but were still unable to return a profit. As we have seen, Harrisons bought these ships on very favourable terms and, despite high running costs, were able to employ them with advantage in their South African trade. Another highly profitable purchase during these years was that of *Merchant*, of 4,500 tons G.R., bought off the stocks from Lithgow's at the then rock-bottom price of £56,000.[2] For Harrisons, this purchase was of some significance as it brought them into contact with a new ship-builder; for Lithgow's, it secured a new customer. Harrisons placed orders with this firm for six new ships before the outbreak of the

1. ibid., 27 April 1932.
2. ibid., 24 April 1935.

second World War and maintained this connection with further contracts in the immediate post-war years.

With the improvement in trading conditions after 1934, the
Managers followed a fairly consistent policy in the ordering of new
ships. In all, a total of eleven were added to the fleet between 1935 and
1939, each ship being of 6,200 tons G.R. By concentrating on this
particular size of ship, it would appear that Harrisons had decided to
abandon the division of their fleet into three traditional classes. As
competition increased it became imperative to increase the speed of
the vessels. Thus, *Settler* (which was the last ship to be delivered before
the outbreak of war) was given additional power by fitting an exhaust
turbine of Bauer-Wach pattern as an alternative to a fourth cylinder,
and the ships of the new Dalesman class were given super-heated
steam with reciprocating engines and Bauer-Wach exhaust turbines,
coal-fired, and with double-ended boilers. This equipment was
designed to produce a speed of 14 knots, an increase of 3 knots on the
usual speed of Harrison ships since the beginning of the century;
in fact *Settler* and *Barrister*, (also of this class,) attained nearly 17 knots
on their trials.

The only other new ship of this period, differing in size, motive
power and appointments from those mentioned above, was the small
passenger liner *Inkosi*.[1] She was built specifically for the West Indian
passenger service, and was fitted with oil-fired quadruple expansion
engines.[2] Finally, as a somewhat sad aside to the ship-building activities
of the Managers, one has to record the abandonment of the Charente
brandy ships. The last of these ships, *Cognac*, was sold in 1935[3] as the
brandy trade had dwindled to such an extent that a new vessel was no
longer justified. For a time, the trade was continued with a ship on
'bare boat' charter to Harrisons, but in 1936 a bargain was made with
Moss Hutchison to carry the cargoes which the Williamson descendants were still obtaining for Harrisons, though the berth rights were
not sold until 1955.[4] This was, indeed, the break in the final link
which tied the Company to its origins.

1. ibid., 21 April 1937.
2. See above.
3. Harrison MSS., Minutes C.S.S.Co., 29 April 1936.
4. Harrison papers, from documents supplied by Eric Carter-Braine.

III

Theoretically, the decision to buy a ready-made ship rather than to lay one down must turn on the relative size of the return from the employment of the capital asset within a given set of circumstances. It would not, for example, have been a worthwhile exercise in 1935 for Harrisons either to have bought or to have ordered ships specifically designed for service on the Calcutta route, because the level of trade and the future prospects of that trade did not justify such outlay. On the other hand, the South African and West Indian services were sufficiently resilient, both to determine and to justify the case for purchase.

The determinants of Harrisons' policy, however, were not only those of a purely national character. They were influenced by the general background of the world shipping situation. A growth in world trade of 35 per cent between 1913 and 1929, coupled with a growth in world shipping tonnage of 45 per cent, and an increase of 20 per cent in the efficiency of the world fleet, should presumably have led to a fall in freight rates. Rising shipping costs both in shipbuilding (which increased by about 35 per cent) over the same period, tended to raise the minimum supply price (i.e. the freight rate at which an owner was indifferent between laying his ship up and keeping it on the berth[1]) generally helped to maintain the level of freight rates above 1913 levels until 1927. After that date the pressure of tonnage on the available quantity of trade asserted itself and freight rates fell accordingly. Professor Sturmey has made an interesting comparison between British, German and Norwegian freight indices[2] adjusted in accordance with changes in exchange rates. His general conclusion is that Norwegian and German shipowners were in a relatively more advantageous position than British shipowners during the 1920s; but that after the de-valuation of sterling in 1931, the German and Norwegian indices show a greater fall than those for Britain. This, perhaps, is too wide a generalization. Some British shipping companies undoubtedly derived benefit from devaluation, but others, such as Harrisons, were hit very hard in particular trades. Recovery to prosperity for shipping as a whole continued to be slow. In 1937, however, as a result of

1. S. G. Sturmey, *British Shipping and World Competition* (1962), p. 64.
2. ibid., p. 64.

expanding world trade and the wholesale scrapping of obsolescent tonnage in the years of depression, a reasonable state of equilibrium between cargo on offer and shipping space available was once again achieved. In 1938 there was a further downturn in world trade and consequently in freight rates, a decline which was only arrested by the outbreak of war in 1939.

Set against these trends in the world shipping situation, the decisions of the Harrison Managers can be given a degree of perspective. Table 10 attempts to show something of the relationship between Harrisons' net earnings and the cost per gross ton of ships laid down, together with the cost of ready made ships bought in 1933, 1934 and 1935.

TABLE 10

HARRISONS' SHIPBUILDING COSTS AND NET EARNINGS
1920–39

Year	Net earnings £000	Index 1924=100	Average cost per gross ton ships laid down £	Index 1924=100	Ships bought: cost per gross ton £
1921	905·6	279	—	—	—
1922	340·7	105	—	—	—
1923	336·4	103	19·1	84	—
1924	324·2	100	22·7	100	12·0
1925	296·0	91	19·3	85	—
1926	333·8	102	18·4	81	—
1927	338·2	104	18·5	81	—
1928	286·6	88	18·4	81	—
1929	314·9	97	19·2	84	—
1930	148·7	45	—	—	
1931	67·4	19	—	—	—
1932	156·0	48	—	—	—
1933	191·1	59	—	—	4·5
1934	234·4	72	15·4	67	12·3
1935	319·5	98	—	—	5·4
1936	383·0	118	—	—	—
1937	716·4	221	30·2	133	—
1938	524·7	161	31·2	137	—
1939	353·3	109	26·3	116	—

The figures indicate that, despite efforts to diversify the company's trade, and the attempts to maintain the fleet in an efficient working order, the net earnings between 1924 and 1929 were relatively stable, though depressed, the violence of the competitive struggle in some trades tending to offset better results on other more profitable routes. The reductions in operating costs which were gained, partly from innovation and improvement, and partly from working the ships harder and faster, were made less effective by the specific and often intensive nature of trade fluctuations. Nevertheless, it is pertinent to enquire whether the Harrison Managers were, in fact, justified in their assessment in 1924 of future prospects, bearing in mind the possibility that shipbuilding costs might fall in the years immediately ahead. What success they had was due in large measure to their wise management of the shipbuilding programme. In contradistinction, the decisions taken in the 1930s were based on a different conception of the use of capital under conditions of extreme economic uncertainty. In both cases, however, whether the policy was directed towards the laying down of ships or to the buying of ready-made ships, there was, given the economic instability of the time, a reasonable rate of return.

In support of the foregoing statements we now propose to make a comparative analysis of the anticipated and the actual returns on specific outlays of capital by the Harrisons. This is one way of testing the soundness of the Managers' judgement in employing the firm's resources. The period from 1925 to 1939 has been chosen for this purpose notwithstanding the fact that a period of twenty or twenty-five years would have enabled a more accurate analysis to be made. The reason for the choice of fifteen years was determined partly by the distortions of the immediate 1914–18 post-war boom, and partly because the years after 1939 were war years and, therefore, not comparable with years of peacetime activity.

In deciding whether or not to invest capital in new ships, the Managers were actuated, as we have already seen, by the desire to maintain an efficient and up-to-date fleet. This desire, in turn, was influenced by three main considerations; the first was the limitation on tonnage imposed by Conference agreements on particular routes, the second was the anticipated profitability of working the ships under fluctuating trading conditions, and the third was the relative rate of

return on capital from other forms of investment. It is this latter
consideration with which we are now concerned.

In 1924 Harrisons held £2.9 million in reserve investments, bank
deposits and other securities on which there was a net return of something less than 3 per cent. In the light of current economic conditions
any decision to invest part of these resources in ships must have turned
on the possibility of securing a return greater than 3 per cent. From
the evidence available it would appear that the Managers were prepared
to lay down ships with a minimum anticipated return of 4 per cent,
and this figure has therefore been used in our calculations. In 1924
Harrisons ordered three new ships; *Inanda*, a ship specially designed
for the West Indian trade, costing £177,000; *Magician* of 5,000 tons
G.R. costing £90,000 and *Wayfarer* of similar size but costing £94,000.
It was anticipated that a ship of 5,000 tons would earn a net annual
profit of approximately £6,000,[1] the expectation being that any
degree of fluctuation would tend to be in an upward rather than in a
downward direction. It might be added, in parenthesis, that this
anticipated earning capacity compared very unfavourably with that
calculated some thirty years earlier for a similar amount of capital.
The reasons for this difference will, however, become apparent in the
following pages. If we, therefore, accept the Managers' estimate as
being reasonably accurate (an average based upon the earnings per
gross ton for the fleet as a whole substantiates this figure), we can
proceed to a comparative analysis of actual earnings and anticipated
earnings.

Assuming that a ship of 5,000 tons costing £90,000 had a working
life of twenty-five years the investment would be justified if, over the
period as a whole, the discounted actual earnings were greater than the
discounted anticipated earnings.[2] As the picture is here presented the
calculation involves a degree of hindsight and, consequently, a range
of knowledge not available to the Managers at the time when the
decision was taken to build the ship. This, however, is not a serious
point as it is the intention of the exercise to examine the foresight of

1. Harrison MSS., Memo on state of trade and earning capacity of ships in the
fleet, December 1923.
2. Merrett and Sykes, op. cit.; also F. E. Hyde and G. L. S. Shackle, *A New Prospect
of Economics* (1959), p. 165. See also the excellent paper by R. O. Goss, 'Economic
Criteria for Optimal Ship Designs' to be published in the *Quarterly Transactions of the
Royal Institution of Naval Architects.*

the Managers in the light of subsequent events. This is exactly the same procedure as that applied to a similar analysis in section IV of chapter 6.[1]

Table 11 shows that, despite the absence of figures extending over a working life of twenty-five years, the actual earnings were falling short of anticipation. The fundamental reason for this was that, between

TABLE 11

HARRISONS' ACTUAL AND ANTICIPATED EARNINGS

Year	Actual earnings £	Actual earnings discounted at 4 per cent £	Anticipated earnings discounted at 4 per cent £
1925	3,026	2,904	5,772
1926	6,125	5,635	5,550
1927	6,214	5,530	5,334
1928	5,140	4,369	5,130
1929	5,710	4,682	4,932
Total 1925–1929	26,215	23,120	26,718
1930	3,025	2,389	4,740
1931	1,610	1,223	4,560
1932	3,625	2,546	4,386
1933	4,126	2,888	4,218
Total 1930–1933	12,386	9,046	17,904
1934	4,680	3,135	4,056
1935	5,510	3,581	3,900
1936	6,745	4,181	3,750
1937	12,240	7,344	3,606
1938	8,670	4,941	3,462
1939	6,340	3,487	3,330
Total 1934–1939	44,185	26,669	22,104
Total 1925–1939	82,786	58,835	66,726

1. See above pp. 116-20.

John Kirk Harrison

Brian Watson Hughes

1930 and 1933, the unprecedented depression in trade resulted in such low returns that even the most pessimistic projection in 1924 could not have anticipated the extent of the fall. If we compare discounted actual earnings with discounted anticipated earnings, certain interesting facts claim attention. It will be seen that between 1925 and 1929 actual earnings were somewhat below the forecast, though in the two years 1926 and 1927 they justified the Managers' decision to invest. This would tend to confirm that, despite intense competition and trade fluctuations, the Company was (taking the longer rather than the shorter view) just about holding its own. In the second period between 1930 and 1933, the disastrous effects of the depression are clearly shown, actual earnings (discounted) falling very far short of anticipated earnings. These figures provide a further measure of the extent to which declining commercial activities caused an under-employment of tonnage. Finally, in the years of recovery after 1934 the actual earnings (discounted) show an increase over anticipated earnings. One significant fact emerging from these figures is that, from 1934 onwards, Harrisons made a rapid and sustained recovery. This is borne out, not only by inference drawn from the operation of one particular type of ship, but from the scale of the annual totals of voyage profits.[1] From this it is reasonable to assume that, all other things being equal, actual earnings, under normal conditions of trade, would probably have been in excess of anticipated earnings over a twenty-five year period. In short, the Managers' decision in 1924 to build 5,000 ton ships costing £90,000 was sound both in expectation of the return on the investment and in the practical use of resources.

In retrospect, the years from 1920 to 1939 were testing years for the Harrison management. By a variety of decisions they attempted to redress the adverse effects of increasing pressures tending to disrupt the normal pattern of their shipping services. The nature and extent of their shipbuilding programme throughout the whole period was undoubtedly justified by subsequent events. It was, perhaps, the intensity of the depression and the dislocation resulting from this depression in 1930, 1931 and 1932 that provided the absolute test of strength. To most shipowners these were dead years. Ships were laid up and those which were kept on the berth were more often than not run at a loss; the impelling reason for working very much reduced fleets

1. See Appendix II.

M

being to maintain skeleton services and thereby an interest in particular routes. Harrisons overcame the difficulties of these years and sustained much less damage to their assets than many other companies. It is true that in 1930 they had fifteen ships laid up; but, by wise management, this idle capacity had been substantially reduced within two years through the simple process of selling off obsolescent ships. The economist might well argue that it was at this precise point that the Managers ought to have used their surplus funds to buy new ships. In the event, the Managers proved that they had made a shrewd assessment of the situation by a practical application of theoretical principles. By the end of 1933 they had taken the decision that an upturn in trade was likely. They thereupon implemented this decision by spending £203,000 in the purchase of 45,000 additional tons and, in the following year, a further £178,000 in the purchase of 31,000 additional tons. Though some of the ships in the 1933 purchase were shortly discarded they had, in fact, increased the carrying capacity of their fleet sufficiently to meet the anticipated improvement in trade at a cost per gross ton of something less than half the current price. This combined with a resumed building programme (totalling 11 new ships between 1935 and 1939), gave them a head start over some of their competitors. The significant point is not so much the use or the extent of the resources in giving practical application to the decision, but in the precise timing of taking money out of the bank and putting it into ships. This was the essence of commercial wisdom; it was a positive result of foresight which strengthened the Company's prospects of future reward from an improving world economic situation.

CHAPTER NINE

The Allocation of Resources and the
Strength of Management

I

THE steps taken by the Harrison Managers to safeguard the resources of the Charente Steam-Ship Company during periods of cyclical fluctuation, coupled with a shrewdly-based investment policy, undoubtedly helped to offset abnormal forms of disturbance to earning capacity. The maintenance of Conference agreements, the establishment of new trades and the general improvement in ship construction and increasing efficiency in working the fleet, were essential elements in the process of securing degrees of stability; stability, that is, which could be achieved through the disposition of forces within the Managers' control. In the 1920s and 1930s, however, the widespread fluctuations in the supply of, and the demand for, tonnage in particular markets induced Governments to safeguard their mercantile marines by various legislative procedures. This generally took the form of a massive reliance upon state subsidization. By contrast with such direct action, British shipping companies were afforded Government help of a somewhat indirect character,[1] and, at times when this was not forthcoming, had to rely on their own initiative and financial strength to meet the competition of foreign state-subsidized lines. We propose, therefore, to examine the source and disposition of the Harrison funds in relation to this problem and, at the same time, to relate such an examination to the exercise of managerial responsibility.

During the years from 1885–1939, the funds at the disposal of the

1. Under a 'scrap and build scheme', the Treasury was empowered, in 1935, to advance funds on guaranteed loans to British owners, who were prepared to scrap two tons of obsolete shipping for every one ton built, or who were prepared to modernize existing fleets. Although this scheme was designed for tramp owners, cargo liner owners were also included within the provisions.

Harrison Managers in any one year were derived from three principal sources; voyage profits, insurance premiums and other receipts (mainly the interest on bank deposits and other reserve investments). From the gross total certain disbursements were made, such as insurance claims, dividends, bonus dividends and taxation; the resulting net amount was the sum available to the Managers for allocation.[1] In the ten years before 1914, voyage profits were seldom less than 75 per cent of the gross total, (there were two exceptional years, 1906 and 1908, when the percentages were 71 and 73 respectively); in the years after 1910 the percentage never fell below 80. Between 1922 and 1939 voyage profits accounted for approximately 62 per cent of the total, though in 1925, 1928 and 1929, they fell just below 60 per cent. During the following three years 1930–2 the percentages reflect the disastrous trading conditions, the figures being 45, 27 and 49. Thereafter, there is a rising proportion until the peak year 1937 when the percentage reached the pre-1914 figure of 87.

Two points emerge from this analysis. In the first place, the figures for voyage profits are net figures after transfers have been made to the Insurance Account. Thus, there is a 'sympathetic' relationship between the totals for voyage profits and insurance premiums. In the second place, the income from bank deposits and reserve investments assumes a more positive place in the calculation of the gross total during the inter-war years. Harrisons rarely had less than £2 million in reserve at this time. This was, in the words of Thomas Harrison Hughes, 'a useful fighting fund' to stave off the effects of foreign subsidized competition and the threat of a take-over at home. Whether or not so large a reserve was necessary for these precise purposes is beside the point in this present context. The benefit lay in the annual income which it conferred upon the Managers. In any given year between 1922 and 1933 this income was never less than £100,000.[2] Before 1929 it accounted for approximately 26 per cent of the gross total of funds available to the Managers, and, in the years of depression, the proportion was over one-third, apart from 1931, when it was almost one-half. With the return of more normal trading conditions after 1934, and with the eventual reorganization of the reserve investments in the late

1. See Appendix II for the annual net figures.
2. ibid.

1930s,[1] the significance of this source of income declined. It is, never-theless, of importance to appreciate the relative levels of these various resources, and mark the generally high net amounts which were at the disposal of the Managers for development purposes. If we ignore the exceptional years of 1924 and 1931, these funds were never less than £110,000 (even in the depressed year 1932 the figure was £137,000), while in the very good years they ranged from £233,000 to well over £400,000. In other words, whatever the nature and extent of adverse influences, money was always available to implement policy decisions. On financial grounds, therefore, there was little hindrance to the Managers in their endeavours to sustain the competitive strength of the Company by various forms of technical innovation and by the purchase of additional tonnage.

In the disposition of their available funds, the Managers had to exercise their discretion between the amounts required for the purchase of ships (this is given as a net figure in Appendix II by deducting the receipts from the sale of old ships from the cost of the new) and any surplus which could be used to buy investments. In any year when both purchases and sales were made this figure is represented as the difference between the two amounts. The annual difference between total assets (i.e. funds available) and total liabilities (i.e. net disposition of funds) provides either a credit or a debit to working capital. Between 1923 and 1929, the bulk of the Company's available funds went into the purchase or the improvement of ships; on the side of share investment during the same period the Managers sold rather more than they purchased. This pattern of disposition is in sharp contrast with what happened during the following four years. From 1930 to 1933, no market investments were either bought or sold and there was a net accumulation of funds, rather than a net disbursement, because ships were being sold or scrapped. Despite very bad trading conditions, therefore, there was a corresponding increase in the annual totals of working capital. After 1934 the full effect of the decision to re-equip the fleet can be seen from the fact that virtually no new investments were bought (in 1934 and 1937 there were substantial sales) and the

1. Appendix II. The writing-down of Harrison investments in 1938 is shown, the figures being £2,593,000 in 1937 and £2,463,000 in 1938. The amount written off was £130,000. (See note (g).) A previous sale of investments in 1934 resulted in a profit of £322,677. (See note (f).).

bulk of the funds available were put to the purchase of new ships.

Much of the above analysis confirms conclusions which have already been arrived at in Chapters 7 and 8. This particular view of the Managers' function adds but another dimension to our understanding of their aims and achievements. It is obvious that, in the disposal of their funds, they placed a high priority on the need to engage the bulk of their resources in ships, except only in short periods of acute depression. Their belief in the efficacy of large reserves was both a source of strength in times of adversity and, through its practical application, a means of providing flexibility when times were propitious. Thus the income from the reserve was wisely used, and the reserve itself provided the additional capital for extended development.

Complementary to this disposition was the division of labour between Harrisons' Liverpool and London offices. This division was not only affected by changes in the voyage patterns of the ships, but was also determined by fluctuations in the share of the United Kingdom's trade taken by Liverpool and London. Most of Harrisons' export cargoes to India had been traditionally based on London; so, too, were some of the services to the West Indies; but the trade to South Africa was almost equally divided between East and West coast ports in the United Kingdom. It is in the import trade, however, that one finds a significant magnitude of change between London and Liverpool. A simple moving average of Liverpool's percentage of the United Kingdom's import trade is sufficient to show that between 1925 and 1931 her share dropped steadily, whereas that of London increased.[1] After 1931 there was an improvement in Liverpool's share which lasted until 1936. Fitting a linear trend to the percentage share of Liverpool shows that she was losing trade to other ports at the rate of 0.2 per cent of the trade of the United Kingdom each year.[2] Liverpool was thus losing about 1 per cent of her own share of the import trade each year. London, on the other hand, gained trade at the rate of 0.4 per cent. It is rather more difficult to assess the extent of fluctuation for other ports, though the general conclusion can be made that Bristol, Hull and Southampton had upward trends while Manchester

1. G. C. Allen, F. E. Hyde, D. J. Morgan and W. J. Corlett, *The Import Trade of the Port of Liverpool*, (1946), pp. 20-24; see also F. E. Hyde, 'The Growth of Liverpool's Trade 1700-1950,' *Merseyside, A Scientific Survey* (1953), pp. 159-60.
2. G. C. Allen, F. E. Hyde, D. J. Morgan and W. J. Corlett, op. cit., pp. 22-23.

had a small downward trend. One cannot escape the fact that Liverpool was losing ground relatively to other ports, and that the strong cyclical influence was acting on this trend, tending to make Liverpool's share lower than that of other ports in years of depression.

Declining trends, of the nature described above, undoubtedly provided the Harrison Managers with difficult problems to solve in the allocation of their resources. Traditional voyage patterns were upset and shipping companies were forced to embark on new ventures in order to hedge their risks. This was achieved in a variety of ways; by entering new markets, by greater efficiency in the sailing of ships, by creating supplementary services to their main activity of shipping, and, through their financial structures, so reorganizing themselves that they were able to deploy vast capital resources in the promotion of new enterprise.

II

The varying threads of the general background to Harrisons' management having been discussed, we can now proceed to an estimation of the success or otherwise of this function. This is undoubtedly a foolhardy thing to attempt, partly because management as such cannot be easily defined, and partly because comparison with other shipping managements is incapable of precise measurement. Nevertheless, the business historian ought to be able to arrive at conclusions and, within the terms of reference which he has set himself, to provide a reasonable answer to his enquiries. These, at best, can only be judgements based on a fairly broad survey of his data; only if the data are amenable to analysis can a more precise definition be made in support of, or as a qualification to, the general thesis.

In the case of a company such as the Charente Steam-Ship Company, one is fortunate in possessing a series of accounts and other material capable of statistical analysis, extending over a period of sixty years. Furthermore, these accounts, because they maintain a consistent form, can be subjected to the scrutiny of the accountant and thus given an additional dimension in their importance and value as evidence. For what purpose, then, have we used this information about

Harrisons? So far the analysis has been directed towards the answering
of three main questions. What was the nature of the activity in which
these men engaged; what was the source and disposition of their
resources and by what means did they foster the growth of those
resources; were they successful in achieving the ends which they set
themselves? It is hoped that the answers, or at least the partial answers
to these questions, will have already been given in a variety of ways
and by the use of a variety of techniques. There remains, however, the
final question of successful management, a question which, in turn,
comprehends the answers to all the questions hitherto asked. Such a
re-definition can only be made in comparative terms.

It is possible that most Liverpool shipowners in the 1920s and 1930s
would have agreed that Richard Durning Holt was an excellent
spokesman for their interests and that he possessed high qualities as an
administrator and as a manager. He gave evidence on behalf of his
fellow shipowners before the Royal Commission on Shipping Rings
in 1908 and also before the Imperial Shipping Committee in 1921-2;
he was Chairman of the Liverpool Steamship Owners' Association in
1923; his shrewd judgement was widely recognized to the extent that
when Elder Dempsters found themselves in serious financial difficulties
following the Kylsant disclosures, it was to Richard Holt that they
turned for help. He became Chairman of Elder Dempsters in 1932 and,
largely as a result of his foresight, the Company was reorganized and
given new life. His control of Alfred Holt and Company was no less
an achievement of skill and good judgement. If we accept Holts, therefore, as a criterion of good management, we can, by comparison, make
some assessment of the Harrisons' managerial capacity.

Such a process of investigation is not entirely devoid of degrees of
measurement. In purely physical terms the Holt fleet was about twice
the size of the Harrison fleet (Table 12) and earnings from voyages were
in approximately the same proportion. As far as can be estimated,
Holts had a lower cost structure than the Harrisons and net earnings
were therefore affected by that margin. Both firms had built up the
strength of their commercial activities on the basis of main line traditional trades; but both had been forced during the 1920s to seek new
routes and new markets as a hedge against undue fluctuation in their
main sources of income. Though they served different areas of the
world, both firms, in carrying heavy engineering and textile products

outwards, and primary products homewards, were affected by the same type of cyclical movement in trade though the magnitude of variation was often different. Nevertheless, even in this kind of comparison there were similarities. Just as the Holts found that in times of acute fluctuation an increase in their trade with China helped to offset falls in the Island and Australian trades, so too, were the Harrisons able to balance an increase in their South African trade against falls in the Indian and other trades. Thus, in general terms, certain adverse trends may be discounted in any comparison between the two firms.

TABLE 12

HARRISONS AND HOLTS
GROSS TONNAGE OF THE FLEETS

Year	Harrisons' gross tonnage	Holts' gross tonnage
1932	226,208	635,806
1933	222,025	607,402
1934	258,870	589,627
1935	285,633	589,464
1936	286,892	561,410
1937	294,321	551,496
1938	292,671	555,199
1939	280,401	549,351

Beginning with a comparison of the net voyage profits (as shown in Table 13) a number of interesting points claim immediate attention. From 1924 to 1926 Holts' and Harrisons' net earnings followed a similar pattern of fluctuation. Between 1927 and 1929, Holts' earnings increased by about 50 per cent above their 1926 level, while those of the Harrison fleet showed a declining trend. In 1930, however, Holts' net earnings dropped to 50 per cent and, in 1931, to 18 per cent of the 1929 level; the comparable percentages for Harrisons were 47 and 21. In the following years (apart from 1935) Holts' net earnings gradually recovered though it was not until 1937 that they passed the peaks of 1928 and 1929. Harrisons, on the other hand, made a quicker and a progressively steadier recovery after 1931, reaching their 1929 level by 1935 and making substantial gains in the three years 1936 to 1938.

It is obvious that there was a fair degree of consistency in the trading patterns of the two firms during the 1920s; the discrepancy between Harrisons and Holts in 1928 was caused almost entirely by the fall in Harrisons' net earnings resulting from the competition of the Thomas interests in their South African trade. The relevant questions which one might ask, therefore, refer to the years after 1931 when differences in

TABLE 13

HARRISONS AND HOLTS
COMPARISON OF NET VOYAGE PROFITS

Year	Harrisons Charente S.S. Company £000	Holts Ocean S.S. Co. and China Mutual S.N. Co. £000
1921	905·6	664·6
1922	340·7	560·1
1923	336·4	n.a.
1924	324·2	560·7
1925	296·0	520·7
1926	333·8	564·2
1927	338·2	651·3
1928	286·6	884·9
1929	314·9	848·8
1930	148·7	423·5
1931	67·4	156·5
1932	156 0	483·2
1933	191·1	583·6
1934	234·4	446·8
1935	319·4	377·8
1936	383·0	567·8
1937	716·4	988·6
1938	524·7	1,160·9
1939	353·3	959·7

the scale of fluctuations begin to emerge. Why, in comparison with the Holts, did Harrisons recover from the years of depression at a faster rate of progress, and, once having recovered so quickly, why did their earnings reach a proportionately higher level?

The comparison of earnings per gross ton given in Table 14 provides a rather more precise measurement of difference. If this table is read in conjunction with that giving the gross tonnages of the two fleets, it will be seen that between 1931 and 1937 Holts reduced the size of their fleet by 85,000 tons while Harrisons *increased* their fleet by 68,000 tons; the net earnings per gross ton of the Holt fleet fluctuated with a downward trend until 1935 after which date there was an upturn, whereas the earnings of the Harrison fleet followed a rising trend until 1937. If we now put these facts against the background of actual trading conditions it may be possible to deduce whether or not Harrisons were as effective in their management of the Charente steamships as Holts were with the Oceans and Mutuals.

TABLE 14

HARRISONS AND HOLTS
COMPARISON OF NET EARNINGS PER GROSS TON

Year	Harrisons Charente S.S. Company £	Holts Ocean S.S. Co. and China Mutual S.N. Co. £
1932	0·68	0·76
1933	0·86	0·96
1934	0·90	0·75
1935	1·11	0·64
1936	1·33	1·01
1937	2·43	1·79
1938	1·79	2·09
1939	1·26	1·74

In their trade with the Far East Holts were able to maintain their earnings, because the China trade, though severely hit, made a more rapid recovery after 1932 than did Malaya's trade. This latter trade, and especially that between Singapore and the East Indian islands, was particularly hard hit by the fall in commodity prices and by the fact that after Britain had abandoned the gold standard the Netherlands East Indies remained on it, a policy which aggravated rather than alleviated the economic difficulties of the area. It is hardly surprising, therefore, that shipping companies such as Holts should have regarded the China trade, despite depression, political unrest and the imminence of war between China and Japan, as the mainstay of their business. Another reason for the relative stability of Holts net earnings during depression was the fact that they had developed a more economical carrier, powered by diesel engines.[1] This innovation enabled them to compete on more favourable terms in a shrinking market. Against the background of falling commodity prices and a deepening of the depression in the United States, which affected adversely the trade between China, Japan and the west-coast ports of America, the Holt managers reported that their company was 'doing no worse than their rivals' and somewhat better than the government-assisted lines of the United States and Japan.[2]

It is, perhaps, surprising that in the years following the depression, Holts did not maintain this satisfactory trading position. Capital costs were, on the whole, not excessive in relation to the return on capital; while working costs in the case of Holts' new ships were reduced by as much as 20 per cent. The unsettled political conditions in the Far East were a potent factor in creating uncertainty and in causing trade fluctuations. Holts were, therefore, hesitant in risking their reserves (amounting to some £5 million invested in the market) in large scale construction, until they had a clearer understanding of the probable course of future events in the struggle between China and Japan. This not only inhibited new investment but reacted adversely on their earning capacity. Nevertheless, in spite of this, the level of Holts' earnings when compared with those of British shipping as a whole, was far higher and subject to a much narrower degree of fluctuation.[3]

From what has already been said in previous pages, it is obvious that Harrisons' shipping interests were equally well managed during the 1920s and 1930s. The Richard Holt of Harrisons was undoubtedly Thomas Harrison (Harry) Hughes. Though senior partner, Hughes preferred, for a variety of reasons, to take charge of the London office, a decision which might appear at first sight to be a little odd; but when considered against the background of the growing strength of the London-based trades it was a decision of the utmost importance. If Harry Hughes was the master mind on matters of policy, he had no less able and loyal lieutenants in John Watson Hughes and John Cecil

1. Minutes O.S.S.Co., 1924–31. These engines were made by Burmaster and Wain of Copenhagen.
2. ibid.
3. Taking the years 1933, 1937, and 1938, British shipping earnings fluctuated by 59:8:29 per cent *below* the 1924 level; the corresponding fluctuation for Holts was 3:76:107 *above* the 1924 level.

Mannings, the latter being mainly responsible for the operation of the Harrison fleet.

The problems which these men had to overcome were, in many respects, similar to those facing the Holts. The decline in Holts' trade with the East Indies was matched by an equally serious decline in Harrisons' trade with India and the Gulf (cotton trade); the balancing factor of strength in Holts' China trade bears favourable comparison with Harrisons' development of their South African trade. Both firms experienced difficulty from the depredations of foreign subsidised tonnage; both firms were equally concerned in the declining trend of Liverpool's import trade. There, however, the comparison ends. Holts were much more keenly alive to the cost advantages of building and using motor vessels than Harrisons though, by the purchase of the four ships of the Prince Line the latter firm was able, without incurring costs of innovation, to use oil-fired vessels as a means of increasing their share of trade in a period of recovery after depression. In general, Holts were more successful on the shipbuilding side of their business (taking into account the potentialities of the trades in which they were engaged); Harrisons were rather more successful than Holts in forecasting trends and thus securing a proportionately larger return on the investment of their capital.

A further indicator of the comparative strength of the Harrison management can be made from dividends paid to shareholders. Table 15 contrasts the Harrison disbursement with that of six other shipping lines, most of which (apart from Holts) had interests, either wholly or in part, in those trades in which Harrisons engaged.[1] Anyone who has knowledge of shipping company accounts will not be tempted to read too much into these figures nor expect them, without considerable qualification, to provide conclusive proof of financial strength. As is well known, the more conservative of British shipping companies paid dividends on a nominal capital which, by virtue of self-financing practice, bore very little relationship to the total value of capital assets. Holts and Harrisons both had such a nominal capital structure and, for this reason, their dividend percentage was, by comparison with other companies not similarly structured, consistently

1. Holt MSS., Minutes O.S.S.Co., 1934-6. Holts ran a South African service homewards from Australia during the 1930s and were thus, to a limited extent, in competition with Harrisons.

TABLE 15

DIVIDENDS OF SELECTED SHIPPING COMPANIES 1932-9

Year	Harrisons (£512,000) %	Holts (£1,010,000) %	Booth (£550,000) %	Clan (£2,102,000)[1] %	Ellerman (£5,450,000)[2] %	P. & O. (£7,632,518) %	Union Castle (£5,480,000) %
Capital							
1932	35·00	26·67	nil	1·83	2·97	1·99	nil
1933	40·00	20·00	nil	4·45	n.a.	n.a.	1·83
1934	30·00	20·00	nil	5·40	4·33	1·99	3·07
1935	35·00	20·00	3·00	3·46	3·47	1·99	1·99
1936	50·00	20·00	nil	8·93	3·47	4·40	2·93
1937	70·00	25·00	nil	9·74	3·47	4·40	2·93
1938	50·00	40·00	3·00	9·74	7·14	6·81	7·04
1939	25·00	40·00	nil	9·74	7·14	5·90	2·93

1. This capital was changed in 1933 to £1,750,000; the 1935 percentage was based on total capital including £500,000 of 5½ per cent Preference and £225,000 Ordinary shares issued in September 1934. After this year the total capital was £1,900,000 until 1937 when it was changed to £2,050,000.
2. This capital was changed in 1934 to £2,180,000.

higher and more profitable to their limited number of shareholders. From 1932 to 1939 Harrisons and Holts were able to pay astonishingly high rates of dividend; as compared with the other companies in Table 15 the magnitude of the difference is phenomenal. It would still have remained so even if the Harrison and Holt dividends had been expressed as a percentage of their employed, rather than as a percentage of their nominal, capital. Undoubtedly the poor showing of the Booth Line reflected that company's waning shipping interests;[1] but the P. and O. and Union Castle Lines, which were in receipt of mail contract subsidies, were generally depressed; the Clan and Ellerman Lines which were on berth with Harrisons in the main trades and might, therefore, have been expected to share equally in the expansion of trade after 1934, showed a rather closer correlation with the Harrison trend. But the great strength of Harrisons' position was undoubtedly created by their ability to anticipate the earning capacity of given amounts of capital; their high rate of dividend and the consistent improvement in their financial and trading position were but reflections of wise and skilful entrepreneurship. Looking at British shipping as a whole during the 1930s, it was a matter of general comment that had shipping companies invested the whole of their funds in gilt-edged securities at 5 per cent (as they could have done), the shareholders would have been much better recompensed. This may have been fair comment, but if so, it is equally certain the Harrisons and Holts were two major exceptions to such comment. To this extent Harrisons can be said not only to have demonstrated their competence as managers, but to have so organized their resources that they could match the endeavours of the most successful and efficient firms in the industry.

III

In 1938, the earning capacity of the Harrison fleet in relation to markets served, was as follows:—[2]

1. A. H. John, op. cit., pp. 144-6.
2. Harrison MSS., Voyage books for 1938. The total of earnings does not agree exactly with the figure given in Appendix II because a small number of voyages remained unclosed.

TABLE 16

Number of voyages		£
24	Calcutta	112,741
1	Calcutta to River Plate	7,500
39	West Indies and Demerara	95,761
27	West Indies and Venezuela	56,541
27	Kingston, Colombia and Gulf	31,208
15	West Coast U.K.—S. Africa	102,994
17	East Coast U.K.—S. Africa	103,811
6	East Africa	20,277
6	Brazil	608
1	Gulf, in ballast	4,015
		535,456

From these figures it will be seen that the earnings from the Calcutta trade were approximately 21 per cent, those from South and East Africa, 42 per cent and those from the West Indies, the Gulf and S. America, 37 per cent of the total. By comparison with other periods in the Company's history these percentages indicate considerable change in the relative position of particular markets. The declining trend in the trade with India and the virtual extinction of that with Brazil, are clearly in evidence, though these adverse figures are offset by the increasing importance of the services to South and East Africa and to the West Indies. Insofar as this static picture of one year's working supports previous conclusions, it reflects the Managers' continuous search for profitable openings for the employment of their resources. To this end, their decisions frequently altered the pattern of the Company's trading activities. Old and established markets gave way to new and prospectively more profitable ones.

It is, nevertheless, a far cry from the widespread engagements of the fleet of some fifty odd ships in 1938, to the first small brandy ships sailing from Liverpool to Charente a century earlier. We have attempted to unravel the threads of this growing progress; we have devised systems of measurement to assist in judging the scale of success, or failure, of the enterprise, at precise periods in the Company's history. What, then, are the conclusions? The evidence, so far as it has been capable of assessment, is reasonably clear. On financial grounds, the growth of resources compared favourably with that of any other British cargo liner company of similar size. The disposition and use of these resources was effective and, bearing in mind the particular nature of some of the Harrison interests, more often than not highly profitable. To have weathered successive depressions in trade without substantial injury, and to have shown such resilience in recovery, must stand testimony to the soundness of the Managers' financial policy. Added to this was the flexibility of their commercial relationships. Harrisons were fortunate in their agents and in the services provided. They, in turn, were generous as principals and shrewd as advisers. The friendship accorded to Alfred Le Blanc is a case in point. These factors, however, were not the only prerequisites of success. Without the tradition and the organiaztion fundamental to good seamanship, the ships might have been run less profitably and, as a consequence, the decisions of the Managers and the services of their agents might have been seriously impaired. A quantitative analysis of the results of men's actions cannot, however, provide an infallible measurement of business behaviour; there must also be a qualitative assessment of influences and motives in the direction of their affairs. Each successive generation of Managers built upon the knowledge and experience of the last, and directed their efforts in accordance with the particular circumstances of their time. In so doing, they created an invisible but accumulating asset which ranked in importance with the increase in the Company's physical growth.

Any retrospective judgement of the impact of men on events must, therefore, acknowledge the insight of Thomas Harrison Hughes in safeguarding the Harrison interests during the difficult years of the 1920s and 1930s; it must also give just recognition to the skill of John Watson Hughes and John Cecil Mannings (with the assistance of Eric Carter Braine in the London Office) in the disposition and the employment of the fleet; and to the prescience of Frank Ward and John Cowan in the diversification of trade routes and services. To these men the present-day Managers, under the chairmanship of Brian Watson Hughes, owe their trusteeship. The further back we go in time, the greater the historical perspective and, therefore, the greater the precision which can be given to individual achievement. Thus, there is a sharper focus to the discipline and foresight of John William Hughes

N

in the over-all direction of business, and to the organisational ability of Thomas Hughes and Frederick James Harrison in opening up new routes to the West Indies, Mexico and Brazil. The success of their work, however, grew out of the wisdom of the founder brothers, Thomas and James Harrison. From them came both the inspirational force and the means for promoting the Company's business. Their husbanding of resources, beginning with the part ownership in the brandy ships to Charente; their foresight in changing from sail to steam, giving new direction and an expanding interest in trans-oceanic trades to Calcutta and New Orleans, were the essential consequences of the rightness of their decisions. So, too, was their reliance on the navigational skill of Richard Pierre Williamson. If we go back even further, beyond the Liverpool of the 1830s where this shipping enterprise began, we come finally to the two marriages in December 1812 between James Harrison and Ann Hodgson at Cockerham, and Richard Williamson and Lucy Pierre in Verdun. The inter-twining family and business relationships which sprang from this conjunction brought continuity of policy in the management of one of Britain's leading shipping companies; and, through the provision of efficient services, had a profound and distinctive influence over the economies of many countries throughout the world.

Appendices

APPENDIX I

CHARENTE STEAM-SHIP COMPANY LTD.
FLEET TONNAGE AND PURCHASE PRICE 1884-1939

Year	ADDITIONS No. of Vessels	ADDITIONS Tonnage	ADDITIONS Purchase Price £000	RETIREMENTS No. of Vessels	RETIREMENTS Tonnage	RETIREMENTS Purchase Price £000	END-YEAR TOTAL No. of Vessels	END-YEAR TOTAL Tonnage	END-YEAR TOTAL Purchase Price £000
1884	22	—	512	—	—	—	22	—	512
5	2	—	42	1	—	23	23	—	530
6	2	—	51	—	—	47	23	—	535
7	1	—	34	2	—	23	23	—	546
8	2	—	67	1	—	23	24	—	590
9	8	—	266	3	—	79	29	—	777
1890	—	—	—	2	—	62	27	—	714
1	3	—	162	2	—	47	28	—	830
2	1	—	98	—	—	—	30	—	928
3	—	—	19	2	—	47	30	—	900
4	2	—	104	2	—	39	28	—	965
5	2	—	118	1	—	23	29	—	1,060
6	2	—	137	1	—	23	30	—	1,174
7	2	—	76	1	—	70	31	—	1,180
8	1	—	160	1	—	81	31	—	1,259
9	2	18,428	207	3	2,667	23	30	—	1,443
1900	2	14,281	223	3	2,623	23	29	111,766	1,643
1	2	14,853	204	1	4,637	61	28	127,527	1,785
2	2	19,954	230	1	—	23	29	138,867	2,015
3	4	14,843	184	2	4,710	44	30	149,083	2,155
4	3	14,218	162	1	7,379	107	31	169,027	2,210
5	3	10,544	124	3	6,890	79	35	179,160	2,255
6	3	10,379	119	1	2,066	23	36	185,999	2,351
7	2	5,882	65	—	—	—	38	189,653	2,416
8	1	9,627	111	2	—	66	38	197,966	2,526
9	2	10,718	119	2	4,136	63	39	203,848	2,579
1910	3	15,287	159	—	5,763	—	40	213,475	2,676
1	2	39,684	403	2	—	—	42	220,057	3,079
2	1	25,739	335	1	8,651	80	43	227,290	3,334
3	10	19,109	277	2	2,983	20	43	266,974	3,592
4	4	16,908	257	1	19,983	219	53	284,082	3,629
2	4						55	300,208	
3	4			4			58	297,133	
4	3						57		

APPENDIX I—continued

CHARENTE STEAM-SHIP COMPANY LTD.
FLEET TONNAGE AND PURCHASE PRICE 1884-1939

Year	ADDITIONS			RETIREMENTS			END-YEAR TOTAL		
	No. of Vessels	Tonnage	Purchase Price £000	No. of Vessels	Tonnage	Purchase Price £000	No. of Vessels	Tonnage	Purchase Price £000
1915	1	3,670	56	7	36,862	424	51	263,941	3,261
6	2	14,762	255	4	20,014	251	49	258,689	3,265
7	2	11,748	304	11	50,226	691	40	220,211	2,878
8	14	77,670	2,411	5	26,952	592	49	270,929	4,698
9	2	7,903	600	3	16,698	134	48	262,134	5,163
1920	13	55,648	2,537	3	17,688	196	58	300,094	7,505
1	—	—	111	1	9,656	71	57	290,438	7,545
2	—	—	25	5	24,682	322	52	265,756	7,248
3	3	14,800	285	4	28,468	318	51	252,088	7,215
4	3	21,300	418	—	—	—	51	273,388	7,633
5	4	15,605	298	7	27,517	812	55	261,476	7,119
6	3	11,200	209	2	8,081	351	51	264,595	6,977
7	5	29,649	543	3	12,904	238	53	281,340	7,282
8	1	5,738	105	2	9,100	407	52	277,978	6,980
9	2	11,600	221	1	3,588	43	53	285,990	7,157
1930	—	—	3	2	6,813	80	51	279,177	7,081
1	—	—	—	—	—	—	51	279,177	7,081
2	—	—	—	10	52,869	1,160	41	226,308	5,921
3	2	12,857	50	3	17,140	653	40	222,025	5,318
4	8	49,290	426	—	—	—	48	271,315	5,744
5	4	31,660	181	4	17,342	345	48	285,633	5,579
6	3	18,400	446	3	17,141	274	48	286,892	5,751
7	2	13,115	381	1	5,686	104	49	294,321	6,028
8	2	12,425	387	3	14,075	321	48	292,671	6,094
9	3	18,941	490	5	31,211	811	46	280,401	5,773

APPENDIX II

CHARENTE STEAM-SHIP COMPANY LTD.

STATEMENTS OF THE SOURCE AND APPLICATION OF FUNDS (in £000)

	1885	1886	1887	1888	1889	1890	1891	1892	1893	1894	1895	1896	1897
SOURCES OF FUNDS													
Voyage Profits	42	53	79	164	225	141	144	72	95	118	98	141	171
Insurance Premiums	53	19	21	23	33	23	29	23	26	28	24	22	26
Other Income	38	—	1	2	2	3	2	2	2	2	2	3	6
	—133	—72	—101	—189	—260	—167	—175	—97	—123	—148	—124	—166	—203
Less:													
Insurance Claims	—	—	—	—	—	—	1	1	1	1	—	—	1
Other Expenses	—	—	2	4	4	8	6	5	4	6	8	6	4
Taxation	—	—	1	1	1	2	3	4	2	2	2	2	2
	—	—	3	5	5	10	10	9	6	8	10	8	7
	133	72	98	184	255	157	165	88	117	140	114	158	196
Less:													
Dividends	31	41	41	92	82	92	41	21	61	61	31	61	72
Bonus Dividends	—	—	10	—	—	—	—	—	—	—	—	—	—
	—31	—41	51	92	82	92	41	21	61	61	31	61	72
	102	31	47	92	173	65	124	67	56	79	83	97	124
Less: Transfer to Provident Fund	—	—	1	1	1	—	—	—	—	1	—	1	1
Funds Available	102	31	46	91	172	65	124	67	56	78	83	96	123

APPENDIX II—continued

CHARENTE STEAM-SHIP COMPANY LTD.

STATEMENTS OF THE SOURCE AND APPLICATION OF FUNDS (in £'000)

APPLICATION OF FUNDS	1885		1886		1887		1888		1889		1890		1891		1892		1893		1894		1895		1896		1897	
Fleet:																										
Purchases	42		51		34		67		266		2		162		98		19		104		118		137		76	
Sales	5	37	10	41	8	26	5	62	50	216	25	(23)	16	146	—	98	11	8	24	80	5	113	4	133	9	67
Investments:																										
Purchases	30		10		1		2		1		41		—		15		—		—		—		—		—	
Sales	—	30	—	10	—	1	—	2	—	1	—	41	37	(37)	—	15	—	—	—	—	—	—	—	—	—	—
Working Capital:																										
Increase	35		—		19		27		—		47		15		—		48		—		—		—		56	
(Decrease)	—	35	(20)	(20)	—	19	—	27	(45)	(45)	—	47	—	15	(46)	(46)	—	48	(2)	(2)	(30)	(30)	(37)	(37)	—	56
Funds Spent		102		31		46		91		172		65		124		67		56		78		83		96		123

CHARENTE STEAM-SHIP COMPANY LTD.

STATEMENTS OF THE SOURCE AND APPLICATION OF FUNDS (in £000)

	1898	1899	1900	1901	1902	1903	1904	1905	1906	1907	1908	1909	1910
SOURCES OF FUNDS													
Voyage Profits	268	241	423	225	196	201	209	213	190	241	165	207	311
Insurance Premiums	24	30	23	47	54	52	58	61	63	60	44	52	42
Other Income	9	7	8	11	12	7	9	8	13	16	16	15	15
	301	278	454	283	262	260	276	282	266	317	225	274	368
Less:													
Insurance Claims	—	—	—	—	—	—	21	26	—	—	1	3	3
Other Expenses	5	6	7	8	8	8	9	34(a)	8	8	6	7	5
Taxation	3	3	5	9	16	16	7	7	7	6	6	8	9
	8	9	12	17	24	24	37	67	15	14	13	18	17
	293	269	442	266	238	236	239	215	251	303	212	256	351
Less:													
Dividends	102	82	174	92	51	38	90	96	77	151	82	123	143
Bonus Dividends	—	—	—	—	—	—	—	—	38	51	31	—	41
	102	82	174	92	51	38	90	96	115	202	113	123	184
	191	187	268	174	187	198	149	119	136	101	99	133	167
Less: Transfer to Provident Fund	—	—	1	—	—	—	—	—	—	1	—	—	5
Funds available	191	187	267	174	187	198	149	119	136	100	99	133	162

APPENDIX II—continued

CHARENTE STEAM-SHIP COMPANY LTD.

STATEMENTS OF THE SOURCE AND APPLICATION OF FUNDS (in £000)

APPLICATION OF FUNDS	1898	1899	1900	1901	1902	1903	1904	1905	1906	1907	1908	1909	1910
Fleet:													
Purchases	160	207	223	204	230	184	162	124	119	65	111	119	159
Sales	—	8	8	37	—	7	25	19	4	—	—	8	10
	—160	—199	—215	—167	—230	—177	—137	—105	—115	—65	—111	—111	—149
Investments:													
Purchases	32	2	1	50	—	—	6	11	—	23	—	3	—
Sales	—	—	—	—	—	—	—	7	—	—	—	—	—
	—32	—2	—1	—50	—	—	—6	—4	—	—23	—	—3	—
Working Capital:													
Increase	—	—	51	—	—	21	6	10	21	12	—	19	13
(Decrease)	(1)	(14)	—	(43)	(43)	—	—	—	—	—	(12)	—	—
Funds Spent	191	187	267	174	187	198	149	119	136	100	99	133	162

APPENDIX II—continued

CHARENTE STEAM-SHIP COMPANY LTD.
STATEMENTS OF THE SOURCE AND APPLICATION OF FUNDS (in £000)

	1911	1912	1913	1914	1915	1916	1917	1918	1919	1920
SOURCES OF FUNDS										
Voyage Profits	393	668	734	582	2,069	3,626	2,104	1,303	2,619	3,196
Insurance Premiums	41	52	65	82	77	96	5	5	82	47
Other Income	14	14	22	25	48	104	289	310	221	323
	448	734	821	689	2,104	3,826	2,398	1,618	2,922	3,566
Less:										
Insurance Claims	4	77	3(c)	5	47	67	4	4	3	117
Other Expenses	8	48(b)	12	13	17	16	13	31	28	129
Taxation	9	10	13	20	40	584	2,303	1,447	831	1,119
	21	135	28	38	104	667	2,320	1,482	862	1,365
	427	599	793	651	2,090	3,159	78	136	2,060	2,201
Less:										
Dividends	82	235	461	256	819	819	512	154	154	205
Bonus Dividends	—	—	—	—	—	—	—	102	1,536	—
	82	235	461	256	819	819	512	256	1,690	205
	345	364	332	395	1,271	2,340	(434)	(120)	370	1,996
Less:										
Transfer to Provident Fund	—	—	10	—	—	50	50	35	—	—
Funds Available	345	364	322	395	1,271	2,290	(484)	(155)	370	1,996

CHARENTE STEAM-SHIP COMPANY LTD.

STATEMENTS OF THE SOURCE AND APPLICATION OF FUNDS (in £000)

APPLICATION OF FUNDS	1911	1912	1913	1914	1915	1916	1917	1918	1919	1920
Fleet:										
Purchases	403	335	277	257	56	255	304	2,411	600	2,537
Sales	—	14	22	35	267	212	1,540	1,546	272	569
	403	321	255	222	(211)	43	(1,236)	865	328	1,968
Investments:										
Purchases	4	36	30	—	481	200	—	—	17	—
Sales	4	1	—	1	1	—	—	85	200	50
	—	35	30	(1)	480	200	—	(85)	(183)	(50)
Working Capital:										
Increase	—	8	37	174	1,002	2,047	752	—	225	78
(Decrease)	(58)	—	—	—	—	—	—	(935)	—	—
Funds Spent	345	364	322	395	1,271	2,290	(484)	(155)	370	1,996

CHARENTE STEAM-SHIP COMPANY LTD.

STATEMENTS OF THE SOURCE AND APPLICATION OF FUNDS (in £000)

SOURCES OF FUNDS	1921	1922	1923	1924	1925	1926	1927	1928	1929	1930
Voyage Profits	906	341	336	324	296	334	338	287	315	149
Insurance Premiums	9	41	37	48	75	62	66	69	75	56
Other Income	264	172	144	149	137	142	143	134	142	121
	— 1179	— 554	— 517	— 521	— 508	— 538	— 547	— 490	— 532	— 326
Less:										
Insurance Claims	4	4	20	6	15	5	28	29	14	4
Other Expenses	32	17	16	19	16	17	25	20	20	23
Taxation	559	1,548	401	166	39	20	25	24	27	19
	— 595	1,569	— 437	— 191	— 70	— 42	— 78	— 73	— 61	— 46
	584	(1,015)	80	330	438	496	469	417	471	280
Less:										
Dividends	77	102	205	307	205	205	307	307	307	166
Bonus Dividends	—	—	—	—	—	—	—	—	—	—
	— 77	— 102	— 205	— 307	— 205	— 205	— 307	— 307	— 307	— 166
Less:										
Transfer to Provident Fund	—	—	—	—	—	—	—	—	—	(1)
	507	(1,117)	(125)	23	233	291	162	110	164	114
Funds Available	507	(1,117)	(125)	23	233	291	162	110	164	115

APPENDIX II—continued

CHARENTE STEAM-SHIP COMPANY LTD.

STATEMENTS OF THE SOURCE AND APPLICATION OF FUNDS (in £000)

APPLICATION OF FUNDS	1921	1922	1923	1924	1925	1926	1927	1928	1929	1930
Fleet:										
Purchases	111	25	285	418	298	209	543	105	221	3
Sales	96	64	75	—	78	38	54	37	12	24
	15	(39)	210	418	220	171	489	68	209	(21)
Investments:										
Purchases	—	—	71	5	2	—	2	—	—	—
Sales	7	—	—	—	50	—	—	72	—	—
	(7)	—	71	5	(48)	—	2	(72)	—	—
Working Capital:										
Increase	499	—	—	—	61	120	—	114	—	136
(Decrease)	—	(1,078)	(406)	(400)	—	—	(329)	—	(45)	—
Funds Spent	507	(1,117)	(125)	23	233	291	162	110	164	115

APPENDIX II—continued

CHARENTE STEAM-SHIP COMPANY LTD.

STATEMENTS OF THE SOURCE AND APPLICATION OF FUNDS (in £000)

	1931	1932	1933	1934	1935	1936	1937	1938	1939
SOURCES OF FUNDS									
Voyage Profits	68	156	191	234	319	383	716	525	353
Insurance Premiums	66	40	35	40	41	30	35	43	45
Other Income	115	122	110	93	89	45	64	85	79
	249	318	336	367	449	458	815	653	477
Less:									
Insurance Claims	4	5	7	8	11	15	11	12	46
Other Expenses	19	18	70(d)	71(e)	21	22	28	43	37
Taxation	4	(17)	(65)	(36)	(11)	12	2	14	92
	27	6	12	43	21	49	41	69	175
	222	312	324	324	428	409	774	584	302
Less:									
Dividends	154	179	205	154	179	256	358	256	128
Bonus Dividends	—	—	—	819	—	—	—	—	—
	154	179	205	973	179	256	358	256	128
	68	133	119	(649)	249	153	416	328	174
Less:									
Transfer to Provident Fund	(1)	(4)	—	26	—	20	2	1	(1)
Funds Available	69	137	119	(675)	249	133	414	327	175

CHARENTE STEAM-SHIP COMPANY LTD.
STATEMENTS OF THE SOURCE AND APPLICATION OF FUNDS (in £000)

APPLICATION OF FUNDS	1931	1932	1933	1934	1935	1936	1937	1938	1939
Fleet:									
Purchases	—	—	50	426	181	446	381	387	490
Sales	—	—	15	—	27	48	30	49	59
	—	—	35	426	154	398	351	338	431
Investments:									
Purchases	—	—	—	—	—	—	4	—	—
Sales	—	(31)	—	326(f)	—	590	—	—	10
	—	(31)	—	(326)	—	(590)	4	—	(10)
Working Capital:									
Increase	69	168	84	—	95	325	59	—	—
(Decrease)	—	—	—	(775)	—	—	—	(11)(g)	(246)
Funds Spent	69	137	119	(675)	249	133	414	327	175

NOTES.—(a) [1905] 'Other expenses £34,000' includes the purchase price of £17,543 of qualifying shares presented by the Company to Mr. J. W. Hughes on his election to the Board of the Suez Canal Company.

(b) [1912] 'Other expenses £48,000' includes the payment of £40,000 for the goodwill of J. T. Rennie & Co.

(c) [1913] 'Insurance claims £3,000' is made up as follows:

Various claims   £33,000
Less: Amount credited to General Account in respect of S.S. *Workman*, lost in 1912   30,000

Net charge   £3,000

(d) [1933] 'Other expenses £70,000' includes the payment of £50,000 towards the purchase of the goodwill of Leyland & Co. Ltd.

(e) [1934] 'Other expenses £71,000' includes a second payment of £50,000 for the purchase of the goodwill of Leyland & Co. Ltd.

(f) [1934] 'Sale of investments £326,000' includes a profit of £322,677 made on the realization of various investments shown under the heading Current Assets in the Balance Sheets. The actual proceeds of the realization are included in the net change in working capital.

(g) [1938] 'Decrease in working capital £11,000' is the net change in working capital after allowing for the writing down of the company's holdings of government securities by £130,000 to their market value of the day, in recognition of 'the serious international situation'.

APPENDIX III

CHARENTE STEAM-SHIP COMPANY LTD.

SUMMARISED BALANCE SHEETS (in £000)

	1884	1885	1886	1887	1888	1889	1890	1891	1892	1893	1894	1895	1896	1897	1898	1899
ASSETS																
Fleet—Cost	512	530	535	546	590	777	714	830	928	900	965	1,060	1,174	1,180	1,259	1,443
Investments—Market	N/k	N/k	N/k	N/k	N/k	N/k	N/k	N/k	N/k	N/k	N/k	N/k	N/k	N/k	N/k	N/k
Cost	—	30	40	41	43	44	86	49	64	64	64	64	64	64	96	98
	512	560	575	587	633	821	800	879	992	964	1,029	1,124	1,238	1,244	1,355	1,541
Net Working Capital	—	35	15	33	60	15	62	77	32	80	77	47	10	65	64	49
Net Assets	512	595	590	620	693	836	862	956	1,024	1,044	1,106	1,171	1,248	1,309	1,419	1,590

APPENDIX III—continued
CHARENTE STEAM-SHIP COMPANY LTD.
SUMMARISED BALANCE SHEETS (in £000)

	1884	1885	1886	1887	1888	1889	1890	1891	1892	1893	1894	1895	1896	1897	1898	1899
CAPITAL EMPLOYED																
Nominal Share Capital	512	512	512	512	512	512	512	512	512	512	512	512	512	512	512	512
Suspense/Reserve Fund	—	30	40	41	43	45	87	64	66	66	66	66	66	66	97	99
General Account	—	12	13	21	59	5	29	1	3	24	46	42	3	42	54	7
Insurance Account	—	23	2	12	1	10	32	61	27	54	29	3	5	20	6	36
Accident Fund	—	—	—	—	—	—	—	—	—	—	—	—	—	1	3	5
Balance Sheet Equity	512	577	567	586	615	572	660	638	608	656	653	623	586	641	672	659
Earnings ploughed back to purchase vessels	—	18	23	34	78	264	202	318	416	388	453	548	662	668	747	931
Capital Employed	512	595	590	620	693	836	862	956	1,024	1,044	1,106	1,171	1,248	1,309	1,419	1,590
'Current Value' of Share Capital: Total (£000)	—	410	410	410	435	512	640	589	640	640	614	589	614	717	768	1,024
Per Share (£)	—	800	800	800	850	1,000	1,250	1,150	1,250	1,250	1,200	1,150	1,200	1,400	1,500	2,000

APPENDIX III—continued

CHARENTE STEAM-SHIP COMPANY LTD.
SUMMARISED BALANCE SHEETS (in £'000)

	1900	1901	1902	1903	1904	1905	1906	1907	1908	1909	1910	1911	1912	1913	1914
ASSETS															
Fleet—Cost	1,643	1,785	2,015	2,155	2,210	2,255	2,351	2,416	2,526	2,579	2,676	3,079	3,334	3,592	3,629
Investments—Market	N/k	N/k	N/k	N/k	[140]	[147]	[143]	[161]	[161]	[162]	[158]	[153]	N/k	[204]	N/k
Cost	98	149	149	149	155	159	158	182	182	184	184	183	218	248	247
Working Capital															
(a) Current Assets															
Treasury Bills	—	—	—	—	—	—	—	—	—	—	—	—	—	—	—
Mersey Docks & Harbour Board Bonds	—	—	—	—	—	—	—	—	—	—	—	—	—	—	—
Loans	—	—	—	—	—	—	50	50	107	—	—	51	—	8	8
Bank Deposits	—	—	—	—	—	—	—	—	—	—	—	—	—	—	—
Owed by Managers	218	236	187	127	158	157	181	254	94	131	144	180	253	396	358
Debtors	3	5	7	5	15	4	4	5	7	123	165	39	119	44	233
Pernambuco Lighters	—	—	—	—	—	—	—	—	—	6	4	—	7	4	11
	221	241	194	132	173	161	235	309	208	260	313	270	379	452	610
(b) Less: Current Liabilities															
Excess Receipts on Open Voyages	38	134	127	40	52	18	42	49	48	44	61	75	212	68	71
Creditors	23	25	42	47	55	76	80	147	51	96	122	118	67	249	254
Bills Payable	60	24	10	9	24	14	39	27	35	26	24	28	43	42	17
Protection Club	—	—	—	—	—	1	1	1	1	1	1	1	1	1	1
	121	183	179	96	131	109	162	224	135	167	208	222	323	360	343
(c) Net Working Capital	100	58	15	36	42	52	73	85	73	93	105	48	56	92	267
Net Assets	1,841	1,992	2,179	2,340	2,407	2,466	2,582	2,683	2,781	2,856	2,965	3,310	3,608	3,932	4,143

APPENDIX III—continued

CHARENTE STEAM-SHIP COMPANY LTD.

SUMMARISED BALANCE SHEETS (in £'000)

	1900	1901	1902	1903	1904	1905	1906	1907	1908	1909	1910	1911	1912	1913	1914
CAPITAL EMPLOYED															
Nominal Share Capital	512	512	512	512	512	512	512	512	512	512	512	512	512	512	512
Reserve Fund	99	149	149	149	159	159	159	184	184	184	184	185	240	250	445
General Account	36	50	4	27	63	43	38	38	55	66	79	27	38	61	14
Insurance Account	59	2	5	4	(30)	4	30	41	11	22	20	13	(11)	22	49
Accident Fund	5	5	5	5	5	5	5	5	5	5	6	6	7	7	6
Balance Sheet Equity	711	718	675	697	709	723	744	780	767	789	801	743	786	852	1,026
Earnings ploughed back to purchase vessels	1,130	1,274	1,504	1,643	1,698	1,743	1,838	1,903	2,014	2,067	2,164	2,567	2,822	3,080	3,117
Capital Employed	1,841	1,992	2,179	2,340	2,407	2,466	2,582	2,683	2,781	2,856	2,965	3,310	3,608	3,932	4,143
'Current Value' of Share Capital:															
Total (£'000)	1,024	1,280	1,024	1,024	1,024	1,024	1,024	1,024	1,024	1,024	1,024	1,280	1,536	1,792	2,048
Per Share (£)	2,000	2,500	2,000	2,000	2,000	2,000	2,000	2,000	2,000	2,000	2,000	2,500	3,000	3,500	4,000

APPENDIX III—continued

CHARENTE STEAM-SHIP COMPANY LTD.
SUMMARISED BALANCE SHEETS (in £000)

	1915	1916	1917	1918	1919	1920	1921	1922	1923	1924	1925	1926	1927	1928	1929
ASSETS															
Fleet—Cost	3,261	3,265	2,878	4,698	5,163	7,505	7,545	7,248	7,215	7,633	7,119	6,977	7,282	6,980	7,157
Investment—Market	[656]	[832]	[843]	[767]	[561]	[464]	[494]	[541]	[610]	[623]	[561]	[566]	[571]	[503]	[488]
Cost less depreciation	658	858	858	773	591	540	529	527	599	603	556	556	558	486	486
Working Capital															
(a) Current Assets															
Treasury Bills	956	2,799	3,114	2,974	3,449	2,705	2,477	1,253	—	—	—	—	—	—	—
Bank Deposits	250	270	—	1,000	—	—	—	1,000	1,400	900	1,000	1,000	1,100	900	900
War Bonds 1922	—	—	770	750	350	—	—	—	—	—	—	—	—	—	—
War Loan 1929–47	—	—	550	550	550	550	550	550	550	550	550	550	550	550	550
Victory Bonds	—	—	—	—	850	850	846	841	841	829	829	824	816	812	803
	1,206	3,069	4,434	5,274	5,199	4,105	3,873	3,644	2,791	2,279	2,379	2,374	2,466	2,262	2,253
Owed by Managers	508	809	605	333	430	586	546	395	137	246	166	140	137	52	83
Debtors	18	100	97	132	71	54	56	40	21	22	19	10	7	9	16
Pernambuco Lighters	8	8	8	8	2	—	—	—	—	—	—	—	—	—	—
African Coasters	—	—	13	13	—	—	—	—	—	—	—	—	—	—	—
	1,740	3,986	5,157	5,760	5,702	4,745	4,475	4,079	2,949	2,547	2,564	2,524	2,610	2,323	2,352
(b) Less: Current Liabilities															
Excess Receipts on Open Voyages	137	334	776	1,666	857	69	39	103	92	57	145	(i)	90	140	80
Creditors	321	319	285	942	1,455	1,215	487	1,099	394	429	289	272	604	155	281
Bills Payable	12	16	23	11	26	19	12	18	12	9	18	22	13	12	19
Protection Club	1	1	4	8	5	5	2	2	—	—	—	—	—	—	—
	471	670	1,088	2,627	2,343	1,308	540	1,222	498	495	452	293	707	307	380
(c) Net Working Capital	1,269	3,316	4,069	3,133	3,359	3,437	3,935	2,857	2,451	2,052	2,112	2,231	1,903	2,016	1,972
Net Assets	5,188	7,439	7,805	8,604	9,113	11,482	12,009	10,632	10,265	10,288	9,787	9,764	9,743	9,482	9,615

APPENDIX III—continued

CHARENTE STEAM-SHIP COMPANY LTD.
SUMMARISED BALANCE SHEETS (in £000)

	1915	1916	1917	1918	1919	1920	1921	1922	1923	1924	1925	1926	1927	1928	1929
CAPITAL EMPLOYED															
Nominal Share Capital	512	512	512	512	512	512	512	512	512	512	512	512	512	512	512
Reserve Fund	730	930	930	845	662	612	600	599	599	603	555	555	558	486	486
General Account	260	271	125	154	290	309	440	246	219	89	46	137	146	182	65
Insurance Account	81	116	121	112	104	36	43	83	102	148	213	270	94	135	195
Accident Fund	6	7	8	8	9	9	9	9	9	9	9	10	10	10	10
Tax Suspense Account	850	2,450	1,944	1,205	1,566	2,469	2,614	1,626	1,224	909	870	803	586	586	586
New Steamers Account	—	400	1,798	1,582	1,000	542	758	821	897	897	975	1,012	1,067	1,104	1,116
Capital Reserve	—	—	—	—	318	—	—	—	—	—	—	—	—	—	—
Balance Sheet Equity	2,439	4,686	5,438	4,418	4,461	4,489	4,976	3,896	3,562	3,167	3,180	3,299	2,973	3,015	2,970
Earnings ploughed back to purchase vessels	2,749	2,753	2,367	4,186	4,652	6,993	7,033	6,736	6,703	7,121	6,607	6,465	6,770	6,467	6,645
Capital Employed	5,188	7,439	7,805	8,604	9,113	11,482	12,009	10,632	10,265	10,288	9,787	9,764	9,743	9,482	9,615
'Current Value' of Share Capital:															
Total (£000)	2,304	3,072	3,584	3,328	2,048	2,048	2,048	1,792	1,792	1,792	2,048	2,048	2,048	2,048	2,048
Per Share (£)	4,500	6,000	7,000	6,500	4,000	4,000	4,000	3,500	3,500	3,500	4,000	4,000	4,000	4,000	4,000

CHARENTE STEAM-SHIP COMPANY LTD.

SUMMARISED BALANCE SHEETS (in £000)

	1930	1931	1932	1933	1934	1935	1936	1937	1938	1939
ASSETS										
Fleet—Cost	7,081	7,081	5,921	5,318	5,744	5,579	5,751	6,028	6,094	5,773
Investments—Market	[492]	[446]	[470]	[499]	[534]	[521]	[122]	[114]	[93]	[87]
Cost less depreciation	484	484	480	480	475	475	90	94	94	84
Benevolent Fund Investments—Market	[222]	[202]	[237]	[246]	[307]	[296]	[315]	[293]	[275]	[266]
Cost	232	232	232	232	262	262	282	282	282	282
Working Capital										
(a) Current Assets										
Bank Deposits	400	200	300	—	—	—	—	—	—	—
War Loan 1929-47	550	550	544	1,036						
4% Consols	803	803	803	805						
2½% Consols	—	254	254	370						
4% Treasury Stock 1934-36	—	—	—	—						
Mersey Docks & Harbour Board Bonds	400	400	400	—						
	2,153	2,207	2,301	2,211	1,762	1,762	2,353	2,593	2,463	2,177
Owed by Managers	59	55	139	309	252	127	244	115	147	242
Debtors	12	10	10	13	14	15	18	18	16	39
	2,224	2,272	2,450	2,533	2,028	1,904	2,615	2,726	2,626	2,458
(b) Less: Current Liabilities										
Excess Receipts on Open Voyages	68	57	56	68	128	113	105	156	110	237
Creditors	46	35	42	30	239	34	428	430	510	471
Bills Payable	2	4	8	7	7	7	7	5	13	3
	116	96	106	105	374	154	540	591	633	711
(c) Net Working Capital	2,108	2,176	2,344	2,428	1,654	1,750	2,075	2,135	1,993	1,747
Net Assets	9,905	9,973	8,977	8,458	8,135	8,066	8,198	8,539	8,463	7,886

APPENDIX III—continued

CHARENTE STEAM-SHIP COMPANY LTD.

SUMMARISED BALANCE SHEETS (in £,000)

	1930	1931	1932	1933	1934	1935	1936	1937	1938	1939
CAPITAL EMPLOYED										
Nominal Share Capital	512	512	512	512	512	512	512	512	512	512
Reserve Fund	484	484	480	480	475	629	629	629	629	630
Profit and Loss Account	123	128	227	343	131	159	102	109	218	154
Insurance Account	247	309	344	372	403	433	448	472	503	502
Accident Fund	10	10	10	10	10	10	8	9	9	8
Tax Suspense Account	586	586	586	486	270	270	—	—	—	—
Steamer Renewal Account	1,141	1,141	1,172	1,187	687	714	762	792	641	449
Taxes Recovered	—	—	—	—	144	—	—	—	—	—
Capital Reserve	—	—	—	—	4	4	211	215	85	85
Balance Sheet Equity	3,103	3,170	3,331	3,390	2,636	2,731	2,672	2,738	2,597	2,340
Earnings ploughed back to purchase vessels	6,569	6,569	5,409	4,806	5,232	5,068	5,239	5,516	5,582	5,261
Benevolent Fund	232	232	232	257	262	262	282	282	282	282
Benevolent Fund Income Account	1	2	5	5	5	5	5	3	2	3
Capital Employed	9,905	9,973	8,977	8,458	8,135	8,066	8,198	8,539	8,463	7,886
'Current Value' of Share Capital:										
Total (£,000)	2,048	1,792	1,972	1,792	1,792	1,536	2,048	2,560	3,072	2,560
Per Share (£)	4,000	3,500	3,500	3,500	3,500	3,000	4,000	5,000	6,000	5,000

GENERAL INDEX

INDEX OF SHIPS

Dates refer to the ordering or acquisition of ships

SECTION ONE : 1800-84

Admiral Grenfell (1854), 9, 10, 16, 34, 45
Alice (1866), 17, 37, 51n.
Amazon (1865), 17, 51n., 52
Anna Dorothea, 35n.
Artist (1864), 35, 35n., 42n.
Astronomer (1860), 35, 35n.
Author (1880), 41
Botanist (1863), 34n., 35, 35n., 42n.
Chancellor (1873), 41
Charente (1862), 13, 13n., 17
Charles Souchay (1845), 4
Chrysolite (1867), 17, 37, 51n.
City of Lincoln (1848), 22
Cognac (1860), first steamship, 12, 12n.
Commander (1877), 41
Cordova (1870), 37
Counsellor (1877), 41
Crescent (1837), 7, 7n.
Dauntless (1846), 51n.
Discoverer (1877), 41
Dragon (1862), 13, 13n., 17
Eagle (1800), Scarborough, captured by
    the enemy 1804, 5, 5n.
Edward Boustead (1852), 51n.
Engineer (1882), 30
Euphemia (1828), 8n.
Explorer, 30, 41
Fire Queen (1866), 18, 18n., 22, 37, 37n.,
    51n.
Gem (1851), 51n.

Geologist (1859), 35, 35n.
Gladiator (1864), 17, 22, 51n., 52, 53, 53n.
Governor (1881), 30
Historian (1870), 37, 41
Inventor (1878), 26, 41
Jane (1836), 7, 7n., 9, 45
Jubilee (1814), Scarborough, 5
King Arthur (1871), 42n.
Legislator (1873), 26, 30, 41
Lightning, purchased from the Black Ball
    Line in 1865, 16, 16n.
Linguist (1876), 42n.
Margaret, 6, 6n.
Mariote (1825), 6
Mediator, 41
Naturalist (1863), 35, 35n.
Olinda (1865), 17, 37, 51n., 52, 53, 53n.
Orator (1877), 41, 106
Orkney Lass, 51n.
Pantheon (1867), 18, 18n.
Philosopher (1857), 35, 35n., 42n.
Sculptor (1882), 106
Senator (1874), 42n.
Sir Colin Campbell (1839), 8
Statesman (1869), 37, 41
Templar (1842), 33, 34n., 51n.
Tom Tough (1829), Scarborough, 7, 8
Urgent (1845), 51n.
Vanguard (1874), 41
Warrior (1874), 26, 41

SECTION TWO : 1885-1939

Actor (1916, delivered 1917), 150
Barrister (1914, delivered 1915), 155
Cognac (1902), 155
Collegian (1898, delivered 1899), 101
Counsellor (1903), 107
Craftsman (1896, delivered 1897), 30, 101
Custodian (1899), 101, 102
Diplomat (1921), 147, 150
Dramatist (1913), 150
Governor (1917), 150
Historian (1895), 118

Huntsman (1921), 147, 150
Inanda (1911), 106n., 129, 150
Inanda (1924), 159
Ingeli (1911), 106n.
Ingoma (1912, delivered 1913), 129
Inkonka (1911), 106n.
Inkosi (1911), 106n., 129, 155
Insizwa (1911), 106n.
Intaba (1911), 106n., 129
Inventor, 107
Inyati (1911), 106n.

207

SECTION THREE : SHIPS OF OTHER COMPANIES